T0399834

Second Homes and Climate Change

This book is the first to address the important interrelationship between second homes and climate change, which has become an increasingly relevant issue for many regions around the world.

Second homes are often a key source of tourist visitation as well as economic benefit for their host communities. The chapters provide an array of international case studies and climate change impacts, including the changing biocultural landscapes in Italy, hazard risks in the mountains of Poland, and the shifting media discussion on second homes and climate change in Finland. Topics covered focus on issues around planning and governance in second home locations, adaptation and mitigation measures implemented by second home owners, and the influence of second home owners' place attachment in relation to second home impacts. It introduces the overall topic of second homes and climate change while also laying the groundwork for future work in this burgeoning area of research.

This book will be of significant interest to upper-level undergraduates, graduate students, and academics in the fields of geography, tourism, planning, housing studies, regional development, environmental management, and disaster management. It would also be of use for professionals who engage with second home communities, particularly planners, government officials, and environmental officers.

Bailey Ashton Adie is Research Affiliate in the Geography Research Unit at the University of Oulu, Finland; Visiting Research Fellow at the Center for Tourism Research, Wakayama University, Japan; and Chair of the Leisure Studies Association. She has a PhD in Management and Development of Cultural Heritage from IMT Lucca, Italy. Her research interests include community resilience, second homes, community-based tourism, World Heritage tourism, tourism and development, and heritage tourism. She is the author of the Routledge book *World Heritage and Tourism: Marketing and Management*. She sits on the editorial boards of the *Journal of Heritage Tourism*, *Tourism Geographies*, *Tourism Management Perspectives*, and *El Periplo Sustentable*. Her work has been published in book chapters as well as in leading journals, including *Annals of Tourism Research*, *Current Issues in Tourism*, and *Journal of Sustainable Tourism*.

C. Michael Hall is Ahurei Professor in the Department of Management, Marketing and Tourism, University of Canterbury, New Zealand; Visiting Professor and Docent in Geography, University of Oulu, Finland; Visiting Professor, School of Business and Economics, Linnaeus University, Kalmar; Guest Professor, Department of Service Management and Service Studies, Lund University, Helsingborg, Sweden; Visiting Professor, CRiC, Taylors University, Kuala Lumpur, Malaysia; and Eminent Scholar, Kyung Hee University, Seoul, South Korea. Co-editor of *Current Issues in Tourism* and Field Editor of *Frontiers in Sustainable Tourism*, he publishes widely on tourism, sustainability, global environmental change, food, and regional development.

Contemporary Geographies of Leisure, Tourism and Mobility
Series Editor: C. Michael Hall
Professor at the Department of Management, College of Business and Economics, University of Canterbury, Christchurch, New Zealand

The aim of this series is to explore and communicate the intersections and relationships between leisure, tourism and human mobility within the social sciences.

It will incorporate both traditional and new perspectives on leisure and tourism from contemporary geography, e.g. notions of identity, representation and culture, while also providing for perspectives from cognate areas such as anthropology, cultural studies, gastronomy and food studies, marketing, policy studies and political economy, regional and urban planning, and sociology, within the development of an integrated field of leisure and tourism studies.

Also, increasingly, tourism and leisure are regarded as steps in a continuum of human mobility. Inclusion of mobility in the series offers the prospect to examine the relationship between tourism and migration, the sojourner, educational travel, and second home and retirement travel phenomena.

The series comprises two strands:

Contemporary Geographies of Leisure, Tourism and Mobility aims to address the needs of students and academics, and the titles will be published simultaneously in hardback and paperback.

Routledge Studies in Contemporary Geographies of Leisure, Tourism and Mobility is a forum for innovative new research intended for research students and academics, and the titles will initially be available in hardback only. Titles include:

Inclusion in Tourism
Understanding Institutional Discrimination and Bias
Edited by Susan L. Slocum

Second Homes and Climate Change
Bailey Ashton Adie and C. Michael Hall

For more information about this series, please visit: www.routledge.com/Contemporary-Geographies-of-Leisure-Tourism-and-Mobility/book-series/SE0522

Second Homes and Climate Change

Edited by Bailey Ashton Adie
and C. Michael Hall

Routledge
Taylor & Francis Group

LONDON AND NEW YORK

First published 2024
by Routledge
4 Park Square, Milton Park, Abingdon, Oxon OX14 4RN

and by Routledge
605 Third Avenue, New York, NY 10158

Routledge is an imprint of the Taylor & Francis Group, an informa business

British Library Cataloguing-in-Publication Data
A catalogue record for this book is available from the British Library

Library of Congress Cataloging-in-Publication Data
Names: Adie, Bailey Ashton, editor. | Hall, Colin Michael, 1961–editor.
Title: Second homes and climate change / edited by Bailey Ashton Adie
    and C. Michael Hall.
Description: Abingdon, Oxon ; New York, NY : Routledge, 2023. |
    Series: Contemporary geographies of leisure, tourism and mobility |
    Includes bibliographical references and index.
Identifiers: LCCN 2022061944 (print) | LCCN 2022061945 (ebook) |
    ISBN 9780367549466 (hardback) | ISBN 9780367549510 (paperback) |
    ISBN 9781003091295 (ebook)
Subjects: LCSH: Second homes—Environmental aspects. | Tourism—
    Environmental aspects. | City planning—Environmental aspects. |
    Climatic changes—Effect of human beings on.
Classification: LCC HD7289.2 .S43 2023 (print) | LCC HD7289.2 (ebook) |
    DDC 643/.12—dc23/eng/20230208
LC record available at https://lccn.loc.gov/2022061944
LC ebook record available at https://lccn.loc.gov/2022061945

ISBN: 978-0-367-54946-6 (hbk)
ISBN: 978-0-367-54951-0 (pbk)
ISBN: 978-1-003-09129-5 (ebk)

DOI: 10.4324/9781003091295

Typeset in Times New Roman
by Apex CoVantage, LLC

Contents

Figures

Tables

Contributors

Bailey Ashton Adie, Center for Tourism Research, Wakayama University, Japan, and Geography Research Unit, University of Oulu, Oulu, Finland.

Andreas Back, Department of Geography, Umeå University, 901 87 Umeå, Sweden.

Adam Czarnecki, Institute of Rural and Agricultural Development, Polish Academy of Sciences, 72 Nowy Świat St., 00–330 Warsaw, Poland.

Aneta Dacko, Department of Agricultural Geodesy, Cadastre and Photogrammetry, Faculty of Environmental Engineering and Land Surveying, 'Hugo Kołłątaj' University of Agriculture in Krakow, 253a Balicka St., 30–198 Krakow, Poland.

Mariusz Dacko, Department of Economics and Food Economy, Faculty of Agriculture and Economics, 'Hugo Kołłątaj' University of Agriculture in Krakow, 21 Mickiewicz Ave., 31–120 Krakow, Poland.

O. Cenk Demiroglu, Department of Geography, Umeå University, 901 87 Umeå, Sweden.

C. Michael Hall, Department of Management, Marketing and Tourism, University of Canterbury, New Zealand; Geography Research Unit, University of Oulu, Oulu, Finland; School of Business and Economics, Linnaeus University, Kalmar, Sweden; Department of Service Management and Service Studies, Lund University, Helsingborg, Sweden; CRiC, Taylors University, Kuala Lumpur, Malaysia; and Kyung Hee University, Seoul, South Korea.

Linda Lundmark, Department of Geography, Umeå University, 901 87 Umeå, Sweden.

Alan March, Faculty of Architecture, Building and Planning, University of Melbourne, Victoria, Australia, and the Bushfire and Natural Hazard Cooperative Research Centre, Australia.

Dieter K. Müller, Department of Geography, Umeå University, 901 87 Umeå, Sweden.

Petter Næss, Department of Urban and Regional Planning, Norwegian University of Life Sciences (NMBU), P.O. Box 5003 NMBU, N-1432 Ås, Norway.

Rasmus Nedergård Steffansen, Department of Planning, Aalborg University, Aalborg, Denmark.

Leonardo Nogueira de Moraes, Faculty of Architecture, Building and Planning, University of Melbourne, Victoria, Australia, and the Bushfire and Natural Hazard Cooperative Research Centre, Australia.

Kati Pitkänen, Environmental Policy Centre, Finnish Environment Institute SYKE, P.O. Box 111, FI – 80101 Joensuu, Finland, and Geography Research Unit, University of Oulu, Oulu, Finland.

Manu Rantanen, University of Helsinki, Ruralia Institute, Lönnrotinkatu 7, FI-50100 Mikkeli, Finland.

Timothy Kevin Richardson, Department of Urban and Regional Planning, Norwegian University of Life Sciences (NMBU), P.O. Box 5003 NMBU, N-1432 Ås, Norway.

Harpa Stefansdottir, Faculty of Planning and Design. Landbúnaðarháskóli Íslands/Agricultural University of Iceland, Keldnaholt, Árleynir 22, 112 Reykjavík, Iceland.

Stefania Toso, Department of Sociology and Social Research, University of Milano Bicocca, Italy.

Mario A. Velázquez García, Colegio del Estado de Hidalgo, Hermosillo, Sonora, Mexico.

Jin Xue, Department of Urban and Regional Planning, Norwegian University of Life Sciences (NMBU), P.O. Box 5003 NMBU, N-1432 Ås, Norway.

Acknowledgements

Second homes have always been a large part of Bailey's life as she grew up going to her family's home every summer in Ocean Beach on Fire Island, New York. While the house has now been sold, the memories remain, and this book is, in many ways, a tribute to her family's history on the island, which spanned five generations of Adies, Briethuts, and Schopps and a myriad of family stories and intergenerational memories. One particularly funny family legend being that Marilyn Monroe once visited her great-grandparents' grocery store and was reprimanded by her great uncle, Bill Adie, for squeezing the tomatoes. These memories, stories, and people form the second home fabric that she still carries with her today.

For this book, Bailey would like to first thank her co-editor Michael whose invaluable work has helped make this book what it is today. Thank you also to the team at Routledge for all of their understanding and help during this process. She would also like to thank her friends and colleagues who have been nothing but supportive, in particular special thanks go out to Cecilia de Bernardi, Ellena Parsons, Brittany Rudacille, Shaina Ungar, Rene G. Cepeda, Jane Parry, and Helen Devereux. She wants to also thank her family for pretending that they remember what this book is about, in particular her parents, Rich and Debbie Adie, and her siblings, Courtney Wagner and Alex Adie. She would also like to thank her grandparents, Richard and Betty Adie, whose second home was the base for her first foray into this field of research and who helped her gain access to the local community. Finally, she would like to thank her husband, André, who has been with her this whole journey and who has provided unwavering support. She couldn't have done it without him.

Michael would like to thank colleagues and friends with whom he has had relevant conversations or conducted research with over the years in relation to this work, some of which are also contributors. In addition to thanking Bailey for co-editing and those friends who have contributed to this book, Michael would like to thank Alberto Amore, Dorothee Bohn, Chris Chen, Tim Coles, Hervé Corvellec, David Duval, Martin Gren, Stephan Gössling, Peter Harinson, Johan Hultman, Tyron Love, Dieter K. Müller, Yael Ram, Jarkko Saarinen, Anna Dóra Sæþórsdóttir, Daniel Scott, Siamak Seyfi, Kimberley Wood, and Maria José Zapata-Campos for their thoughts on tourism and the world, as well as for the stimulation of Beirut, Paul Buchanan, Nick Cave, Bruce Cockburn, Elvis Costello, Stephen Cummings,

David Bowie, Ebba Fosberg, Mark Hollis, Aimee Mann, Larkin Poe, Vinnie Reilly, Henry Rollins, Emma Swift, TISM, Henry Wagons, *The Guardian*, BBC6, JJ, and KCRW – for making the world much less confining. Special mention must also be given to the Malmö Saluhall; Packhuset and Postgarten in Kalmar; and Hotel Lasaratti in Oulu. Michael would also like to very gratefully acknowledge Jody Cowper-James for her proofreading of much of the book as well as her contribution to Michael's work over the years.

Finally, they would both like to thank their authors for dealing with COVID and life-related delays to this book and to Emma and all at Routledge for continuing to support this project despite the stresses of the last few years.

List of abbreviations

CO_2	Carbon dioxide
GHG	Greenhouse gas
GWh	Gigawatt hours

1 Second home tourism and climate change

An introduction

C. Michael Hall and Bailey Ashton Adie

Introduction

Second homes are an increasingly important driver of tourism mobility (Hall, 2018c; Müller & Hall, 2018). Second home tourism is characterised by the temporary relocation of people in travelling between a permanent place of residence and a secondary dwelling (Hoogendoorn & Fitchett, 2018; Müller & Hall, 2018). Although there are urban second homes, escaping from cities is the main motivation for temporary mobility between cities and rural and peri-urban areas in which most second homes have long been located (Coppock, 1977; Hall & Müller, 2004, 2018a; Hiltunen, 2007; Müller & Hoogendoorn, 2013; Müller, 2021).

Several reasons have been provided for growth in both the number of second homes and second home related tourism. As urbanization processes continue to grow and more people live in cities than ever before, a lack of green areas such as gardens, parks, and outdoor places in big cities have been identified as encouraging people to travel to exurban areas to compensate for the absence of such green space (Hall & Page, 2014; Strandell & Hall, 2015). A temporary change of residence has also been identified as being a part of what has been described as a recreational lifestyle (Hall, 2005).

Second home ownership is also embedded in the cultural context of a number of countries. For example, Marjavaara and Müller (2007) argue that among the Swedish population, it is generally regarded as desirable to have a second home, with a similar culture also existing in Finland (Adamiak et al., 2016). Næss et al. (2019) state that possessing a second home is part of the perception of how Norwegian life should look. Second home tourism represents a significant proportion of domestic tourism in Australia, New Zealand, Russia, North America, Europe, and the Nordic countries in particular (Pitkänen et al., 2020). However, despite their important role in tourism and regional development, and long held concerns over their environmental impact, definitions of second homes differ between and sometimes within countries, making international comparisons difficult (Hall & Müller, 2018a).

Hall and Müller (2004) argue that the notion of a 'second home' is often used as an umbrella for numerous terms related to the use of secondary dwellings. The boundaries between there various terms are blurred and often reflect different forms of planning, housing, and taxation governance as well as assumptions about

DOI: 10.4324/9781003091295-1

permanency and mobility in everyday life (Hall, 2015; Hall & Müller, 2018b). Defining a primary and second home or 'home' and 'away' context becomes problematic in many cases. The availability and difference in national data, relative relationships to property, use of second homes as an investment vehicle, inherited properties, empty properties, absentee owners, and long-term rent agreements significantly contribute to confusion in research on second home mobility (Müller & Hall, 2018). Müller and Hall (2018) point out that the debates on the definition and what to attribute to a second home make investigation and understanding of its impacts difficult. Second homes therefore have multiple dimensions such as temporal, functional, evolutionary, geographical, physical, political, and psychological which makes their analysis extremely complex (see Müller & Hall, 2018) and will affect any analysis of their contribution to climate change.

The multiple roles of second homes as well their significance also became noticeable during the COVID-19 pandemic when many people moved from urban areas to a second dwelling in order to 'escape' the outbreak (Gallent, 2020; Müller, 2021; Pitkänen et al., 2020; Zoğal et al., 2022). While international tourism was substantially affected by the pandemic (Gössling et al., 2020; Hall et al., 2020), domestic second home tourism became extremely popular along with a growth in caravanning and mobile homes (Gallent, 2020; Pitkänen et al., 2020). Pitkänen et al. (2020) claim that second homes have served as a shelter for isolation in low-risk locations. The effects of such movement was substantial. For example, the population of Paris was estimated to have decreased by 11% in 2020 as people moved to safer countryside or seaside second home destinations (Seraphin & Dosquet, 2020). Such changes to mobility patterns are substantial in the short term but may become even more significant in the longer term with respect to sustainability concerns (Seyfi et al., 2022). However, at this stage we do not fully know the implications of working from second homes with respect to the work and recreational purposes of primary and secondary homes and, importantly for transport emissions, the effects on climate change.

As any form of tourism-related mobility, second home tourism contributes significantly to climate and environmental change through transportation (Adamiak et al., 2016; Næss et al., 2019), construction work and land use change (Gallent et al., 2005; García-Andreu et al., 2015), and water and electricity use (Hiltunen, 2007; Hiltunen et al., 2016). Air and car travel are among major factors contributing to greenhouse gas emissions (Gössling, 2002; Hall et al., 2015; Scott et al., 2012) with second home tourism being potentially significant contributors of tourism-related mobility (Williams & Hall, 2002). However, second homes not only contribute to climate and environmental change but they may also be substantially affected by it, especially because of the location of many second homes in amenity environments such as coastal destinations, forests, and mountain areas that are at risk from climate change. Therefore, the development of an improved understanding of the relationships between second homes and climate change would appear to be important from several perspectives including destination adaptation, management, marketing and planning; mitigating second home related emissions; and the potential of domestic second home tourism to substitute for long-haul travel (Adamiak et al., 2016; Næss et al., 2019; Seyfi et al., 2022).

Second tourism and climate change impacts

Concern with the impacts of second home tourism is longstanding (Coppock, 1977) and is typically viewed through economic, social, and environmental dimensions (Müller et al., 2004). Although early research on second homes did consider their environmental impacts, it was not approached in terms of emissions but rather environmental change and pressure, especially in relation to seasonal visitation. For example, Dower (1977) and Priddle and Kreutzwiser (1977) focused on issues such as construction, planning standards, indicators, seasonal pressures, and environmental carrying capacity in relation to fauna and flora and the effects of mass second home development.

From an environmental point of view, the location of second homes is significant since they are usually situated in relatively natural environment settings (Hoogendoorn & Fitchett, 2018). These areas are often mountain (Kaltenborn et al., 2007; Kaltenborn et al., 2008) or shorefront areas with access to water such as lakes, seas, and rivers (Marjavaara & Müller, 2007), which may make them more susceptible to some of the effects of climate change. In terms of adaptation issues, it is noticeable that remote areas have more limited opportunities to deal with increased pressure of second home tourism and related consequences (Hall, 2018b). For example, the coastal areas of south-eastern France have become greatly urbanised due to the development of second home tourism with subsequent effects on the environment as well as the social fabric of the region (Rey-Valette et al., 2015). However, Marjavaara and Müller (2007) and Hall (2014) point out that second home tourism provides stable and sometimes substantial tourist flows. In addition, it is vital to consider the potential long-term implications of second home tourism and their connection to lifestyle, amenity, and retirement migration as second homes become permanent homes (Hall, 2014). Nevertheless, research on the environmental impacts of second homes remains surprisingly limited (Müller & Hoogendoorn, 2013).

The literature on climate change impacts of second homes is relatively scarce (Hall, 2018c). Debates on whether second homes possess environmental threats are ongoing (Hall & Saarinen, 2021; Hiltunen et al., 2016; Long & Hoogendoorn, 2014; Müller et al., 2004). Müller (2004) stresses that converted second homes may not introduce additional environmental impacts. In addition, the development of second home tourism contributes to the local economies and supports rural communities (Marjavaara & Müller, 2007; Müller, 2002, 2004). Moreover, it is argued that second home owners sense themselves as environmentally friendly (Hiltunen et al., 2016; Long & Hoogendoorn, 2014). Nevertheless, second homes put pressure on local infrastructures, communities, and the environment, especially where there is relatively limited taxation paid by second home owners to the jurisdiction in which the second home is located (Müller & Hall, 2003; Hall, 2018c). However, it is recognised that second home usage increases the use of electricity (Dubois, 2005), water (Long & Hoogendoorn, 2014), contributes to CO_2 emissions (Adamiak et al., 2016; Næss et al., 2019), but a comprehensive understanding of second homes' environmental impacts is difficult as these impacts are dispersed and not well understood by individuals (Hiltunen et al., 2016) or government (Müller et al., 2004).

The limited literature that exists demonstrates two main viewpoints on second home tourism and related climate change impacts. The first perspective on the problem is the risks that climate change brings for second home tourism, particularly for owners and/or users (Hall & Saarinen, 2021). This area covers topics regarding hazards such as temperature rise (Hall, 2018b), sea-level rise (Hall, 2018a), drought and heat waves (Hoogendoorn & Fitchett, 2018), storms (Cheong, 2018; Hall & Prayag, 2023), and flooding (Hall & Prayag, 2023). Climate change and second home research also touches upon policy and planning implications due to the increasing pressure on public infrastructure and utilities by climate change (Hall, 2018c). The risk perceptions of second home owners and users can be attributed to this category as well (Adie, 2020; Adie & de Bernardi, 2020; Hiltunen et al., 2016; Johansen, 2019; Rey-Valette et al., 2015). The second view is the contribution of second home tourism to climate change (Hiltunen et al., 2016). This group analyses greenhouse gas emissions due to traveling between dwellings (Adamiak et al., 2016), impacts of new building construction (García-Andreu et al., 2015; Hiltunen, 2007), the increased use of non-renewable energy, uncontrolled water use, and waste production (Hiltunen et al., 2016). The two approaches to the relationships between second homes and climate change are discussed in greater detail in the following section.

Risks for second home owners: climate change, policy, and perceptions

Climate change induced risks

Second homes are often found in coastal and mountain areas that are prone to natural threats (Adie, 2020; Hall, 2014). While second home owners are frequently considered as a privileged group, the research underlines how vulnerable they are to natural hazards and disasters (Cheong, 2018; Hall, 2018a; Hall & Prayag, 2023; Hao et al., 2020; Hoogendoorn & Fitchett, 2018). Hao et al. (2020) stress that coastal communities in North Carolina are vulnerable to erosion, sea-level rise, and storms. The main concern is that these communities are dependent on tourism given that second home owners make up the majority of the population. Hall (2018a) demonstrates how crucial it is to consider sea-level rise for the future of second homes on Banks Peninsula, New Zealand, near Christchurch, given the importance of second homes to the area's tourism economy. Sea-level rise is seen as a major natural hazard as it will greatly affect coastal infrastructure, heritage, and properties. Rey-Valette et al. (2015) also point out that sea-level rise and flooding are great threats to coastal second home communities in France.

Hoogendoorn and Fitchett (2018) argue that second home tourism is highly exposed to climate change. They underline that desirable remote locations with 'untouched' environments have limited capital and have significant issues in adapting to climate change hazards such as flood, drought, wildfire, and cyclones (Hoogendoorn & Fitchett, 2018). Cheong (2018) investigates the consequences of the Sandy Superstorm in Ortley Beach, New Jersey where the majority of the population is represented by second home owners. The houses have been damaged due to high winds and dune failure, as they had not been properly maintained and looked after. Without the support of a local government, second home owners abandoned their houses and chose to relocate (Cheong, 2018) (see also Adie, 2020, and Chapter 5, this volume). Hall (2014, 2018b) also emphasises the significance of climate change hazards such as temperature, sea-level rise, and storms with it being a growing threat to many second home destinations.

Planning/policy

The changing climate conditions require planning both for second home owners and local governments (Hall, 2018b). The literature emphasises that fluctuating populations, such as the seasonal nature of many second homes, may bring stress to public services at second home destinations due to an increase in water use, waste production, and other public services (Hall, 2014, 2018c). Also, environmental concerns have a significant impact on the distribution of infrastructure costs and its maintenance between local permanent residents and second home owners (Hall, 2015). The issue of costs is extremely significant when some form of protection is necessary for coastal locations due to sea-level rise and weather events (Scott et al., 2012) and especially the issue of who should pay for adaptation measures (Hall, 2018a).

Second home tourism and ownership have a major policy and planning impact in such vulnerable destinations (Hall, 2015). It is vital to include second home owners in policy and the decision-making process although processes may not be appropriately set up to accommodate this, given that lack of residency can prevent the capacity to participate in democratic processes (Hall, 2015). Osbaldiston et al. (2015) discuss some of the planning and policy issues surrounding climate change and second homes in coastal Australia. Especially of interest with respect to future adaptation is that they note that equivocal government policies towards climate change significantly influences second home owners' environmental concerns and perceptions. Furthermore, as in other jurisdictions where studies have been conducted, the exclusion of second home owners from planning processes leads to ambivalent policies, despite the significance of second homes in the governance and resource management of coastal areas in Eastern Victoria (Osbaldiston et al., 2015). Such issues reflect Müller et al's (2004) argument that permanent and second home owners have substantial distinctions which need to be taken into account by local governments. Since the two groups use the dwellings differently, it has implications on the obligations and functions of local governments. In fact, 48 out of 58 surveyed councils in New Zealand identified that second homes create significant planning issues to communities. Councillors struggle to identify second homes and often do not see the reasons why they need to keep records of such dwellings. While second home tourism introduces waste, water, infrastructure problems, the determination of second home impacts is difficult in such settings (Müller et al., 2004), while a failure to identify second homes results in a lack of councils' recognition of their role and impact.

Second home owners are often excluded from the research and public debates on community and regional futures with this group often ignored as this is not their primary place of residence (Cheong, 2018; Hao et al., 2020). A refusal to identify second home groups carries risks for communities, especially where a large proportion of the population at certain times of year is represented by second home owners. In the case of the Superstorm Sandy, Cheong (2018) shows that the government was not willing to support second home owners because that was not their primary place of residence. On the other side, second home owners were not willing to return and rebuild their second homes without financial support. As a result, the local community was hit the most with abandoned houses and the relocation of second home owners influencing community demographic and rebuilding with subsequent economic impacts (Cheong, 2018). This situation highlights the importance of considering second home owners as a group to be included in local government decision-making.

Risk perceptions

Planning and policy making are complicated by differences between local residents and second home owners in perceptions of climate change induced risks. There is some evidence that second home owners do not treat any climate change threats seriously (Adie, 2020; Cheong, 2018; Hall, 2018a). One of the major problems in the governance of the effects of climate change is the balance between short- and long-term costs. For example, some short-term implications are that second home owners will have to pay higher insurance premiums (Hall, 2018a). However, second home owners may believe that paying for insurance is not necessary as major cataclysms are unlikely to happen (Cheong, 2018). Moreover, potential natural hazards have little impact on second home ownership or place decisions (Adie, 2020).

Second home owners often underestimate or deny environmental risks (Adie, 2020). Long and Hoogendoorn (2013, 2014) argue that second home owners in Hartbeespoort, South Africa contribute to climate change, but they do not recognise these contributions nor believe that they are not responsible for climate change impacts. Rey-Valette et al. (2015) investigate second home owners' perceptions towards climate change risks and climate change adaptation policies. They highlight that second home owners are less concerned and sensitive to climate change threats but are more concerned about the application of any policies (Rey-Valette et al., 2015). Hiltunen et al. (2016) echo findings regarding second home owners' perceptions of climate change risks. In investigating second home owners in Finland, they note that second home owners are least concerned about environmental impacts, even if they acknowledge these impacts to some extent. Paradoxically second home owners may create the same disturbances they are escaping from in urban areas. Second home owners are more concerned about the area development, noise, and environmental pollution rather than the environmental harm that second homes bring (Kaltenborn et al., 2009).

While remote communities need development initiatives, they are more vulnerable and have higher costs of climate mitigations strategies (Hall, 2018b). The investigation of second home owners' perceptions is essential as it allows the understanding of attitudes towards evacuation, managed retreat, changes in property values, and mitigation and adaptation strategies (Hall, 2018a; Hao et al., 2020). Research on second home owners' perceptions with respect to climate change are therefore integral to planning, taxation, and effective governance.

Contribution of second home tourism to climate change: mobility, consumption, and construction

Mobility

Second home tourism contributes primarily to climate change through mobility (Hiltunen et al., 2016), consumption (Gössling, 2002; Hiltunen, 2007), and construction (García-Andreu et al., 2015) and associated land use change. Travelling to and from second dwellings is the major concern regarding the climate change impacts mainly because of fossil fuel consumption and production of GHG emissions. It is argued sometimes that second home tourism is more environmentally friendly since people travel shorter distances domestically instead of long-haul trips abroad (Adamiak et al., 2016; Hall, 2018c; Hall & Saarinen, 2021; Hiltunen, 2007; Seyfi et al., 2022). However, this depends on whether it is a substitute for more energy intensive travel or is in addition to.

While there is limited research regarding emissions and second home tourism, existing studies are not optimistic. Second home owners and users represent a highly mobile group of travellers which implies higher GHG emissions (Adamiak et al., 2016; Hall & Saarinen, 2021; Hiltunen, 2007; Næss et al., 2019). Hiltunen (2007) investigated several Lake District communities in Finland. The study shows that second home owners travel abroad as well as to a second dwelling. Travelling by car is the main way of moving between dwellings. Findings reveal that a trip by car to a second home produces approximately the same amount of CO2 as seven trips by bus to the same destination. Also, these trips are equal in CO2 emissions to two round trips from Helsinki to a Mediterranean resort by air in a year. Therefore, the ownership of a second home does not necessarily lead to CO2 reduction or substitution of long-haul international travels. Furthermore, the study indicated that people will keep using primary and secondary dwellings in the foreseeable future (Hiltunen, 2007).

Hiltunen's (2007) examination of the environmental impacts of rural second home tourism in Finland estimated that on average, 1264 kg CO_2 was emitted per year per car and 599 kg CO_2/year per person. Also in Finland, Ahlqvist et al. (2008) estimated that 1999 trips to second homes resulted in 0.4 million tons of CO_2 with trips to second homes accounting for 7 percent of all distance travelled by private cars. Interestingly, in analysing data from 2004–5, Ahlqvist et al. (2008) suggested that the annual energy consumption of second home related mobility was approximately 1070 GWh, equivalent to about 0.26 million tons of CO_2. In contrast, the use of electricity at second homes was only 500–900 GWh a year, highlighting the importance of mobility as a factor in second home related GHG emissions.

In a study of CO2 generation by second home tourism in Finland, Adamiak et al. (2016) found that second home owners visit second homes on average 25.9 times a year and users 10.3 times a year with the mean distance between the place of permanent residence and the second home being 167 km for second home owners and 229 km for users. Importantly, with respect to GHG emissions reduction, Adamiak et al. (2016) posed the question as to whether short domestic trips replace long-haul mobility, which would reduce the amount of emissions (see also Seyfi et al., 2022). They found that trips to second homes do not replace overseas trips. While there is some difference between owners, users, and non-users of second homes, all travellers make overseas trips with equal frequency. Trips to second homes by one owner are roughly equal in the CO2 emissions to a round-trip from Finland to Europe. Second home owners are therefore hypermobile travellers in comparison with users or non-users. However, non-users do travel to other destinations within a country (Adamiak et al., 2016). Therefore, in Finland, second home ownership or use do not make people infrequent travellers. On the contrary, ownership reflects more travel, which, in addition to trips abroad trips, produces more emissions.

The issue of second home tourism related CO2 emissions is highlighted when considering ownership of a second home abroad (Honkanen et al., 2016; Næss et al., 2019). Næss et al. (2019) reveal that overseas trips of Oslo residents to second homes contribute greatly to climate change. Travelling to a second home abroad has substantial impacts due to the travel distances and use of airplane as the main travel mode generating nearly 1650 kg CO_2 per capita over the 12-month period of the study. As Næss et al. (2019) note, the per capita CO_2 emissions of Oslo residents participating in the study and travelling to second homes overseas produce one-quarter of the mean of total CO2 emission per capita and is four times higher than people who travel to second homes domestically in Norway. However, travelling to second homes domestically contributes significantly to GHG emissions due to the numbers of trips and accounted for about 240 kg CO_2 emissions per year per respondent in Naess et al.'s (2019) survey. The intensity of domestic trips does not provide for compensation of international trips. Travelling by car is the prevailing mode of transportation between a permanent place of residence and a second home. Moreover, some people have a car just for travelling to a second home. Contrariwise, the absence of a second home stimulates international trips (Næss et al., 2019), highlighting some of the difficulties in curtailing emissions from tourism and the significance of understanding substitution effects (Seyfi et al., 2022).

Consumption

The second area of climate change contribution is related to consumption induced by second home tourism. While mobility between dwellings contributes to emissions of greenhouse gasses, the use of second homes possesses risks through the increased use of electricity and water (Hiltunen et al., 2016), waste production (Long & Hoogendoorn, 2013), and pollution of the natural environment (Long & Hoogendoorn, 2014), all of which can have implications for emissions. Hiltunen et al. (2016) suggest that the use of electricity, water, and production of waste are significant concerns for small communities in remote areas (Hiltunen et al., 2016). Remote areas, where second homes are usually located, often have scarce resources of water and poor infrastructure, so the seasonal increase of residents may create additional pressure on a limited resource base, leading to pollution and/ or inefficient use. Similarly, Long and Hoogendoorn (2014) speculate that second home tourism substantially affects water, sewage system, and electricity use in some South African destinations. For example, the recreational purpose of second homes implies higher usage of electricity. The major issue with electricity consumption is that the source is primarily coal-powered electric stations which produce significant emissions (Long & Hoogendoorn, 2014).

The use of utilities in second homes that are vacant is another area of concern. In Finland, some second homes consume electricity by keeping them warm throughout the year (Hiltunen et al., 2016). In Hartbeespoort, South Africa, Long and Hoogendoorn (2014) reason that second homes use water and electricity while being vacant. Systems such as water sprinklers, alarm security, electrical fencing are the major power consumers in empty houses. Additionally, the temporal occupation of second homes brings fire risks in the dry climate due to the uncontrolled growth of gardens (Long & Hoogendoorn, 2014).

Construction

Another worrying area of second home tourism is the construction of new dwellings. The construction of new homes has become an income source for local governments in many remote mountain and coastal areas (Kaltenborn et al., 2008). While Müller (2004) argues that converting old homes may not create unwanted environmental impacts, Gallent et al. (2005) state that conversion or building of new properties does present threats. Also, the construction of new homes can disturb the environment (Hiltunen, 2007). Considering the locations of second homes in coastal and mountain areas, Hiltunen (2007) stresses that development in such areas implies negative impacts since new developments change the landscape and the soundscape (Hiltunen, 2007). In addition to landscape alterations, García-Andreu et al. (2015) state that second home development increases water demand and noise pollution in Alicante, Spain. Hence, the aesthetic appeal of natural areas degrades and introduces new demand for local natural and public resources due to the development of new dwellings.

In many places, construction of second homes has become a part of local and regional investment strategies (Hall, 2018c). Paris (2018) argues that the purpose of owning a second home is shifting to a hybrid form of leisure and commercial use. While the weekend use of second homes contributes to carbon dioxide emissions due to the frequency of motorised and air trips both domestically and internationally, the situation potentially gets worse in the light of investment properties which may also be used as rental accommodation. Initially, the seasonal use of second homes for recreational purposes not only involves consumption of utilities but also increases demand for additional services including special infrastructure which in turn makes people travel more often to the attractive areas (Aall, 2011). Short-term and medium-term lettings highlight the issues of mobility, consumption, and construction of second homes even more. If an owner is not using a second home and opts to let it, the remote areas become accessible to a wide range of local and international tourists. For example, a second home may be used to escape to urban areas for a weekend. In the case of letting, the use of second home shifts from a weekend gateway to any available day throughout the week. Furthermore, the availability of peer-to-peer platforms for short-term lettings increases the mobility of people. This may not be a concern if it is a substitute for longer distance travel, but as noted earlier in this chapter, there is no evidence to show that this is the case. In addition, building second homes for commercial use adds environmental concerns and may raise realty prices and have unwanted flow-on effects in communities which may influence their capacity for change. Additionally, communities where the majority of the population are second home owners may suffer if owners suddenly decide to sell their properties (Hoogendoorn & Fitchett, 2018). The constant changing temporary population, comprised of different owners or tourists, may therefore place substantial stress on community cohesion and identity and alter behaviours, attitudes, and sense of place in relation to the environment.

Conclusions

It is often argued that tackling second home tourism related climate impacts requires changing the behaviour of owners and users of second homes. Næss et al. (2019) suggest strategies aiming to reduce the number of privately owned and used second homes in favour of collective dwellings. However, the substitution of a second home with a collective cabin of the Norwegian Trekking Association arguably contradicts the idea of second home holidays for most Norwegians, especially with respect to notions of place. Hiltunen (2007) suggests reducing tourists' mobility by increasing fuel prices or providing opportunities to work from home. Of course, in the case of the latter, it may be possible to work from both homes. The opportunity to restrict physical mobility and work from home was provided by lockdowns in 2020/2021 due to the COVID-19 outbreak. In Norway, Jacobsen et al. (2021) found that despite lockdown restrictions, there were limited impacts on people's future behaviour to spend Easter holidays differently. The motivation to escape a daily routine and have holidays remains strong (Jacobsen et al., 2021). Physical restrictions of mobility to change people's behaviour represents a utopian idea. For example, the possibility of being locked in a small apartment in urban areas encouraged many people to flock to second homes in the UK, the US, Greece, Spain, Italy, and other countries (Gallent, 2020; Pitkänen et al., 2020; Seraphin & Dosquet, 2020). The situation suggests that as long as people are willing to keep travelling and use second homes, then they will (Hiltunen, 2007). Applying the 'polluter pays' principle (Hall, 2008) may not work since the costs will fall on second home owners and users, who may then travel elsewhere instead or change their travel behaviour in such a way that it negatively affects second home destinations. Demarketing of second home use or vacations may only shift the spending to more environmentally harmful choices of tourism with more emissions (Hall &

Wood, 2021; Seyfi et al., 2022). Promotion of strategies to reduce emissions need to provide 'green' alternatives (Hall, 2018b) that still meet second home users' expectations of ease of access in order to be likely to succeed. However, second home areas are often in rural areas with poor public transport access that could offer an alternative to private cars.

Second home tourism is a significant form of regular tourism mobility in many countries and is a potentially significant aspect of tourism's contribution to climate change. However, there is a relative dearth of research in this area compared to other aspects of tourism (Hall, 2018c). Nordic studies dominate in second home tourism research (Müller, 2021) and constitute three of the chapters in the present volume. But there is a need to extend research to a wider geographical base (Hoogendoorn & Fitchett, 2018).

Mobility, consumption, and construction areas cover questions of whether second home tourism provides more climate-friendly tourism opportunities. Nevertheless, there is limited knowledge of many areas in second home tourism and climate change research (Hall, 2018c; Scott et al., 2023). Further research may extend the knowledge of second home owners' and users' behaviour, especially in regards to the difference between internationally and domestically owned second homes. The commercial use of second homes also represents a new angle from which to view climate change impacts, especially in the light of highly accessible and unregulated letting online platforms which serve to encourage further mobility. Additionally, researchers need to better understand mobility within second home destinations while also considering both the short- and long-term effects of climate change. This book therefore addresses a number of significant issues with respect to the relationship between second homes and climate change. However, many more remain in the desire to lessen tourism's contribution to climate change and improve second home tourism related mitigation and adaptation.

References

Aall, C. (2011). Energy use and leisure consumption in Norway: An analysis and reduction strategy. *Journal of Sustainable Tourism*, *19*(6), 729–745. https://doi.org/10.1080/09669 582.2010.536241

Adamiak, C., Hall, C. M., Hiltunen, M. J., & Pitkänen, K. (2016). Substitute or addition to hypermobile lifestyles? Second home mobility and Finnish CO_2 emissions. *Tourism Geographies*, *18*(2), 129–151. https://doi.org/10.1080/14616688.2016.1145250

Adie, B. A. (2020). Place attachment and post-disaster decision-making in a second home context: A conceptual framework. *Current Issues in Tourism*, *23*(10), 1205–1215. https://doi.org/10.1080/13683500.2019.1600475

Adie, B. A., & de Bernardi, C. (2020). 'Oh my god what is happening?': Historic second home communities and post-disaster nostalgia. *Journal of Heritage Tourism*. https://doi.org/10.1080/1743873X.2020.1828429.

Ahlqvist, K., Santavuori, M., Mustonen, P., Massa, I., & Rytkönen, A. (2008). *Vapaa-ajan asumisen ekotehokkuus (VAPET) Mökkeily elämäntapana ja ekotehokkaiden käytäntöjen hyväksyttävyys* [Eco-efficiency of leisure housing (VAPET) Summer cottages lifestyle and the acceptability of ecoefficient practices]. TTS tutkimuksen raportteja ja oppaita 36. Työtehoseura.

Cheong, S.-M. (2018). Second homes and vulnerability after superstorm Sandy in Ortley Beach, New Jersey. *The Professional Geographer*, *70*(4), 583–592. https://doi.org/10.10 80/00330124.2018.1432369

Coppock, J. T. (Ed.). (1977). *Second homes: Curse or blessing?* Pergamon.

Dower, M. (1977). Planning aspects of second homes. In J. T. Coppock (Ed.), *Second homes: Curse or blessing?* (pp. 155–164). Pergamon.

Dubois, G. (2005). Indicators for an environmental assessment of tourism at national level. *Current Issues in Tourism*, *8*(2–3), 140–154. https://doi.org/10.1080/13683500508668210

Gallent, N. (2020). COVID-19 and the flight to second homes. *Town & Country Planning*, *89*(4/5), 141–144.

Gallent, N., Mace, A., & Tewdwr-Jones, M. (2005). *Second homes: European perspectives and UK policies*. Routledge. https://doi.org/10.4324/9781315243580

García-Andreu, H., Ortiz, G., & Aledo, A. (2015). Causal maps and indirect influences analysis in the diagnosis of second-home tourism impacts. *The International Journal of Tourism Research*, *17*(5), 501–510. https://doi.org/10.1002/jtr.2017

Gössling, S. (2002). Global environmental consequences of tourism. *Global Environmental Change*, *12*(4), 283–302. https://doi.org/10.1016/S0959-3780(02)00044-4

Gössling, S., Scott, D., & Hall, C. M. (2020). Pandemics, tourism and global change: A rapid assessment of COVID-19. *Journal of Sustainable Tourism*, *29*(1), 1–20. https://doi.org/1 0.1080/09669582.2020.1758708

Hall, C. M. (2005). *Tourism: Rethinking the social science of mobility*. Pearson.

Hall, C. M. (2008). Tourism and climate change: Knowledge gaps and issues. *Tourism Recreation Research*, *33*(3), 339–350. https://doi.org/10.1080/02508281.2008.11081557

Hall, C. M. (2014). Second home tourism: An international review. *Tourism Review International*, *18*(3), 115–135.

Hall, C. M. (2015). Second homes planning, policy and governance. *Journal of Policy Research in Tourism, Leisure and Events*, *7*(1), 1–14. https://doi.org/10.1080/19407963. 2014.964251

Hall, C. M. (2018a). Case Study New Zealand: Planning responses to coastal climate change risks: the case of Christchurch and the Akaroa Harbour, New Zealand. In A. Jones & M. Phillips (Eds.), *Global climate change and coastal tourism: Recognizing problems, managing solutions and future expectations* (pp. 231–246). CABI.

Hall, C. M. (2018b). Climate change and its impacts on coastal tourism: Regional assessments, gaps and issues. In A. Jones & M. Phillips (Eds.), *Global climate change and coastal tourism: Recognizing problems, managing solutions and future expectations* (pp. 27–48). CABI.

Hall, C. M. (2018c). The future of second homes. In C. M. Hall & D. K. Müller (Eds.), *The Routledge handbook of second home tourism and mobilities* (pp. 355–360). Routledge.

Hall, C. M., Amelung, B., Cohen, S., Eijgelaar, E., Gössling, S., Higham, J., Leemans, R., Peeters, P., Ram, Y., & Scott, D. (2015). On climate change skepticism and denial in tourism. *Journal of Sustainable Tourism*, *23*(1), 4–25. https://doi.org/10.1080/09669582.2014.953544

Hall, C. M., & Müller, D. K. (Eds.). (2004). *Tourism, mobility, and second homes: Between elite landscape and common ground*. Channel View Publications. https://doi.org/10.21832/9781873150825

Hall, C. M., & Müller, D. K. (Eds.). (2018a). *The Routledge handbook of second home tourism and mobilities*. Routledge.

Hall, C. M., & Müller, D. K. (2018b). Governance and planning for second homes. In C. M. Hall & D. Müller (Eds.), *The Routledge handbook of second home tourism and mobilities*. Routledge.

Hall, C. M., & Page, S. J. (2014). *The geography of tourism and recreation: environment, place and space* (4th ed.). Routledge.

Hall, C. M., & Prayag, G. (Eds.). (2023). *Tourism, cyclones, hurricanes, and flooding.* Channelview.

Hall, C. M., & Saarinen, J. (2021). 20 years of Nordic climate change crisis and tourism research: A review and future research agenda. *Scandinavian Journal of Hospitality and Tourism*, *21*(1), 102–110. https://doi.org/10.1080/15022250.2020.1823248

Hall, C. M., Scott, D., & Gössling, S. (2020). Pandemics, transformations and tourism: Be careful what you wish for. *Tourism Geographies*, *22*(3), 577–598. https://doi.org/10.108 0/14616688.2020.1759131

Hall, C. M., & Wood, K. J. (2021). Demarketing tourism for sustainability: Degrowing tourism or moving the deckchairs on the titanic? *Sustainability*, *13*(3), 1585. https://doi. org/10.3390/su13031585

Hao, H., Eulie, D., & Weide, A. (2020). An integrative approach to assessing property owner perceptions and modeled risk to coastal hazards. *ISPRS International Journal of Geo-Information*, *9*(4), Art. 275. https://doi.org/10.3390/ijgi9040275

Hiltunen, M. J. (2007). Environmental impacts of rural second home tourism – Case Lake District in Finland. *Scandinavian Journal of Hospitality and Tourism*, *7*(3), 243–265. https://doi.org/10.1080/15022250701312335

Hiltunen, M. J., Pitkänen, K., & Halseth, G. (2016). Environmental perceptions of second home tourism impacts in Finland. *Local Environment*, *21*(10), 1198–1214. https://doi.org/ 10.1080/13549839.2015.1079701

Honkanen, A., Pitkänen, K., & Hall, C. M. (2016). A local perspective on cross-border tourism. Russian second home ownership in eastern Finland. *The International Journal of Tourism Research*, *18*(2), 149–158. https://doi.org/10.1002/jtr.2041

Hoogendoorn, G., & Fitchett, J. M. (2018). Perspectives on second homes, climate change and tourism in South Africa. *African Journal of Hospitality, Tourism and Leisure*, *7*(2), 1–18.

Jacobsen, J. K. S., Farstad, E., Higham, J., Hopkins, D., & Landa-Mata, I. (2021). Travel discontinuities, enforced holidaying-at-home and alternative leisure travel futures after COVID-19. *Tourism Geographies*, 1–19. https://doi.org/10.1080/14616688.202 1.1943703

Johansen, K. (2019). Local support for renewable energy technologies? Attitudes towards local near-shore wind farms among second home owners and permanent area residents on the Danish coast. *Energy Policy*, *132*, 691–701. https://doi.org/10.1016/j. enpol.2019.04.027

Kaltenborn, B. P., Andersen, O., & Nellemann, C. (2007). Second home development in the Norwegian mountains: Is it outgrowing the planning capability? *The International Journal of Biodiversity Science & Management*, *3*(1), 1–11. https://doi. org/10.1080/17451590709618158

Kaltenborn, B. P., Andersen, O., & Nellemann, C. (2009). Amenity development in the Norwegian mountains Effects of second home owner environmental attitudes on preferences for alternative development options. *Landscape and Urban Planning*, *91*(4), 195–201.

Kaltenborn, B. P., Andersen, O., Nellemann, C., Bjerke, T., & Thrane, C. (2008). Resident attitudes towards mountain second-home tourism development in Norway: The effects of environmental attitudes. *Journal of Sustainable Tourism*, *16*(6), 664. https://doi. org/10.2167/jost792.0

Long, D., & Hoogendoorn, G. (2013). Second home owners' perceptions of a polluted environment: The case of Hartbeespoort. *South African Geographical Journal*, *95*(1), 91–104. https://doi.org/10.1080/03736245.2013.806112

Long, D., & Hoogendoorn, G. (2014). Second home owner perceptions of their environmental impacts: The case of Hartbeespoort. *Urban Forum*, *25*(4), 517–530. https://doi.org/10.1007/s12132-013-9208-y

Marjavaara, R., & Müller, D. K. (2007). The development of second homes' assessed property values in Sweden 1991–2001. *Scandinavian Journal of Hospitality and Tourism*, *7*(3), 202–222. https://doi.org/10.1080/15022250601160305

Müller, D. K. (2002). Second home ownership and sustainable development in Northern Sweden. *Tourism and Hospitality Research*, *3*(4), 343–355. https://doi.org/10.1177/146735840200300406

Müller, D. K. (2004). Mobility, tourism and second homes. In A. A. Lew, C. M. Hall, & A. M. Williams (Eds.), *A companion to tourism* (pp. 387–398). Blackwell.

Müller, D. K. (2021). 20 years of Nordic second-home tourism research: A review and future research agenda. *Scandinavian Journal of Hospitality and Tourism*, *21*(1), 91–101. https://doi.org/10.1080/15022250.2020.1823244

Müller, D. K., & Hall, C. M. (2003). Second homes and regional population distribution: On administrative practices and failures in Sweden. *Espace Populations Sociétés*, *21*(2), 251–261.

Müller, D. K., & Hall, C. M. (2018). Second home tourism: An introduction. In C. M. Hall & D. K. Müller (Eds.), *The Routledge handbook of second home tourism and mobilities* (pp. 3–14). Routledge.

Müller, D. K., Hall, C. M., & Keen, D. (2004). Second home tourism impact planning and management. In C. M. Hall & D. K. Müller (Eds.), *Tourism, mobility, and second homes: Between elite landscape and common ground* (pp. 15–32). Multilingual Matters. https://doi.org/10.21832/9781873150825-004

Müller, D. K., & Hoogendoorn, G. (2013). Second homes: Curse or blessing? A review 36 years later. *Scandinavian Journal of Hospitality and Tourism*, *13*(4), 353–369, http://doi.org/10.1080/15022250.2013.860306

Næss, P., Xue, J., Stefansdottir, H., Steffansen, R., & Richardson, T. (2019). Second home mobility, climate impacts and travel modes: Can sustainability obstacles be overcome? *Journal of Transport Geography*, *79*, 102468. https://doi.org/10.1016/j.jtrangeo.2019.102468

Osbaldiston, N., Picken, F., & Duffy, M. (2015). Characteristics and future intentions of second homeowners: A case study from Eastern Victoria, Australia. *Journal of Policy Research in Tourism, Leisure and Events*, *7*(1), 62–76. https://doi.org/10.1080/1940796 3.2014.934689

Paris, C. (2018). Australian holiday homes: Places of escape and sites of investment. In C. M. Hall & D. K. Müller (Eds.), *The Routledge handbook of second home tourism and mobilities* (pp. 152–166). Routledge.

Pitkänen, K., Hannonen, O., Toso, S., Gallent, N., Hamiduddin, I., Halseth, G., Hall, C. M., Müller, D. K., Treivish, A., & Nevedova, T. (2020). Second homes during Corona – Safe or unsafe haven and for whom?: Reflections from researchers around the world. *Finnish Journal of Tourism Research*, *16*(2), 20–39.

Priddle, G., & Kreutzwiser, R. (1977). Evaluating cottage environments in Ontario. In J. T. Coppock (Ed.), *Second homes: Curse or blessing?* (pp. 165–180). Pergamon.

Rey-Valette, H., Rulleau, B., Hellequin, A.-P., Meur-Férec, C., & Flanquart, H. (2015). Second-home owners and sea-level rise: The case of the Languedoc-Roussillon region (France). *Journal of Policy Research in Tourism, Leisure and Events*, *7*(1), 32–47. https://doi.org/10.1080/19407963.2014.942734

Scott, D., Gössling, S., & Hall, C. M. (2012). International tourism and climate change. *Wiley Interdisciplinary Reviews. Climate Change*, *3*(3), 213–232. https://doi.org/10.1002/wcc.165

Scott, D., Hall, C. M., Rushton, B., & Gössling, S. (2023). A review of the IPCC Sixth Assessment and implications for tourism development and sectoral climate action. *Journal of Sustainable Tourism*, https://doi.org/10.1080/09669582.2023.2195597.

Seraphin, H., & Dosquet, F. (2020). Mountain tourism and second home tourism as post COVID-19 lockdown placebo? *Worldwide Hospitality and Tourism Themes*, *12*(4), 485–500. https://doi.org/10.1108/WHATT-05-2020-0027

Seyfi, S., Hall, C. M., & Saarinen, J. (2022). Rethinking sustainable substitution between domestic and international tourism: A policy thought experiment. *Journal of Policy Research in Tourism, Leisure and Events*. https://doi.org/10.1080/19407963.2022.2100410.

Strandell, A., & Hall, C. M. (2015). Impact of the residential environment on second home use in Finland – Testing the compensation hypothesis. *Landscape and Urban Planning*, *133*, 12–23. https://doi.org/10.1016/j.landurbplan.2014.09.011

Williams, A. M., & Hall, C. M. (2002). Tourism, migration, circulation and mobility. In C. M. Hall & A. M. Williams (Eds.), *Tourism and migration: New relationships between production and consumption* (pp. 1–52). Springer Netherlands. https://doi.org/10.1007/978-94-017-3554-4_1

Zoğal, V., Domènech, A., & Emekli, G. (2022). Stay at (which) home: Second homes during and after the COVID-19 pandemic. *Journal of Tourism Futures*, *8*(1), 125–133.

2 Tourism development and climate change adaptation

Second homes, connectivity and building resilience to wildfires in Wye River, Australia

Leonardo Nogueira de Moraes and Alan March

Introduction

This chapter explores the interfaces between second home tourism and climate change adaptation (CCA) from the perspective of broader community integration and resilience to natural hazards and disasters, to include those staying at second homes and investment properties – their owners and their guests. It also identifies some of the additional challenges and opportunities for emergency management (EM) in dealing with those staying at second homes, who can exhibit a broad spectrum of skills, knowledge of and connection to place.

Findings presented in this chapter emerged from the research project *Wildfire Disaster Preparedness, Response and Recovery in Coastal Tourist Destinations: the case of Wye River, Australia.* The project's broader aim was to explore the effects of tourism development on local resilience to natural-hazard disasters, especially those exacerbated by climate change, such as wildfires. This chapter specifically addresses the following research questions: *How does second home tourism interplay with CCA and EM in a Victorian coastal destination located in a wildfire-prone area? What relevant implications do research findings bring to tourism and second home studies?*

Wye River (38°38'5.18"S 143°53'25.79"E) is a small coastal town in Victoria, Australia with a population of 63 residents and 199 dwellings recorded in the 2016 Australian Census. The relatively low proportion of residents for Wye River's housing stock highlights the number of investment properties offered for short-term rentals to visitors and of second homes (holiday houses) owned by metropolitan and regional dwellers who voluntarily and temporarily relocate to this town for retreat and recreation at certain times of the year. On 25 December 2015, extreme wildfires forced the emergency evacuation of Wye River residents and visitors, interrupting the Christmas celebrations of many. While the bushfire resulted in no human casualties, 98 houses were lost (Inspector-General for Emergency Management (IGEM), 2016), about half of the township's housing stock recorded in 2016 (ABS, 2018). This number rises to 116 if impacted houses from neighbouring Separation Creek are accounted for.

Data collection involved fieldwork for direct observation during the township's recovery phase, ten semi-structured interviews with representatives from

DOI: 10.4324/9781003091295-2

governmental and non-governmental organisations operating at local, regional, state and national levels, and desktop research for the sourcing of news media, meeting minutes, reports, Australian Bureau of Statistics (ABS) 2016 Census Data, Tourism Research Australia (TRA) National Visitor Survey (NVS), and International Visitor Survey (IVS) statistical data, and relevant documents published by community and government organisations. The project employed qualitative data analysis following a Grounded Theory approach supported by the development of interactive timelines for data visualisation.

Second homes, short-term rentals, and climate change

To explore the interfaces between second home tourism and CCA is a relevant task because second home owners' investment in the destination can be multidimensional, inclusive of an emotional nature that is "reflected in the expression of a strong attachment to place" (Blondy et al., 2018, p. 242). When they feature as places of repeated family reunions across several years, these second homes can become primary sources of memorable events and experiences that bring together different generations. And when its generational character is brought alongside first-hand experience of climate change related impacts upon places of secondary residence, they bring opportunities for building climate change awareness and action that could benefit both the areas of second and primary residence.

Importantly, second homes constitute surplus housing stock that can become part of disaster relief if temporarily made available for those helping with relief efforts or who have lost their homes. With the advent of short-term rental platforms such as AirBnB, this possibility has been promoted as a way of supporting affected communities during the 2019–2020 Australian summer bushfires. Through a program called Open Homes, the platform sought to encourage the offering of free accommodation between 1 January 2020 and 16 January 2020 for those "displaced or [. . .] helping with relief efforts" (AirBnB, 2020).

Short-term rentals also play a significant role outside times of disaster, bringing complexity to the nature and impacts of second homes on local communities. By shifting the focus on property from emotional to financial investment, short-term rentals may become the primary purpose of second homes over time, stimulating the development of financial investment property markets and potentially driving displacement of local residents, especially long-term renters who are traditional residents. In other words, visitors' greater spending capacity can translate as price increases for local year-round renters, thus increasing the rent gap and affecting housing affordability for local residents (Yrigoy, 2018). For more on the *rent gap* and its implications, see Clark (2018).

The platform-enabled peer-to-peer nature of sharing economy services such as AirBnB can translate as challenging to regulate (Gurran et al., 2018) but has not stopped different responses from local communities and policymakers. These can range from banning the advertisement of properties on the platform altogether (Christiania, Copenhagen, Denmark) to imposing limits on the number of guests that can be hosted per year, or limits to yearly nights that can be offered as short-term rentals (Nieuwland & van Melik, 2018). Nevertheless, the potential for significant negative externalities associated with the rise of short-term rentals in popular tourist destinations is a critical part of the debate and research on overtourism (Dodds & Butler, 2019; Milano et al., 2019), also flagged as a pressing planning research agenda (Gurran, 2017).

Crucially, attachment to place and knowledge of local conditions will differ greatly between generational second home owners (and their families and friends) and one-off visitors staying in short-term rentals. This can shift the landscape of challenges and opportunities for CCA in the context of disaster response (Nogueira de Moraes & March, 2020a, 2020b), potentially affecting overall settlement resilience (Leonard et al., 2016; Nogueira de Moraes & March, 2020a, 2020b) and bringing to light questions of disaster justice (March et al., 2020).

The significance of second home tourism and the growth of short-term rentals in Australia

The concept of second home tourism has been defined by Hall and Müller (2004, 2018) as complex and multidimensional with 'second home' being an umbrella term for many specialisations. Second homes are a significant part of Australian domestic intrastate tourism and, in the case of Victoria, shape a "belt along the coast between 80 and 200 kilometres either side of the City of Melbourne" (Frost, 2004, p. 162).

Second homes also feature as a significant housing surplus stock, with ABS (2016) data pointing to 9.1% of Australia's dwellings being unoccupied on Census night in 2016. In that same year, TRA recorded 84,799,277 international and 131,387,000 domestic overnights in private accommodation or that owned by their family or friends, respectively representing 33.64% and 40.73% of total international and domestic overnights for 2016. In 2019, absolute numbers have respectively decreased 0.1% and increased 22.8%. In sharp contrast, overnights in short-term rentals have increased 16.8% for international visitors (from 95,192,179 to 111,232,000) and 28.3% for domestic visitors (from 27,794,000 to 35,651,000) over that same period (TRA, 2021a, 2021b). Figure 2.1 illustrates this trend since 2005 for international visitors.

Hall and Müller (2004) suggest that, in addition to non-mobile homes such as houses and apartments, second homes also comprise semi-mobile camping structures such as trailers, recreational vehicles (RVs), tents and caravans. In 2019, TRA recorded this segment as accounting for 4,962,277 or 1.81% of total domestic overnights (TRA, 2021b).

Second homes and climate change disaster risk reduction in the context of COVID-19

In 2020, international tourism was brought to a halt due to COVID-19, and domestic tourism, especially interstate, decreased considerably due to border restrictions and metropolitan areas undergoing lockdown. The challenges brought by

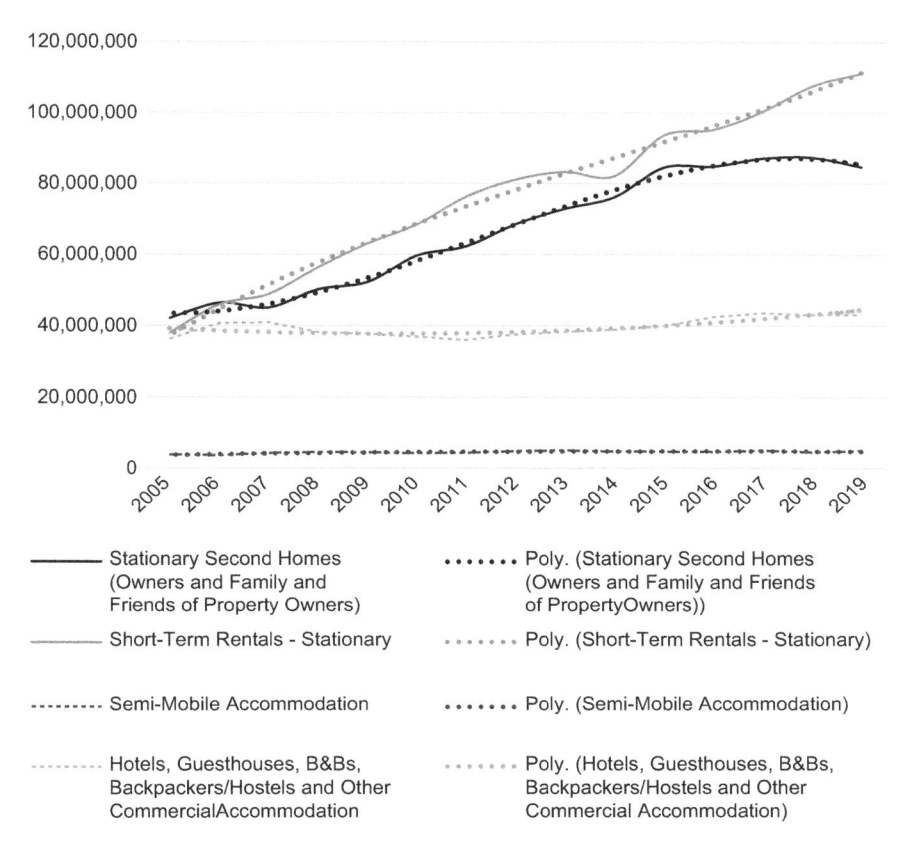

Figure 2.1 International visitor overnights by type of accommodation per calendar year (based on data from TRA, 2021a)

lockdowns and COVID-19 restrictions and the opportunities brought by working-from-home arrangements also translated as an urban exodus, resulting in increased demand for housing in regional areas. Coastal areas such as Victoria's Surf Coast experienced this trend more significantly, reaching a 0% vacancy rate in December 2020 and a median property value of $1,038,253, representing an increase of 5.8% in 12 months (Terzon, 2021).

In that context, second homes may help buffer COVID-19-induced increases in housing demand in regional areas by being made available for rent or purchase. However, there is also the question of whether they may act as a gateway for the displacement of local coastal communities by former metropolitan residents. This is from the standpoint that they can allow a quick demographic shift from seasonal to permanent populations, with implications to year-round demand for infrastructure and specific products and services. As new residents keep their metropolitan city jobs and pay rates while working remotely, they are likely to have greater spending capacity for renting and buying regional properties, driving property prices and long-term rents higher. While they also bring increased demand for services and products that are likely to result in new local employment and business opportunities, it is unclear whether these are being captured by those residents with longer histories of attachment to and engagement with these places.

When it comes to EM arrangements, COVID-19 brought additional layers of complexity to the interplay between second homes and CCA. This complexity was highlighted by the overlapping of responding to the pandemic and bushfire season preparedness efforts. In October 2020, the state of Victoria was still battling its second wave of COVID-19 infections, with most of them concentrated within a ring-fenced Metropolitan Melbourne under strict levels of lockdown. As part of the effort to reduce fuel levels within and around properties, owners are required to "carry [. . .] out fire prevention work such as mowing, trimming and clearing gutters" to ensure their properties are fire-ready. In this context, Metropolitan Melbourne dwellers with second homes in regional Victoria who were required to carry out fire prevention work were able to apply for a special permit to travel outside of ring-fenced areas for that purpose (Colac Otway Shire, 2020). This was especially relevant to settlements with a large number of holiday homes in *bushfire-prone areas* (those in the State of Victoria that have been formally assessed as prone to wildfires and, as a consequence, are subject to specific building and planning controls aimed at reducing disaster risk), such as Wye River in Victoria.

Contemporary EM, CCA, DRR and resilience-building in Australia

Australia's long history of natural hazard management includes indigenous cultural practices of controlled landscape burning as part of *Caring for Country* (Weir, 2020). Following European settlement, successive significant wildfire events such as Black Thursday (1851), Black Friday (1939) and Ash Wednesday (1983) have been critical for the ongoing development of contemporary EM arrangements across all governance levels. Australia's close engagement with the UN's International Decade for Natural Disaster Reduction in the 1990s and subsequent formulation of the Hyogo and Sendai Frameworks meant not only an early national adoption of disaster risk reduction (DRR) principles and practices but an active contribution to its development at the international level.

More recently, the 2009 Victorian bushfires and the 2019–2020 Australian summer fires had a profound impact on many communities, businesses and economies across the country, triggering critical State and Commonwealth Commissions of Inquiry. Notably, the 2009 Victorian Bushfires Royal Commission of Inquiry called for a *shared responsibility* approach (Teague et al., 2010) that was later reinforced by the 2011 National Strategy for Disaster Resilience (Council of Australian Governments, 2011), also providing the necessary platform for contemporary national resilience-building arrangements.

Following the devastating Australian 2019–2020 summer fires, the 2020 Royal Commission into National Natural Disaster Arrangements (NNDA) included a significant focus on inquiring into arrangements in place in 2019 and 2020 in light of climate change. Previously, the 2018 National Disaster Risk Reduction Framework was a critical national document seeking to integrate climate change action and EM through DRR and resilience-building (RB).

However, evolving through rather separate paths that would only occasionally acknowledge crossovers, CCA and EM have developed their own terminology, principles and framings, which still challenge a broader integration between the two. When it comes to CCA, Australian efforts and discourse seem to focus on coastal hazard and drought-prone areas, whereas for EM, the emphasis has been traditionally on wildfire-prone and flood-prone areas.

In that context, framing CCA and EM using a disaster resilience perspective highlights the former is largely focused on addressing increasing chronic stresses, whereas the latter has done the same for acute shocks. Notwithstanding, acute shocks such as wildfires have been acknowledged to grow in frequency and intensity because of climate change related stressors such as extended droughts and rising temperatures (NNDA, 2020). For coastal towns that are in wildfire-prone areas and undergoing climate-related coastal changes such as Wye River, there is an opportunity to bring CCA and EM concepts together through DRR and RB initiatives.

Victoria

The State of Victoria is Australia's southernmost mainland state, covering approximately 227,495.6 sq km, with a population of 5,926,624 recorded in the 2016 census. By December 2019, Victoria was estimated to have 6,658,771 inhabitants (ABS, 2020a) and to have hosted 3,137,432 international visitors and approximately 29,748,000 domestic overnight trips over that same year (TRA, 2021a, 2021b), the second greatest numbers in Australia.

Victoria's capital city, Melbourne, is an international tourist destination in its own right, an important gateway to Australia and renowned for hosting significant international events such as the Australian Open tennis tournament and the Melbourne Formula One Grand Prix. It is home to a number of Australian universities of international significance and, pre-COVID-19, featured as one of the leading hosts for a large number of international students arriving in Australia every year. In 2019, it accounted for 309,483 international students or 32.3% of all international students enrolled in Australia that year (956,773) (Department of Education, Skills and Employment (DESE), 2020).

Domestically, Greater Melbourne is an important visitor market. In 2019, it comprised a resident population of 5,078,193 people (ABS estimate for 2020, roughly 20% of Australia's population) in comparison to 1,517,846 people in the rest of Victoria (ABS, 2020a). Recording a median total income of A$50,648 (excluding government pensions and allowances) in the 2017–2018 financial year, Greater Melbourne residents earnt 1.7% more than the average Australian (A$49,805) and 12.6% more than those residing in the rest of Victoria (A$44,967) (ABS, 2020b). In 2017, greater Melbourne residents accounted for 12,756,000 trips or 26% of all intrastate trips in Victoria (49,226,000) (TRA, 2021b). This included respectively

10,679,000 and 954,000 visits from the Melbourne and Peninsula Victorian tourism regions, and 1123,000 from the Melbourne East Victorian tourism sub-region. Due to misalignment between Victorian tourism region boundaries and the ABS boundaries for Greater Melbourne, there is a portion of residents from the Macedon, Goulburn, and Upper Yarra tourism subregions whose trips are not accounted in this total but who would be considered part of Greater Melbourne by ABS.

Barwon South West

Administratively, the 48 regional and rural council areas across Victoria are divided into five regions and ten regional cities. The Barwon South West administrative region covers the State's West coast and Southern Grampians and includes all municipalities that form the Great Ocean Road tourism region in addition to the Greater Geelong Regional City and the Borough of Queenscliff. (For destination marketing reasons, Victorian tourism regions do not always align with regional administrative boundaries.)

In terms of EM arrangements, Barwon South West's Regional Emergency Management Plan (REMP) (Barwon South West Regional Emergency Management Planning Committee (REMPC), 2020), released in late 2020, outlines a response strategy to natural hazards based on risk assessment and management principles prescribed in the National Emergency Risk Assessment Guidelines (NERAG) (Australian Institute for Disaster Resilience, 2020). As part of the EM reforms triggered by the 2009 VBRC, an integrated all-hazards approach has been emphasised with the implementation of Emergency Management Victoria and the State Crisis and Resilience Council. These reforms also resulted in the development and implementation of an EM planning framework that instituted state, regional and municipal EM planning committees responsible for the formulation and implementation of state, regional, and municipal emergency management plans. The REMP supports the Victorian State Emergency Management Plan (SEMP) (Emergency Management Victoria (EMV), 2020) and is complemented by nine multi-hazard Municipal Emergency Management Plans (MEMPs) (Borough of Queenscliffe, 2019; City of Greater Geelong, 2018; Colac Otway Shire Council, 2014; Corangamite Shire Council, 2019; Glenelg Shire Council, 2019; Moyne Shire Council, 2020; Southern Grampians Shire Council, 2016; Surf Coast Shire Council, 2019; Warrnambool City Council, 2017). Importantly, REMPs are aligned with Victoria's administrative regions, which also play a role in operationalising the formulation of Climate Adaptation Plans.

Based on Municipal Climate Adaptation Plans, regional climate adaptation priority risks for the next five and fifty years were proposed by the Climate Resilient Communities of the Barwon South West project. These priority risks comprise those related to wildfires, coastal erosion and sea-level rise, heat stress, floods, pressure on water supplies and tourism.

In relation to tourism, the Regional Climate Adaptation Priorities Report lists "increased summer community and tourist participation in outdoor activities" (ARUP, 2017a, p. 9) as a priority risk for council to control at the municipal level, while also acknowledging an increase from low to high risk of wildfires and heatwaves, damaging tourism attractions/facilities and reducing tourism opportunities/visitation and regional revenue (ARUP, 2017a). When it comes to wildfire risk to community homes and residential properties, this is identified as more pronounced, being listed as high in the next five years and as extreme for the next fifty (ARUP, 2017a).

Released in late 2020, Barwon South West's Bushfire Management Strategy, deals specifically with wildfires. This strategy supplements the 2011 Regional Strategic Fire Management Plan, which was effective when the 2015 Wye River Separation Creek fires occurred. While the recent strategy makes a clear link between climate change and increased bushfire disaster risk, the 2015 strategy only marginally refers to climate change listing "appropriate mitigation and adaptation to the potential impacts of climate change" as one of 11 key drivers for fire management in the Barwon South West Region. The same applies to Barwon's South West REMP, whose only reference to climate change are in two listed projects that have been funded by the Barwon Regional Partnership Climate Adaptation Project – Local Government and Emergency Management – one on development of a Human Life Loss Probability Framework associated with the impacts of bushfires, and another on the development of a Bushfire House Loss Model. However, regardless of this distinction, both the 2015 and the 2020 strategies address CCA through their proposed actions, using EM terminology.

The 2015 Wye River Christmas Day fires feature as a significant wildfire event in the 2020 strategy, which also acknowledges cascading consequences that can increase vulnerability to other climate-related natural hazards such as heavy rain. On that note, following the 2015 Wye River Fires, "there were up to 100 landslips in Wye River and Separation Creek" resulting in road closures that "caused up to 300 accommodation cancellations, affecting profits for local business" (Department of Environment, Land, Water and Planning (DELWP), 2018b, p. 6). As part of the Victorian State Government investment in CCA, A\$53 million was committed "to fund geotechnical hazard mitigation work along the Great Ocean Road" (DELWP, 2018b, p. 6).

The Great Ocean Road tourism region

For the Victorian government, the Great Ocean Road Tourism Region is a "flagship tourism destination which is vital to Victoria's visitor economy" (DELWP, 2021a). While the road itself is only 243 kilometres long and links Torquay (Surf Coast Shire) and Allansford (Warrnambool City), the Great Ocean Road Tourism Region is marketed as comprising multiple destinations along the road and within its surroundings, including the municipalities of Surf Coast Shire (Torquay, Anglesea, Aireys Inlet and Lorne), Colac Otway Shire (the Otways and Apollo Bay), Corangamite Shire (12 Apostles Coast and Hinterland) and Warrnambool City (Warrnambool), and extending further into Moyne Shire (Port Fairy) and Glenelg Shire (Portland) (Great Ocean Road Regional Tourism (GORRT), 2021).

"Like many international tourist destinations, the Great Ocean Road is challenged by increasing numbers of visitors, forces of nature – and the impacts of climate change" (D'Ambrosio, 2018). In 2019, the Great Ocean Road welcomed 1,046,347 international visitors, equivalent to 12% of all international visitors to Australia. In that same year, it ranked as the fourth Victorian international tourist attraction, only behind Melbourne's CBD shopping district (1,980,683), Queen Victoria Market (1,369,904) and Federation Square (1,188,590) (TRA, 2021a).

As one of the most visited regional destinations in Victoria, the Great Ocean Road has been the focus of concern when it comes to the need to manage its tourism development in an integrated manner. As part of the Great Ocean Road Action Plan, new legislation and governance arrangements are being implemented by the Victorian state government, including the institution of a statutory authority to "protect and manage coastal Crown land along the length of the Great Ocean Road" (DELWP, 2021a). Incorporating the former Great Ocean Road Coast Committee and the Otway Coast Committee, the authority's "primary purpose is to protect and manage visitation of the Great Ocean Road Coast and Parks" (DELWP, 2021a). The implementation of the Great Ocean Road Action Plan is expected "to draw on the experience of cooperative efforts during the Wye River Bushfire Reconstruction process" (DELWP, 2021b).

Otway fire district

Within the Great Ocean Road tourism region, the Otway Forest spreads over the municipalities of Surf Coast Shire, Colac Otway Shire, and Corangamite Shire, with the second concentrating the forest's core. Considering the forest's high level of wildfire risk (highlighted in the plan as one of the most bushfire-prone areas in Australia and the world (Otway District Bushfire Planning Collaboration, 2017)) and the need to better integrate fire management planning and acknowledge landscape boundaries in administrative arrangements, from 2017, individual municipal fire management plans for each shire were replaced and superseded by a single Strategic Fire Management Plan for the Otway District. Based on fire spread modelling, the plan's assessment of bushfire risk profiles places Wye River as one of the top two localities in the district with the highest level of overall risk, the highest tourism factor and a very high score in potential house loss in comparison to total houses in town (Otway District Bushfire Planning Collaboration, 2017).

According to the report, the tourism factor refers to

The relative degree to which tourism is a feature of each town, understanding that tourists are likely to be more vulnerable and large visitor numbers can pose additional risk – e.g., traffic issues.

(Otway District Bushfire Planning Collaboration, 2017, p. 31)

It further explains it as:

The degree to which the usual population of the town expands during the summer months, which also coincides with higher fire danger ratings – ranked. As another major component of susceptible people, in some areas tourists form a substantial proportion of the population and this leads to those areas having a higher risk.

> (Otway District Bushfire Planning Collaboration, 2017, p. 60)

Colac Otway Shire

The Wye River settlement is part of the Colac Otway Shire. With an area of 3437.5 sq km, the Shire was the primary home to 21,564 residents in 2019 (ABS, 2020a) and comprises the core districts of Colac Central, East and West and Elliminyt, its surrounding rural north and rural south districts and its only coastal district, the Great Ocean Road Otways, in its very south. In the 2016 census, 8.8% of its employed population was working with accommodation and food services, an industry representing 134 businesses in that same year (up to 149 in 2019). Medium sale prices for houses in Colac Otway were estimated at A\$350,000 in 2019, an increase of 25% from 2015 prices (A\$280,000) (for a total of respective 384 and 334 transfers) (ABS, 2018).

Developed as part of the Climate Resilient Communities of Barwon South West project, the Colac Otway Shire Council Climate Change Adaptation Plan acknowledges regional climate change projections will translate as an "increase in number of days that emergency services must be fire-ready" (ARUP, 2017b, p. 1), the requirement for increased pre-wildfire-season preparedness and the "increased vulnerability of those in [wildfire] prone areas" (ARUP, 2017b, pp. 1–2). It also highlights that "high terrain areas of the Shire, along the Great Ocean Road, will be the wettest areas" and that the "Wye River Caravan Park is also expected to be affected by inundation" (ARUP, 2017b, pp. 1–2) due to sea-level rise.

"Building community awareness" is listed as the first wildfire priority risk action, including "working with tourism operators and holiday rental owners to raise awareness and build capacity of the sector to understand [wildfire] risk" (ARUP, 2017b, p. 13). That, coupled with the promotion of fire resilient landscaping and "information about retrofitting homes to meet relevant standards" (ARUP, 2017b, p. 13), are actions directly relevant to second homes and short-term rental investment properties. In terms of coastal inundation, the plan seeks to establish foundations for future adaptation actions by ensuring the completion of the Local Coastal Hazard Assessment, the incorporation of "climate change projections into future flood studies" (ARUP, 2017b, p. 13) and their consideration for new developments.

Responding to the experience of the 2015 Wye River fires, adaptation plan activities include "research steps to mitigate bushfire risk to homes" and the development of "materials for tourism operators to ensure the sector and tourists are aware of what to do in an emergency (especially [wildfires])" (ARUP, 2017b, pp. 15–16) with the key performance indicator (KPI) of "20 holiday rentals hav[ing] emergency procedures in place" (ARUP, 2017b, p. 15) by December 2020.

The Otways Region and the Otway Coast Hamlets

The Otway Coast Hamlets destination is a distinct part of the Otways region, comprising a section of the scenic coastline of the Great Ocean Road. Located between Lorne and Apollo Bay, the Otway Coast Hamlets stretch from Mount Defiance to Petticoat Creek, including the townships of Separation Creek, Wye River, and Kennett River as well as Grey River, Wongarra, and Sugarloaf. West of the Hamlets, the Otways region coastline extends to include Apollo Bay (Apollo Bay is marketed both as part of the Otways as well as alongside it), Cape Otway and its light station, as well as Johanna. Inland, the Otways region accounts for vast areas of hinterland and some farmland, featuring the Great Otway National Park and a few regional towns and villages including Beech Forest, Birregurra, Colac, Deans Marsh, Forrest, Gellibrand, Lavers Hill and Pennyroyal. Importantly, the Otway Coast Hamlets and Cape Otway are marked by extensive forested areas that overlap a rugged and steep coastline along the Great Ocean Road, representing areas where the Otway Forest is at its closest to the Tasman Sea and the Southern Ocean.

As part of the recovery from the 2015 Wye River fires and following severe landslides exacerbated by bushfire vegetation clearing, Otway Hamlets Tourism (representing local tourism businesses and formerly known as the Otway Coast Tourism Association) played a critical role in liaising with the wider tourism industry organisations, government agencies and departments for investment on upgrades to vulnerable sections of the Great Ocean Road. Alongside relevant local and regional organisations (including the Wye River Progress Association, the Wye River Country Fire Authority Auxiliary, the Wye River Community Volunteers, the Otway Coast Committee, the Community Resilience Committee and the Community Connections and Wellbeing Committee), Otway Hamlets Tourism also played a significant role in the development of the Otway Coast Hamlets Destination Action Plan. "[F]acilitated by Great Ocean Road Regional Tourism Ltd (GORRT) . . . [the plan was] funded via Regional Development Victoria (RDV) as part of the recovery program for the 2015–2016 Bushfire" (GORRT, 2017, p. 2). Its vision highlights the importance of visitor experience management and ensuring community and visitor experiences are harmonic. "The visitor experience is seamlessly managed and supports sustainability of flora and fauna. The experience of visitors and local community members is symbiotic and mutually respectful" (GORRT, 2017, p. 5). Responsible tourism, environmental sustainability, respect for nature and resilience are listed as values; and the region's "uncommercialised coastal villages" (GORRT, 2017, p. 6) and the communities' connection with nature are highlighted as collective strengths. Among identified challenges, there are concerns about the threat of overtourism, potential processes of gentrification and climate change impacts, including: "Mass visitation management"; "Coastal inundation and erosion"; "Lack of community/holiday owners/involvement"; "Potential hostility/ tension between locals and industry"; "Cultural awareness and sensitivity – locals/ visitors" (GORRT, 2017, p. 7). Its Priority 4 focuses exclusively on Risk Management and targeting the preparation of "a Risk Management Plan for the local and visitor community, linked to the Colac Otway Disaster Management Plan . . . [that] consider[s] the impact of climate change" (GORRT, 2017, p. 15).

Concerns with increased visitation are not without reason. Compared to the overall Great Ocean Road region, the Otways have experienced a greater accumulated growth in domestic visitor nights since 1998 (59% versus 41%), reaching 1,151,579 nights in 2019 or about 15% of domestic visitor nights spent in the Great

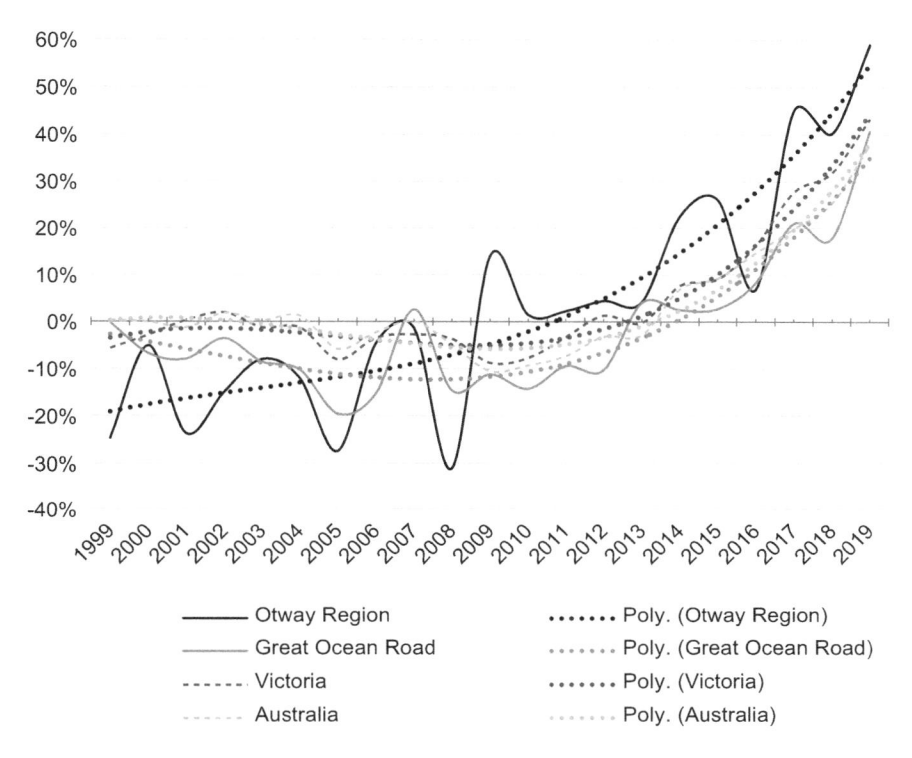

Figure 2.2 Accumulated growth of domestic visitor nights per calendar year since 1998–1999 (based on data from TRA, 2021b)

Ocean Road region. The Otways' accumulated growth is also higher than the Victorian and Australian averages over that same period (respectively 43% and 38%).

Wye River

Wye River is a small coastal settlement on forested steep terrain spreading on both sides of the Wye River valley as it meets the Great Ocean Road, between Separation Creek and Kennett River. The combination of fresh and calm river waters with a beach that normally offers gentle waves suitable for those learning to surf makes Wye River a very attractive destination to urban and countryside dwellers, including families with children.

In 2016, 63 residents were accounted in the census, representing less than 2% of the estimated population for the Otways region (3,429). In that same year, it accounted for 199 private dwellings or 5.44% of the region's total (3,652). Covering approximately 2.38% of the Otways region, Wye River's land area (35.87 sq km) is dominated by parkland (98.23%), with only 1.77% being classified by ABS (2018) as residential (0.6341 sq km). Table 2.1 highlights the high proportion of unoccupied dwellings on Census night in Wye River (75.88%) and the Otway Coast

Table 2.1 Wye River key population census data in the context of its micro and macro tourist regions, Local Government Area (LGA), state and national estimates (based on data from ABS, 2018)

Level	Statistical area	sq km	Residents	Median age	Families	All private dwellings	Average people per household	Occupied dwellings on Census night	Unoccupied dwellings on Census night (and % of total)
Suburb (SSC)	Wye River	35.9	63	50	7	199	1.3	48	151 (75.88%)
Tourist sub-region	Otway Coast Hamlets	151.7	174	50	36	500	1.5	118	382 (76.40%)
SA2 (LGA district)	the Otways region	1,506	3,429	52	838	3,652	2.1	1,632	2,020 (55.31%)
LGA	Colac-Otway Shire	3,438	20,972	45	5,275	11,625	2.3	9,118	2,507 (21.57%)
Tourist region	Great Ocean Road region	21,219	136,127	43	35,062	70,646	2.4	56,236	14,410 (20.40%)
State	Victoria	227,496	5,926,624	37	1,532,077	2,520,912	2.6	2,279,470	241,442 (9.58%)
National	Australia	7,688,126	23,401,892	38	6,070,316	9,901,496	2.6	9,000,727	900,769 (9.10%)

Hamlets (76.40%) in relation to the Otways region (55.31%), the Great Ocean Road region (20.40%), the State of Victoria (9.58%) and across Australia (9.10%). These data suggest a very high concentration of second homes and investment properties in Wye River and the Hamlets, which can be verified by the expressive number of short-term rental property listings online. In 2016, Wye River's housing stock represented two-fifths of that available in the Otway Coast Hamlets and the largest among all its suburbs.

The median age higher than 50 reported for Wye River and the Otways as a whole could also suggest that second homes in these areas may become their own-ers' primary homes once they retire and relocate there from areas with greater job opportunities within the region or from Metropolitan Melbourne. About 45% of res-idents fall into the 55 to 74 years bracket, with no residents in the 75 years or older bracket being recorded in 2016 (community profile data). Census data on mobility and internal migration highlight this trend, identifying that approximately 25.4% of Wye River residents with a primary address in Wye River in 2016 had a different primary address elsewhere in Australia in 2011, in comparison to 31.8% nationwide (ABS, 2018). Of these, the majority relocated from within the Otways region (about four-fifths) and the remaining from Metropolitan Melbourne (ABS, 2018).

Relatively, these numbers increase when a one-year period prior to the 9 August 2016 Census night is considered, for which 22.2% reported a different address elsewhere in Australia (in comparison to only 13.4% nationwide), and, from those, about seven eighths relocated from within the Otways region (ABS, 2018). This may be explained by 98 Wye River dwellings destroyed in the 2015 Christmas fires (IGEM, 2016), and the clean-up of affected lots only being completed in June 2016 (WyeSep Connect, 2016), roughly two months before Census night. Table 2.2 highlights that this is reinforced by the high rate of Wye River resident respondents who answered the Census from alternate addresses – 33.3% in comparison with a national average of 4.9%.

Table 2.2 Location of Census respondents on Census night (based on data from ABS, 2018)

Scale	Area	At home	Elsewhere in Australia
National level	Australia	95.1%	4.9%
Australian state or territory – STE	Victoria	95.5%	4.5%
Victorian administrative Region	Barwon South West Region	93.9%	6.1%
Victorian tourist region	Great Ocean Road Tourist Region	93.0%	7.0%
Local Government Area – LGA	Colac-Otway (S)	92.7%	7.4%
Statistical area level 2 – SA2 / LGA District	Otway	87.0%	13.0%
Victorian tourist sub-Region	Otway Coast Hamlets Tourist Sub-Region	77.8%	18.9%
Australian suburb – SSC	Wye River	61.9%	33.3%

Second homes in Wye River

Only about 162 km from Melbourne's CBD or roughly a two-hour, 20-minute drive, Wye River offers an accommodation stock for non-primary residents (in this chapter, primary resident refers to anyone who has spent more than six months in Wye River over the preceding 12 months) which is broadly comprised of:

- Several private properties that are both/either second homes and/or investment properties for short-term rental.
- Two caravan parks on the flatlands on the bottom of the Wye River Valley on both sides of the Great Ocean Road.

  - North of the Great Ocean Road, one privately owned and operated caravan park business on leased Crown land: BIG4 Wye River Holiday Park.
  - South of the Great Ocean Road, one publicly managed campground on Crown land: Great Ocean Road Coast and Parks Authority's Wye River Beachfront Campground (formerly the Otway Coast Committee's Wye River Foreshore Camping Reserve).

Currently, no accommodation hotels are listed on the official visitor webpage for Wye River in the Great Ocean Road Regional Tourism website (according to the Wye Beach Hotel (2021) website, it currently only offers food and beverages). Non-primary residents staying overnight in Wye River mostly fall into one of these categories (This classification takes into account the questions of ownership and its commercialisation and excludes traditional accommodation services such as hotels, motels, and hostels. Properties listed on platforms such as AirBnB fall into the category of short-term rentals.):

- Owners of second home stationary properties, or their families and friends.
- Families and friends of primary residents staying in their properties.
- Short-term renters of second home/investment stationary properties such as houses, apartments, cottages or self-contained units.
- Short-term renters of semi-mobile properties such as caravans, camper vans, cabins (in this context, a cabin is a moveable small wooden house sitting on a caravan park lot under an annual rent agreement), or tents that are already in Wye River or that they bring to Wye River with them.
- Owners of second home semi-mobile properties (such as caravans, camper vans, cabins or tents) that are already in Wye River or that they bring to Wye River with them; and their family and friends.

The last two categories may temporarily or quasi-permanently station their semi-mobile homes on private properties, on a commercial caravan park operating on leased Crown land, on designated areas within national parks and reserves with on-site and off-site management or on permitted parking spaces and roadsides.

In addition to hosting overnight visitors, Wye River is also a stopover or transit area for some of those touring the Great Ocean Road on daytrips or for overnight visitors staying in neighbouring destinations such as Lorne and Apollo Bay. TRA (2021b) data point to 335,537 daytrip domestic visitors to the Otway Region in 2019, in comparison to roughly four million to the Great Ocean Road. While many day trips originating in metropolitan Melbourne are likely to reach as far as the Surf Coast, the Twelve Apostles in Port Campbell is also a key driver of visitation to the Great Ocean Road and likely to generate transit through the Otway Region.

TRA's most granular NVS data highlight the importance of second homes for the Otway region over the years and the growth of short-term rentals and semi-mobile accommodation. (For the purpose of outlining the importance of second

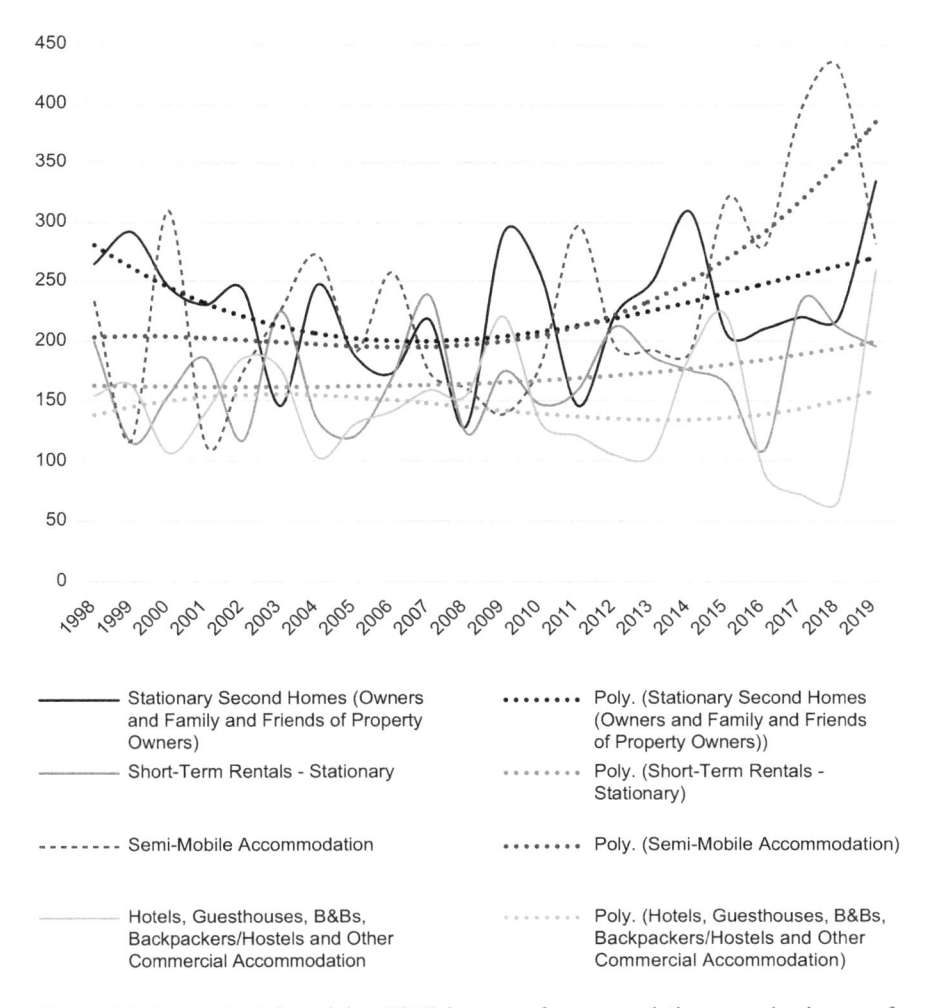

Figure 2.3 Domestic visitor nights ('000) by type of accommodation per calendar year for the Otways (based on data from TRA, 2021b)

home tourism to Wye River, this chapter uses the definitions of 'accommodation' and 'accommodation providers' in the *International Recommendations for Tourism Statistics 2008: Compilation Guide* (UN, 2016, pp. 156–159), in conjunction with TRA's data from the NVS and the IVS, while also acknowledging the complexity in defining and measuring second home tourism pointed out by Hall (2014) and Müller and Hall (2018)).

Currently, NVS's accommodation classification makes no distinction between owned and rented semi-mobile accommodation, but it makes a distinction between those camping or parking in commercial properties and those staying on crown land or non-commercial private properties. While it is common for RVs to be both privately owned for personal use or commercially rented for short terms, when it comes to glamping, a commercial accommodation classification introduced to the NVS in 2019, there seems to prevail the commercial model rather than the privately owned equipment for one's own personal use.

While places like Rottnest Island in Western Australia offer glamping through a local operator who is responsible for both the tents and the site, in Wye River, a commercial business offers the equipment rental and set up for stays in a caravan park that constitutes a separate business requiring a separate booking. This illustrates the difficulty in categorising visitors with the intent to profile second home tourism. While a camper who owns their own gear and who is a weekend regular at a campsite may consider the tent and the site as their second home for recreational purposes, those glamping as a one-off experience who hire both their gear and site may be closer to visitors staying in boutique hotels than to second home traditional campers.

Findings on degrees and nature of place attachment in second home induced mobility

Semi-structured interviews suggested the concept of 'tourist' can be blurred, tourists sometimes being perceived as only those without a history of regular visitation and local engagement. Primary residents may see all or some of those staying at second homes as tourists, whereas second home owners and their families who are regulars to Wye River may only consider non-regular visitors, or those without strong place attachment, as such. Similarly, the term 'visitor' is sometimes replaced by the term 'regulars' when it refers to specific groups. These multiple perspectives challenge the very idea of 'second home tourism' and absolute statistical definitions of tourist and tourism, rather offering the possibility to reflect upon categories that express a spectrum of attachment to place.

Previous research by Stedman (2006) suggests that, albeit portraying distinct features, high degrees of place attachment can be found in both seasonal and year-round residents. In that respect, Aronsson's research (2004) supports the idea that attachment to place might better profile second home groups rather than the exclusive reliance on the assessment of ownership of land and/or accommodation of physical structures permanently or temporarily sitting on them.

A nuanced understanding of attachment to place is relevant to CCA because it allows the exploration of expanded notions of home, and broader understandings of climate change impacts and root causes, helping highlight how agency in places of primary residence can be linked to conditions in places of second home. Potentially, these larger-scale notions of home may also reinforce individual and collective duty to the protection and the building of resilience to environmental change in areas that are neither of primary nor secondary residence.

Places where commons constitute important public spaces that are valued by regular and non-regular visitors, and by permanent residents with varying historical attachments to place, seem to positively contribute to extended notions of home. In the case of Wye River, that encompasses the beach, the river, the forest and the trails, but also the community as a whole and meeting places in venues such as the local hotel (in this case, the hotel is a pub without accommodation services, a rather common Australian feature), the café, the general store and the Wye River Surf and Life Saving Club. For caravan park regulars, whether they are used to staying on caravan parks run by commercial businesses or on public campgrounds managed by an independent statutory authority, notions of second home can also encompass park grounds and the regular visiting communities attached to them. These conditions have proved fertile ground for volunteering, community-building and engagement initiatives that link to disaster risk reduction (Nogueira de Moraes & March, 2020a, 2020b) but also potentially to climate action.

Location, density, accommodation size and the sharing of space and facilities may explain the important role that caravan park and camping grounds have in promoting Wye River's internal and external connectivity. That, in association with long-term community associations that link different groups connected to Wye River, may explain the relatively successful response to (insofar as no human lives were lost) and ongoing recovery from the 2015 Christmas fires. On that note, semi-structured interviews also suggested that one-off visitors staying on camping grounds may have a better chance to engage more widely with the overall holiday community than those staying in short-term rental stationary properties without onsite assistance or family/friendship ties with property owners. In that respect, the communal nature of camping ground environments could be an important factor in facilitating such engagement, which can be an important part of preparing for, responding to and recovering from disasters.

Conclusion

This chapter explored interfaces between second homes and CCA by interrogating the case of Wye River, Australia and the context in which it is embedded. It highlighted the complex multi-level and geographically overlapping governance arrangements that apply to this small settlement and the way these arrangements start to integrate CCA, EM and tourism development from the perspective of second homes, helping to illustrate the concept of polycentricity: "a governance system in which there are multiple interacting governing bodies with autonomy to make and enforce rules within a specific policy arena and geography" Schoon et al. (2015, p. 226)), as a principle for building resilience (Simonsen et al., 2014).

From a social-ecological systems perspective, connectivity and diversity also surfaced as critical principles in building resilience to disasters (Biggs et al., 2015) in the Wye River case. This is supported by the suggestion that specific conditions shaping a diverse spectrum of attachment to place may promote connectivity between different groups, resulting in increased resilience when it comes to preparing for, responding to and recovering from a disaster.

Findings also illustrated the challenges posed by seeking to define and operationalise the concept of second home (as previously raised by Hall (2014) and Müller and Hall (2018)), when it comes to understanding its contributions and impacts on managing disaster risk and building the resilience of local communities, calling for a critical reflection on how we define tourism, tourists and visitors more broadly so as to incorporate questions of attachment to and knowledge of place.

The Wye River case also evidences the role of learning from past disaster events across geographical, administrative and thematic domains in seeking to reduce future disaster risk and continue to build community resilience. In that respect, learning is acknowledged as a key component of complex adaptive systems and one of seven principles of building resilience proposed by the Stockholm Resilience Centre (see Simonsen et al., 2014). Analysis of the Wye River case shows increasing cross-fertilisation between CCA and EM arrangements with due acknowledgement of interfaces between tourism development and disaster risk and resilience in a community that is highly diverse in its degrees and forms of mobility and attachment to place. Whether these conditions will continue to translate as successful CCA in the long-term is yet to be observed.

These conclusions bring the opportunity to pose new questions around the disaster vulnerability of short-term renters without on-site assistance, the link between attachment to place/local knowledge and better disaster preparedness, and the role of visitor profile diversity (in terms of attachment to place and mobility) in the integration between visitors and residents for disaster risk reduction. In the context of COVID-19, there is also the extent to which second homes may constitute a powerful leverage accelerating processes of destination gentrification and local population displacement. Being relevant to tourism studies more broadly, these questions hold great potential to feed from and contribute to second home studies. Notwithstanding, findings presented here suggest that tourism research looking at second homes can highlight critical attachment to place nuances that could otherwise be overlooked.

Acknowledgements

The development of the research underpinning this chapter and the presentation of an early version of its findings in the 8th Nordic Geographers Meeting were made possible by the award of an Early Career Researcher Grant and a Conference Travel Grant by the University of Melbourne and its Faculty of Architecture, Building and Planning.

References

AirBnB. (2020). *Airbnb open homes – Bushfire – Find emergency housing in New South Wales*. Retrieved January 5, 2020, from www.airbnb.com.au/openhomes/disaster-relief

Aronsson, L. (2004). Place attachment of vacation residents: Between tourists and permanent residents. In C. M. Hall & D. K. Müller (Eds.), *Tourism, mobility and second homes: Between elite landscape and common ground* (pp. 75–86). Channel View.

ARUP. (2017a). *Climate resilient communities of the Barwon South West. Regional climate adaptation priorities report*. www.swclimatechange.com.au/resources/CRC%20BSW%20Regional%20Climate%20Adaptation%20Priorities%20Report%202017.pdf

ARUP. (2017b). *Colac Otway Shire Council. Climate change adaptation plan 2017–2027. Climate resilient communities of the Barwon South West*. www.swclimatechange.com.au/resources/Colac%20Otway%20Shire%20Climate%20Change%20Adaptation%20Plan.pdf

Australian Bureau of Statistics (ABS). (2018). *2016 census of population and housing*. www.abs.gov.au/websitedbs/censushome.nsf/home/tablebuilder

Australian Bureau of Statistics (ABS). (2020a). *Estimated resident population by local government area – 2001–2019*. http://stat.data.abs.gov.au

Australian Bureau of Statistics (ABS). (2020b). *Personal income in Australia 2017–2018*. www.abs.gov.au/statistics/labour/earnings-and-work-hours/personal-income-australia/latest-release

Australian Institute for Disaster Resilience. (2020). *National emergency risk assessment guidelines* [NERAG]. www.aidr.org.au/media/7600/aidr_handbookcollection_nerag_2020-02-05_v10.pdf

Barwon South West Regional Emergency Management Planning Committee (REMPC). (2020). *Barwon South West regional emergency management plan* [REMP]. https://files.emv.vic.gov.au/2021-05/Barwon%20South%20West%20Regional%20Emergency%20Management%20Plan_Redacted.pdf

Biggs, R., Schluter, M., & Schoon, M. L. (Eds.). (2015). *Principles for building resilience: Sustaining ecosystem services in social-ecological systems*. Cambridge University Press.

Blondy, C., Plumejeaud, C., Vacher, L., Vye, D., & Bontet, C. (2018). Do second home owners only play a secondary role in coastal territories? A case study in Charente-Maritime (France). In C. M. Hall & D. K. Müller (Eds.), *The Routledge handbook of second home tourism and mobilities* (pp. 233–244). Routledge.

Borough of Queenscliffe. (2019). *Municipal emergency management plan 2019–2021*. www.queenscliffe.vic.gov.au/files/assets/public/documents/for-residents/public-health/boq-municipal-emergency-management-plan-2019-21.pdf

City of Greater Geelong. (2018). *Municipal emergency management plan 2017–2019*. https://geelongaustralia.com.au/em/management/documents/item/8cb3337e450a096.aspx

Clark, E. (2018). Making rent gap theory *not* true. In A. Albet & N. Benach (Eds.), *Gentrification as a global strategy: Neil Smith and beyond* (pp. 74–84). Routledge.

Colac Otway Shire. (2020, October 21). *COVID restrictions update for Colac Otway Shire: Letter of approval to travel for fire preparation*. www.colacotway.vic.gov.au/News-media/COVID-Restrictions-Update-for-Colac-Otway-Shire

Colac Otway Shire Council. (2014). *Colac Otway Shire Municipal emergency mangement plan (MEMP)*. http://memp.colacotway.vic.gov.au/ch01s01s01.php

Corangamite Shire Council. (2019). *Municipal emergency management plan 2019–2021*. www.corangamite.vic.gov.au/Council/Publications/Plans-Strategies#section-5

Council of Australian Governments. (2011). *National strategy for disaster resilience: Buiding the resilience of our nation to disasters*. www.aidr.org.au/media/1313/nationalstrategyfordisasterresilience_2011.pdf

D'Ambrosio, L. (2018). Minister's foreword. In *Department of Environment, Land, Water and Planning (DELWP), Great Ocean Road action plan: Protecting our iconic coast and parks*. www.planning.vic.gov.au/__data/assets/pdf_file/0026/394271/GreatOcean-Road_ActionPlan.pdf

Department of Education, Skills and Employment (DESE). (2020). *International student data 2019*. https://internationaleducation.gov.au/research/international-student-data/Pages/InternationalStudentData2019.aspx#Pivot_Table

Department of Environment, Land, Water and Planning (DELWP). (2018b). *Regional adaptation snapshot: Barwon South West*. www.climatechange.vic.gov.au/?a=392919

Department of Environment, Land, Water and Planning (DELWP). (2021a). *Great Ocean Road action plan*. www.planning.vic.gov.au/policy-and-strategy/great-ocean-road-action-plan?fbclid=IwAR1nh9POWBquece7kjatfTasLzATogwXd_SlN5zV3aukkptYzPxZ8GmXz6o

Department of Environment, Land, Water and Planning (DELWP). (2021b). *Policies and initiatives*. www.planning.vic.gov.au/policy-and-strategy/great-ocean-road-action-plan/tab-pages/documents

Dodds, R., & Butler, R. W. (Eds.). (2019). *Overtourism: Issues, realities and solutions*. De Gruyter.

Emergency Management Victoria (EMV). (2020). *Victorian State emergency management plan* [SEMP]. https://files.emv.vic.gov.au/2021-05/Victorian%20State%20Emergency%20Management%20Plan%20SEMP%20_0.pdf

Frost, W. (2004). A hidden giant: Second homes and coastal tourism in south-eastern Australia. In C. M. Hall & D. K. Müller (Eds.), *Tourism, mobility and second homes: Between elite landscape and common ground* (pp. 162–173). Channel View.

Glenelg Shire Council. (2019). *Glenelg Shire Municipal emergency management plan 2019–2022*. www.glenelg.vic.gov.au/files/EmergencyManagement/ECM_2576536_v1_PUBLIC_VERSION_ECM_2576536_v1_Glenelg_Municipal_Emergency_Management_Plan_2019-2022_Audit_26_March_2.pdf

Great Ocean Road Regional Tourism (GORRT). (2017). *Otway Coast Hamlets. Separation Creek, Wye River, Kennett River & Wongarra. Destination action plan 2017–2020*. https://greatoceanroadtourism.org.au/wp-content/uploads/2020/03/Otway-Coast-Hamlets-Destination-Action-Plan.pdf

Great Ocean Road Regional Tourism (GORRT). (2021). *Towns and villages. Victoria's great Ocean Road region. Meet the locals*. www.visitgreatoceanroad.org.au/towns-and-villages/#

Gurran, N. (2017). Global home-sharing, local communities and the Airbnb debate: A planning research agenda. *Planning Theory & Practice*, *19*(2), 298–304. https://doi.org/10.1080/14649357.2017.1383731

Gurran, N., Searle, G., & Phibbs, P. (2018). Urban planning in the age of Airbnb: Coase, property rights, and spatial regulation. *Urban Policy and Research*, *36*(4), 399–416. https://doi.org/10.1080/08111146.2018.1460268

Hall, C. M. (2014). Second home tourism: An international review. *Tourism Review International*, *18*(3), 115–135. https://doi.org/10.3727/154427214x14101901317039

Hall, C. M., & Müller, D. K. (2004). Introduction: Second homes, curse or blessing? Revisited. In C. M. Hall & D. K. Müller (Eds.), *Tourism, mobility and second homes: Between elite landscape and common ground* (pp. 3–14). Channel View.

Hall, C. M., & Müller, D. K. (Eds.). (2018). *The Routledge handbook of second home tourism and mobilities*. Routledge.

Inspector-General for Emergency Management (IGEM). (2016). *Review of the initial response to the 2015 Wye River–Jamieson Track fire*. www.igem.vic.gov.au/reports-and-publications/igem-reports/review-of-the-initial-response-to-the-2015-wye-river-0

Leonard, J., Opie, K., Blanchi, R., Newnham, G., & Holland, M. (2016). *Wye River/Separation Creek Post-bushfire building survey findings. Report to the Victorian Country Fire Authority.* http://wyesepconnect.info/wp-content/uploads/2016/05/Wye-River-Separation-Creek-final-V1-1.pdf

March, A., de Moraes, L. N., & Stanley, J. (2020). Dimensions of risk justice and resilience: Mapping urban planning's role between individual versus collective rights. In A. Lukasiewicz & C. Baldwin (Eds.), *Natural hazards and disaster justice: Challenges for Australia and its neighbours* (pp. 93–115). Palgrave Macmillan.

Milano, C., Cheer, J. M., & Novelli, M. (Eds.). (2019). *Overtourism: Excesses, discontents and measures in travel and tourism.* CABI.

Moyne Shire Council. (2020). *Municipal emergency management plan.* www.moyne.vic.gov.au/Emergencies

Müller, D. K., & Hall, C. M. (2018). Second home tourism: An introduction. In C. M. Hall & D. K. Müller (Eds.), *The Routledge handbook of second home tourism and mobilities* (pp. 3–14). Routledge.

Nieuwland, S., & van Melik, R. (2018). Regulating Airbnb: How cities deal with perceived negative externalities of short-term rentals. *Current Issues in Tourism, 23*(7), 811–825. https://doi.org/10.1080/13683500.2018.1504899

Nogueira de Moraes, L., & March, A. (2020a). Disaster risk reduction beyond command and control: Mapping an Australian wildfire from a complex adaptive systems' perspective. In P. P. Santos, K. Chmutina, J. Von Meding, & E. Raju (Eds.), *Understanding disaster risk: A multidimensional approach* (pp. 205–224). Elsevier.

Nogueira de Moraes, L., & March, A. (2020b). Disasters, planning and Australian tourism. *Pursuit.* https://pursuit.unimelb.edu.au/articles/disasters-planning-and-australian-tourism

Otway District Bushfire Planning Collaboration. (2017). *Strategic fire management plan – Otway District. 2017–2020. Shires of Corangamite, Colac Otway and Surf Coast.* https://nla.gov.au/nla.obj-2962554923/view Royal Commission into National Natural Disaster Arrangements (NNDA). (2020). *Royal Commission into national natural disaster arrangements: Report.* https://naturaldisaster.royalcommission.gov.au/publications/royal-commission-national-natural-disaster-arrangements-report

Schoon, M. L., Robards, M. D., Meek, C. L., & Galaz, V. (2015). Principle 7: Promote polycentric governance systems. In R. Biggs, M. Schluter, & M. L. Schoon (Eds.), *Principles for building resilience: Sustaining ecosystem services in social-ecological systems* (pp. 226–250). Cambridge University Press.

Simonsen, S. H., Biggs, R., Schlüter, M., Schoon, M., Bohensky, E., Cundill, G., Dakos, V., Daw, T., Kotschy, K., Leitch, A., Quinlan, A., Peterson, G., & Moberg, F. (2014). *Applying resilience thinking: Seven principles for building resilience in social-ecological systems.* Stockholm Resilience Centre. www.stockholmresilience.org/download/18.1011 9fc11455d3c557d6928/1459560241272/SRC+Applying+Resilience+final.pdf

Southern Grampians Shire Council. (2016). *Municipal emergency management plan.* www.sthgrampians.vic.gov.au/Page/Page.aspx?Page_Id=2548

Stedman, R. C. (2006). Understanding place attachment among second home owners. *American Behavioral Scientist, 50*(2), 187–205. https://doi.org/10.1177/0002764206290633

Surf Coast Shire Council. (2019). *Municipal emergency management plan 2019–2022.* www.surfcoast.vic.gov.au/About-us/Council/Policies-plans-strategies-and-reports/Plans-and-strategies#section-3

Teague, B., McLeod, R., & Pascoe, S. (2010, July). *Final report. Summary.* 2009 Victorian Bushfires Royal Commission. www.royalcommission.vic.gov.au/finaldocuments/summary/HR/VBRC_Summary_HR.pdf

Terzon, E. (2021, January 8). Rental vacancy rates hit zero in Australian coastal towns as they hit COVID capacity. *ABC News*. www.abc.net.au/news/2021-01-08/surf-coast-rentals-at-zero-vacancy/13037172

Tourism Research Australia (TRA). (2021a). *IVS trips database*. http://traonline.tra.gov.au

Tourism Research Australia (TRA). (2021b). *NVS overnight trips database*. http://traonline.tra.gov.au

UN. (2016). *International recommendations for tourism statistics 2008 compilation guide*. https://unstats.un.org/unsd/tourism/publications/E-IRTS-Comp-Guide%202008%20For%20Web.pdf

Warrnambool City Council. (2017). *Municipal emergency management plan*. www.warrnambool.vic.gov.au/emergency-planning

Weir, J. (2020). Bushfire lessons from cultural burns. *Australian Journal of Emergency Management*, *35*(3), 11–12. https://knowledge.aidr.org.au/media/7810/ajem_05_2020-07.pdf

Wye Beach Hotel. (2021). *Wye Beach Hotel*. www.wyebeachhotel.com.au/

WyeSep Connect. (2016). *Clean-up zones: Wye River and Separation Creek*. www.wyesepconnect.info/clean-up/index.html

Yrigoy, I. (2018). Rent gap reloaded: Airbnb and the shift from residential to touristic rental housing in the Palma Old Quarter in Mallorca, Spain. *Urban Studies*, *53*(13), 2709–2726. https://doi.org/10.1177/0042098018803261

3 Impacts of climate change on Swedish second home tourism

O. Cenk Demiroglu, Dieter K. Müller,
Andreas Back, and Linda Lundmark

Introduction

The phenomenon of second home tourism has been labelled the 'hidden giant' of tourism (Frost, 2004) indicating the great number of second homes not least in amenity-rich mountain, lake, and coastal regions (Adamiak et al., 2017; Back & Marjavaara, 2017; Barke, 1991, 2007; Lundmark & Marjavaara, 2005; Müller, 2005, 2006; Opačić & Koderman, 2018; Ragatz, 1970; Shellito, 2006; Wolfe, 1951). However, even though the relationship between tourism and climate change has been in focus for quite a while, little has been said about the impacts of climate change on second home tourism. Generally speaking, second homes are privately owned residences, primarily for the recreational use of their owners (Hall & Müller, 2004). Although Hall (2015) notes that awareness for environmental issues in the second home literature is growing, focus is on protecting from negative impacts of second homes. Hitherto research on environmental dimensions of second home tourism has mostly regarded them as a cause of environmental disturbance in relation to landscape aesthetics and land use (Kaltenborn et al., 2008; Langdalen, 1980), ecology (Hiltunen et al., 2013; Kondo et al., 2012; Nellemann et al., 2010), or transport-related CO_2 emissions (Adamiak et al., 2016; Hiltunen, 2007). Furthermore, Kaltenborn et al. (2009), Hiltunen et al. (2016), Long and Hoogendoorn (2013), and Huhtala and Lankia (2012) address how second home owners and residents relate to environmental dimensions of second home tourism.

Thus, second home properties have not been approached as potential objects affected by environmental and climate change with a few notable exceptions such as Hoogendoorn and Fitchett (2018) who are using case studies to illustrate potential consequences of climate change on second home locations in South Africa, and Rey-Valette et al. (2015) assessing the perception of risk in relation to sea-level rise in France. Adie (2020) and Adie and de Bernardi (2020) add a post-disaster perspective to the topic, analysing how second home owners react when climate change has affected their properties. To add to the knowledge in this open and underexplored field, this chapter contributes a national perspective form Sweden. The objective is to assess the Swedish second home stock's exposure to risk caused by climate change.

DOI: 10.4324/9781003091295-3

Second homes and climate change

Second homes are not scattered randomly but, rather, the pattern mirrors geographies of settlements and amenity-rich areas, usually mountains, lakesides, and seashores (Müller, 2005, 2006). Often such locations are highly valued and regarded as attractive (Back & Marjavaara, 2017; Marjavaara & Müller, 2007). Besides visually attractive locations, these areas offer ample opportunities for outdoor recreation such as hiking and skiing, leisure activities on the beach, and water sports. In Sweden, a polarization towards these environments can be detected in overall statistics on second homes (Müller, 2002).

As shown in recent research, planners seldom address second homes as a matter for planning, and indirectly this means that they do not regard them as requiring any special treatment (Back, 2020). Exceptions are related to building restrictions, for example, to meet environmental objectives like the protection and accessibility of shorelines (Goble et al., 2014; Persson, 2015) or a mountain landscape (Brida et al., 2009; Kaltenborn et al., 2007; Langdalen, 1980). This lack of interest regarding second homes could in fact add to the vulnerability of second homes. The preferred shoreline and mountain locations coincide with those areas that are expected to be affected by the impacts of climate change in various ways (Swedish Meteorological and Hydrological Institute (SMHI), 2020). Even though the impacts of climate change differ among landscape types, they could cause similar socio-economic impacts (Table 3.1).

Table 3.1 Impacts of climate change on different second homes according to landscape type

Landscape type	Primary impacts	Secondary impacts
Coastal areas	Thermal comfort Heatwaves Sea-level rise Coastal erosion Storm surge Sea ice changes Sea temperature changes Eutrophication Salinization	Material impacts • Housing destruction • Infrastructure destruction • Changing property values • Heating/cooling related energy use • Biodiversity changes
Riverine areas	Thermal comfort Flooding Erosion Lake temperature Lake ice Brownification	
Mountain areas	Thermal comfort Erosion Avalanches Landslides Snow cover changes Snowfall intensification Floods Water stress	Emotional impacts • Sense of loss (sense of place) • Fragmented/lost community • Values attached to place are destroyed or diminished
Forest areas	Thermal comfort Fire	
Urban areas	Flooding Heatwaves	

Impacts of climate change are not equally distributed in neither time nor space. Particularly the occurrence of extreme weather events is difficult to predict and can hit seemingly random places with unforeseen force. This has, for example, been the case with Hurricane Sandy, a tropical cyclone, that in October 2012 swept over the US Atlantic coast with dramatic consequences for the impacted region. Halverson and Rabenhorst (2013) distinguish five impacts of the storm. Strong winds accelerated when hitting the coastline, also affecting the hinterlands. Consequently, high waves hit the coast but were also detected as far away as in the Great Lakes region. Heavy precipitation and early snowfall owing to the collision of air masses with great temperature differences and extreme temperatures were further impacts. In addition, the storm destroyed 540,000 buildings (Halverson & Rabenhorst, 2013).

Although this is an example of an extreme event, coastlines and buildings are affected even in more temperate climatic zones, where coastline erosion caused by storm and volatile sea level remoulds the topography of shorelines, eventually affecting buildings. Łabuz (2015) notes that climate change in the Baltic Sea region results in sea-level rise, storm surges, land erosion and habitat loss, precipitation and river discharge, and ice cover melt during wintertime. Particularly land erosion causes loss of economic value and private property and increasing cost to society in terms of coastal protection measures. Furthermore, Adie and de Bernardi (2020) report on the emotional costs of such change, not only relating to aesthetic values.

Similarly, riverine environments can be affected by flooding. For the UK, climate experts expected a climate change induced risk for flooding to increase by a factor of 30 (Ashley et al., 2005). Liu et al. (2015) assessed the related risk for property damages to increase dramatically, too. In their study of the US Midwest, they expected the risk for property damage to increase up to 17% during the coming two decades. However, they note that this increase is also due to the growth of housing units in the vicinity of the streams. Obviously, extreme weather events and erosion are additional impacts of climate change, also affecting riverine zones.

Climate change impacts have been studied intensively in relation to snow reliability and skiing (Demiroglu et al., 2013; Steiger et al., 2019). Projections show substantial impacts in the future, making skiing seasons shorter and more dependent on technical snow, which, however, contributes to erosion, too (Pintaldi et al., 2017). Because of alpine skiing, mountain areas are prominent locations for second homes (Flognfeldt & Tjørve, 2013; Lundmark & Marjavaara, 2005; Müller, 2005; Nepal & Jamal, 2011). This implies that second homes are constructed in areas that are exposed to erosion and landslides, and occasionally to flooding along small mountain creeks. Ski-in/ski-out opportunities further entail the construction of second homes in slope areas, particularly sensitive to climate change.

The impacts of climate change on second homes as discussed previously do not only affect the properties as physical structures. Infrastructure connecting the sometimes remotely located second homes to various supporting networks is also at risk. Finally, previous impacts can affect the market value of the properties simply because potential buyers disregard such locations or are not willing to pay the high prices. However, emotional impacts are additional responses caused by climate change (Adie, 2020; Adie & de Bernardi, 2020).

Despite an awareness of climate change, economic goals are often a priority when considering different development options. Hence, in a Canadian context, planners did not consider sea-level rise as a reason for action (Karim, 2019). And indeed, in Norway, second home construction in mountain areas has left increasing imprints on the mountain landscape, also because of a limited planning capacity in the affected municipalities (Kaltenborn et al., 2007, 2009). An explanation for this, it has been argued, is that second home tourists are an 'invisible population' for planners who are used to dealing with local inhabitants and their needs only (Back & Marjavaara, 2017; Czarnecki & Frenkel, 2015; Müller, 2007; Müller & Hall, 2003). This means that local administration often has poor knowledge on second homes as well as second home owners. Because of this, the potential impact of climate change on the total second home stock and its regional distribution has not been considered, and the problems that municipalities and second home owners alike are now starting to see are largely unknown.

Geographical distribution of second homes in Sweden

Sweden is among those countries where second homes are part of the national folklore and tradition (Marjavaara et al., 2019; Müller, 2007). With nearly 700,000 second home properties, apartments not included, more than 50% of the population have access to a second home (Müller, 2013; Back & Marjavaara, 2017). The geography of second home tourism in Sweden mirrors the spatial distribution of population and amenities, implying that most households actually have their second homes close by (Müller, 2006). Major concentrations of second homes are thus to be found around urban centers, while other concentrations can be found along the coastline and in the mountains (Lundmark & Marjavaara, 2005; Müller, 2004, 2005). It has been shown that interest is concentrating to rural locations that also function as major tourist destinations for domestic and Nordic markets (Back & Marjavaara, 2017; Marjavaara & Müller, 2007; Müller, 2002, 2011). This means that many Swedish second homes can be found in mountain and coastal resorts and locations, and that pressure to build new second homes is the greatest in these spots.

Based on the micro register data used by Back and Marjavaara (2017), we present a closer look at the distribution of second homes in Sweden. Considering an inventory of 667,843 second homes (limited to detached houses), the densest areas are found along the coastline, especially in close proximity to the three largest cities, as well as around the most visited ski resorts, exceeding 100 homes per square kilometre at certain clusters (Figure 3.1a). These clusters also coincide well to fall under the 'purpose-built vacation home' category (Figure 3.1b), which, following the original typology by Müller et al. (2004), is defined by Back and Marjavaara (2017) as a region that is not only dense with second homes that are far away (more than 80 km in Euclidean distance) from the primary residences of their owners but also observes an upward trend in the number of second homes which outnumber other detached houses, keeping the average second home age relatively new – below and including the sample median of 32 years.

From an amenity perspective (Figure 3.1c), 34% (n: 229,140) of the second homes are within a five km buffer from the sea coast, including islands, and 37%

(n: 248,460) lie within only one kilometre from lakes and major rivers. Running a service area analysis, based on a transport network dataset provided on ArcGIS Online (Esri, 2021a, 2021b), we also determine the share of second homes within a 20-minute rural driving time, which takes account of the travel on unpaved roads, to a lift-based ski area, including those in the non-mountainous regions, to be 26% (n: 173,552). As another significant amenity aspect, the share of second homes within urban areas is 21% (n: 137,499). Last but not least, 92% (n: 615,169) of the second homes are found to be located either within or just one km away from forest areas, while it should be noted that Sweden is an extensively forested country with 59% of its land cover classified as broad-leaved, coniferous, or mixed forests (European Environment Agency (EEA), 2020).

A critical variable that indicates the patterns of second home localizations is the assessed property tax value (in SEK). While the data is from 2012, it is still consistent across the census for comparisons. After a normalization by dividing each second home's value by its respective living space (m^2), an economic landscape was obtained (Figure 3.1d). Once again, coastal areas, especially in the vicinity of the larger cities, as well as the surroundings of the major ski resorts, become highlighted with high values. However, it should be noted that, due to a large extent of missing values for the property value and/or the living space, the sample size is restricted down to 405,104, and the map displays the results for an average of these values per square kilometre to maintain anonymity of the individual properties.

A further elaboration on the spatial determinants of unit property values is then carried out with a regression analysis. While the results can explain only a small fraction ($R^2 = 10\%$, $p<0.01$) of the variance in the values – which is quite expected as there would be many other spatial and non-spatial attributes to consider for valuation – the estimated coefficients (all significant with $p<0.01$) indicate the direction and the magnitude of the effects of second home locations on their values (1). Accordingly, a location within 5 km from the sea coast adds 8,967 SEK/m^2 to the second home property tax value while 10 SEK/m^2 is lost for each additional rural driving minute away from a ski lift. Presence within an urban area also has a positive effect on the value with an increment of 15 SEK/m^2 per 1,000 inhabitants – here, the population acting as a proxy for the degree of urbanization to further distinguish the magnitude of added value. Proximity (1 km buffer) to a major water source or a forest, as well as presence within a forest, are associated with second homes with relatively lower assessed property tax values per square metre. This resonates the significance of the urban/rural divide in the Swedish second home landscapes (Figure 3.1b and 3.1c) but does not necessarily reject the popularity of lake/riverside and forest areas for second home development, as these places still contain 37% and 92% of the second homes in Sweden, respectively, as mentioned previously.

$$Property\,Tax\,Value(SEK)/Living\,Space(m^2) = 8,967 Coastal\_$$
$$Location + 0.015 Urban\_Population - 10 Distance\_to\_Ski\_Lift -$$
$$722 Lake\_River\_Location - 2,307 Forest\_Location + 14,076$$

(1)

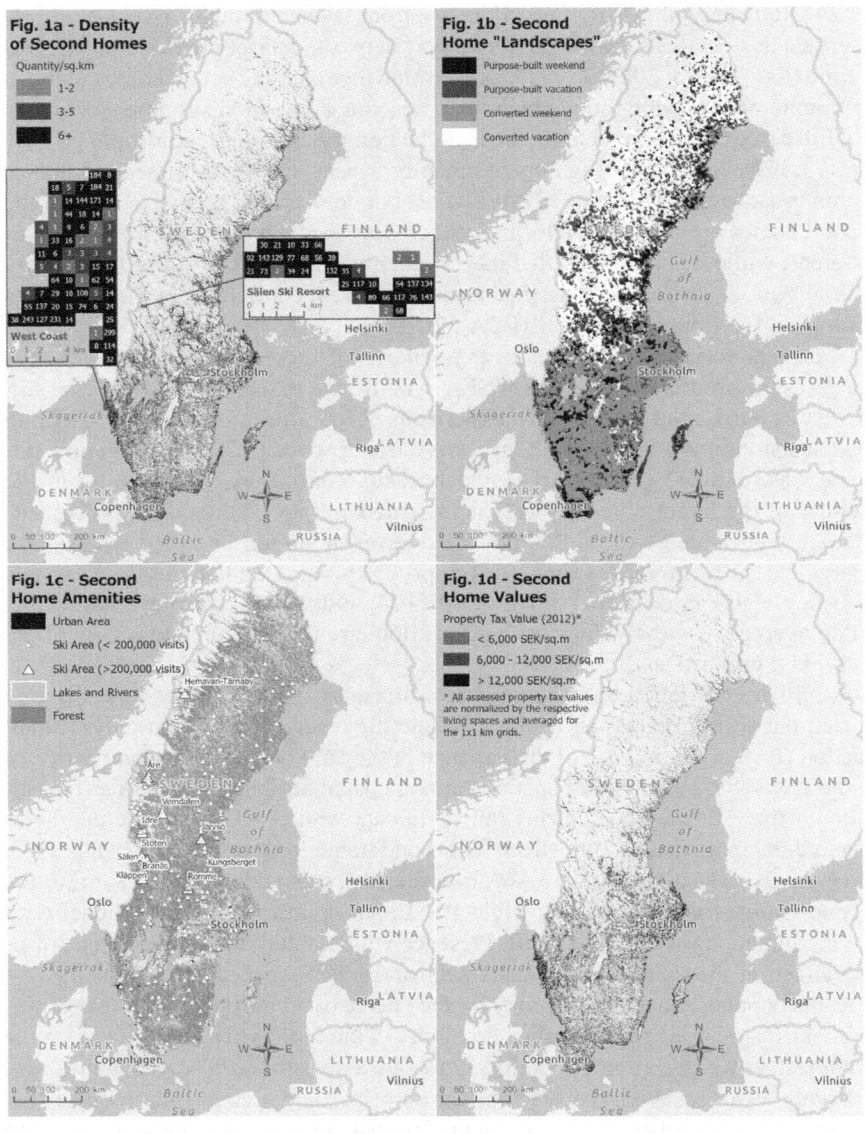

Data Sources: Back & Marjavaara, 2017; Demiroglu et al., 2019; EEA, 2020; SCB, 2021   Projected Coordinate System: SWEREF99 TM
Base Map: ArcGIS Pro "Light Gray Canvas" from Esri, HERE, Garmin, FAO, NOAA, USGS   Cartographer: O. Cenk DEMIROGLU, 2021

Figure 3.1 Distribution patterns of second homes in Sweden according to (a) density, (b) 'landscapes', (c) amenities, and (d) assessed property tax values

Climate change impacts on the amenity-based landscapes of second homes in Sweden

As seen previously, certain amenity clusters act among the major determinants of localisations and valuations of second homes in Sweden. In this respect, ongoing and future impacts of climate change should be well understood primarily in terms of the said amenity-based landscapes. Here, the Swedish Portal for Climate Change Adaptation, maintained by the Swedish Meteorological and Hydrological Institute (SMHI, 2020), provides a valuable resource to reveal both the general and the regional trends as well as to visualize the risks at more local levels (Figure 3.2 and Figure 3.3).

Rising surface temperatures is a prominent consequence of global warming. This impact is amplified around the Arctic, as well as some high mountains, since the albedo effect becomes weaker with the loss of cryosphere elements such as sea ice, glaciers, and snow cover, resulting in increased absorption of heat. In Sweden, a general increase trend in annual average temperatures is projected throughout the 21st century (Figure 3.2). The highest anomalies would take place in the north and during the winters (Sjökvist et al., 2015), and especially along the RCP 8.5 scenario, which is a representative concentration pathway where no policy-driven mitigation is in action, and thereby a radiative forcing of 8.5 W/m^2 by the end of the century is expected with respect to the pre-industrial conditions. RCP 8.5 is the future scenario where emission levels and climate impacts become most severe. On the contrary, a 4.5 W/m^2 radiative forcing is anticipated for the more optimistic RCP 4.5 scenario that takes account of mitigation policies at a moderate level and thus results in relatively lesser impacts, especially in the second half of the 21st century as the mitigation action starts paying off (van Vuuren et al., 2011).

With increased temperatures, and in combination with changes in humidity and wind conditions, touristic climatic comfort would be significantly affected. An earlier study by the European Commission (Amelung & Moreno, 2009; Ciscar et al., 2009) had revealed that 'very good' to 'ideal' climatic conditions for summer tourism could shift from the Mediterranean basin to Northern Europe by the end of the century and boost the touristic expenditures in favour of the latter. The reasons for that were due to both an improvement in the supply of the North and a 'too hot' summer in the Mediterranean, which together would keep vacationers of the tourist-sending countries in their own culture Rutty and Scott (2010) also found that temperatures above 37°C, which would be considered unacceptably hot by the Northern European beach travellers to the Mediterranean, would be common by the end of the century, but not in the immediate future. Demiroglu et al. (2020a), on the other hand, showed that comfort tolerance could be much higher than the stated, as visits to Antalya peaked during July and August months when the humidex values went above the 'too hot' threshold of the HCI: Beach index (Rutty et al., 2020) in the 2007–2015 period. In the case of Swedish arrivals to Antalya for the same period, high maximum temperatures that easily exceeded the previously stated tolerance limits were among the top estimators of visits (*r:* 0.86, p < 0.001). Such empirical findings call for more research on what is generally regarded as too hot and the inconsistencies of stated versus revealed preferences.

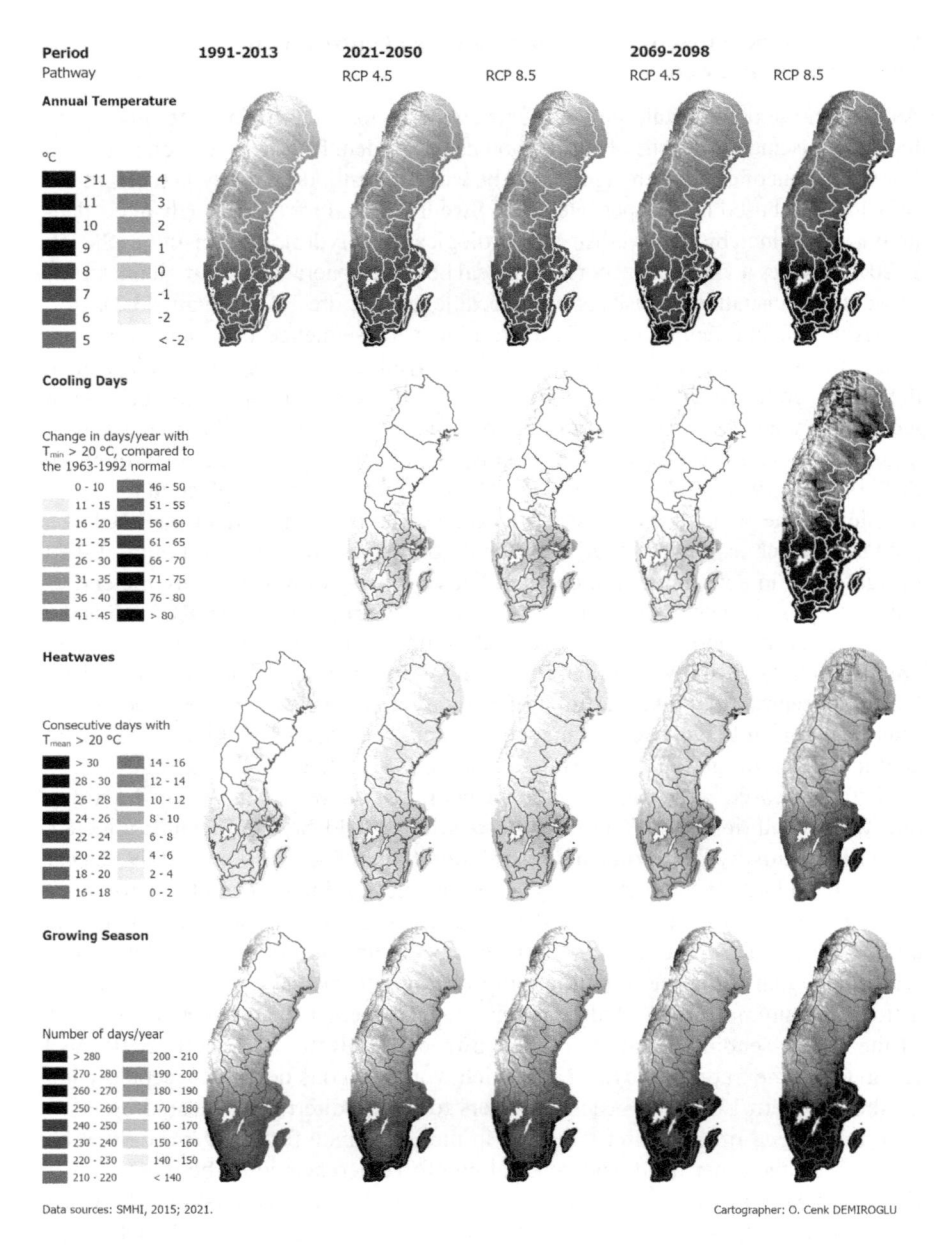

Figure 3.2 Climate change in Sweden according to selected temperature indices

Therefore, it is not easy to conclude that the rising temperatures, especially along the Swedish coastline (Figure 3.2), could bring in any significant competitiveness. Other external factors, such as the COVID-19 pandemic, could, however, be more of a dominant force to popularize domestic second home tourism for not only the coastline but the entire second home landscape, especially regarding those at weekend getaway distances (Figure 3.1b), to best practice social distancing and proximity tourism at the same time. While such trends may jeopardize regional resilience, that is, due to lack of carrying capacity (Willberg et al., 2021), they may also lead to a higher appreciation or acceptance of the domestic amenities against their (currently) more competitive substitutes abroad.

Projections on the spatiotemporal trends and patterns of temperature indices (Figure 3.2) would have different implications for mountain tourism, compared to coastal tourism, especially during the summer seasons. A visitor survey in Northern Norway (Førland et al., 2013), for instance, reveals a preference towards warmer summers in the usually cool regions and concludes that the projected increases in the number of warmer days would meet such demand. In Sweden, a sharp increase in the number of cooling days, also known as 'tropical nights' when the daily minimum temperature does not drop below 20°C, becomes most visible by the second half of the century and under the RCP 8.5 scenario. Extreme changes are found even around the mountain lakesides of Arctic Sweden (Figure 3.2), although a possible overestimation should be noted for the rough mountainous terrains, as these models are based on a four km horizontal resolution (Sjökvist et al., 2015) that may smooth out the higher and normally cooler elevation bands.

Contrary to the demand for warmer summers on the mountains (and other traditional cooler summer destinations), there is growing debate about how the uncomfortably warming tourist origins and the conventional destinations such as the coastline could push the demand further to the relatively cooler mountains. Even if such claims remain as speculations without much scientific evidence (Abegg & Steiger, 2011), the rumour itself might be enough to start driving second home development beyond the already dense ski resort towns of the Swedish mountains. Indeed, heatwave events in Sweden are projected to increase all along the coast and the forest areas, and especially around the metropolitan areas even under the more moderate RCP 4.5 scenario, by the end of the century (Figure 3.2). Wilcke et al. (2020) predict that extremely warm summers characterized by persistent heatwaves, such as the one in 2018, will not be uncommon in the future. The consequences of such conditions on human comfort and health and the impacts such as increased forest fires and changing vegetation patterns then also need to be taken into account by all means, and not least from a second home tourism perspective. For instance, Figure 3.2 provides a visible positive correlation among heatwave and growing season patterns. In this respect, an interesting result of the unusually warm summer of 2018 has been a record high productivity for the relatively marginal wine production in Sweden (The Local, 2018, 2019). Some experts claim Sweden to be the future 'wine hotspot' in a changing climate (Rhys, 2021). With careful product and destination branding, second home supply and price development may be inevitable around these so-called hot spots, which are currently at their infancy stage in Scania and the islands of Gotland and Öland.

The Swedish summer of 2018 was an exceptional one also in terms of the unprecedented frequency of fire events taking place throughout the forest areas – which are home to almost the entirety (92%) of the second homes in Sweden.

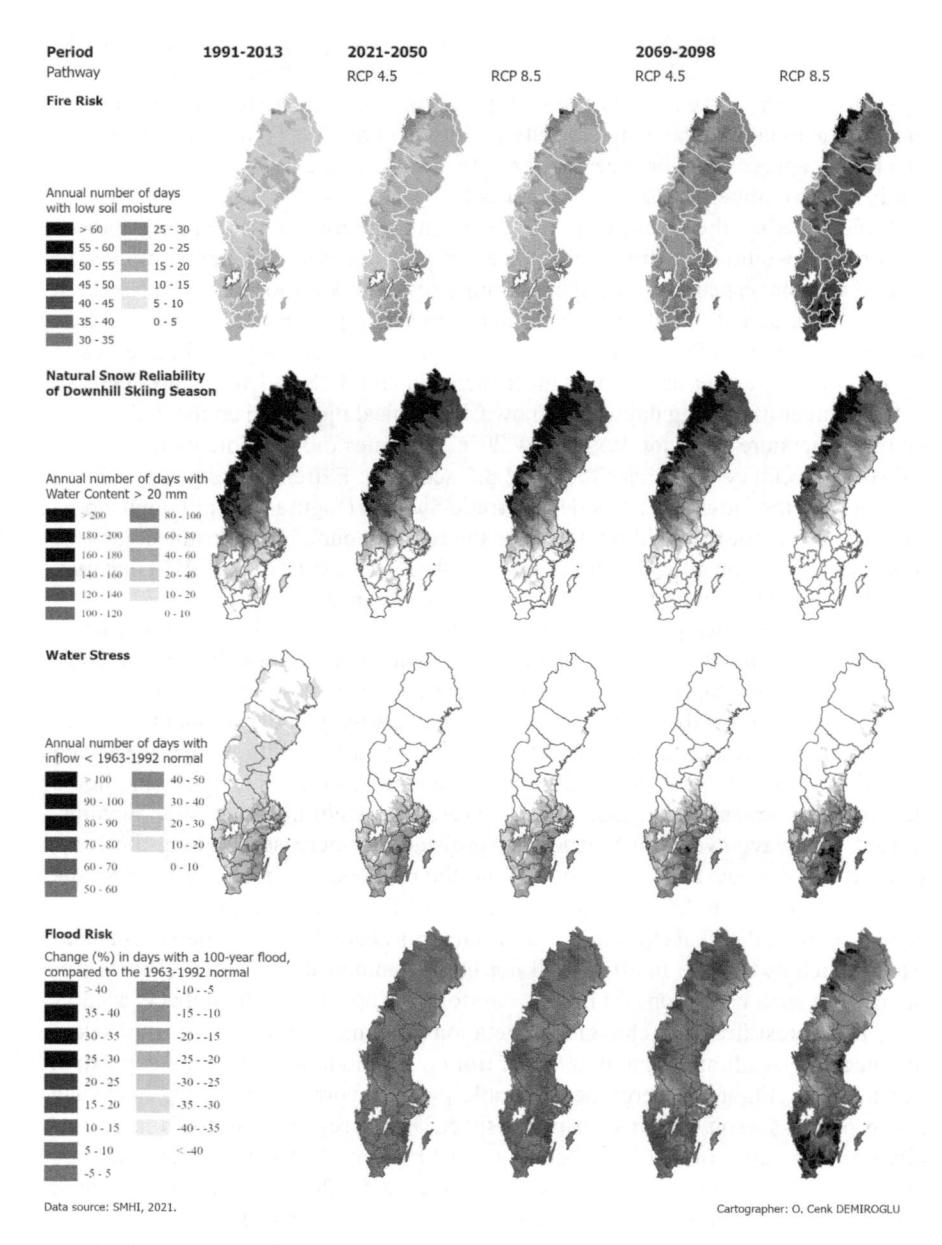

Figure 3.3 Climate change in Sweden according to selected hydrological indices

Krikken et al. (2019) attribute such increase to current global warming and also project a doubling of the forest risk for Sweden even under a 2°C temperature rise, compared to the pre-industrial levels, while the decreasing soil moisture (Figure 3.3) could also add up to the risk especially by the end of the century. Indeed, on an Arctic scale, the European Centre for Medium-ranged Weather Forecasts (ECMWF) (2019a, 2019b) had already detected an unprecedented increase in the spatiotemporal extent and the intensity of wildfire events throughout the summer of 2019 as well. Such trends make Swedish second homes much more vulnerable to climate change, as it is not only the loss or change in forest-based amenity value due to biodiversity change but also a direct exposure to increased fire danger which would destabilize future resilience.

In Sweden, while a general increase in the precipitation amounts is projected for the future, especially on the West Coast and the mountains along the Norwegian border (Sjökvist et al., 2015), a shortening of the snow durations is also significant, especially regarding a depth threshold of a water content above 20 mm – as a proxy for the downhill skiing season (Figure 3.3). Likewise, the weakening snow and ice cover could also indicate a threat over the sustainability of other popular recreational sports and activities such as cross-country skiing, snowmobiling, and ice-fishing. Such a change, along with increasing frequency and intensity of landslides, avalanches, storms, floods, and permafrost thaw, could easily lead to loss of property values (or gain) (Butsic et al., 2011; Galinato & Tantihkarnchana, 2018). While the mountain resorts hold the advantage, coastal ski resorts and areas, even in the higher latitudes, risk their snow reliability. The superior snow reliability of Arctic Sweden's mountainous landscapes, on the other hand, could witness ski tourism and related property development in the future yet along with some land use conflicts with conservation measures (Demiroglu et al., 2020b). Another area of conflicts could arise due to increasing snowmaking requirements to keep the ski resorts and properties viable – in a future where water resources for drinking and irrigation become scarcer (Figure 3.3). Moreover, both the developed and the potential ski locations along the mountains, along with the southern coastline, become more prone to flood risks (Figure 3.3), thus, they may lose the anticipated value gain from the relative snow reliability. The coastline, on the other hand, will also be severely impacted by coastal erosion triggered by sea-level rise and storm surge – especially around the sensitive beach areas in the south (SMHI, 2020), where also some of the densest and the most valuable second home zones exist (Figure 3.2). These far effects of sea-level rise, however, will be minimized or even eliminated especially in the northern parts of the country due to the ongoing glacial isostatic adjustment (Vestøl et al., 2019).

Conclusion

This chapter aimed to provide an overall picture of how climate change may impact second home tourism development in Sweden in accordance with the most climate-sensitive amenity landscapes that are also vital in determining second home locations and economic values. The preliminary results indicate a complex impacts chain that takes effect among different tourism types, origins, and destinations and needs to be studied within a more Nordic, or even international, context, as most of the amenities studied here are also a great reflection of Sweden's general touristic potential. Further research should also look into the adaptive capacities of second home destinations, taking account of the current lack of planning interests, to better understand the overall vulnerabilities and resilience. Besides lack of a public sector interest in planning, the loosening communities may also amplify the only real adaptation impetus at second home dominated regions (see other chapters in this volume). Implications for the financial and insurance sectors should also be made part of a systematic approach to vulnerability assessments. Likewise, mitigation aspects should also be on the agenda as the impacts for the later futures diverge significantly according to different greenhouse gas concentration trajectories. In this respect, sustainable accessibility and housing for second homes become more interesting, especially in Sweden where cooling and heating requirements will be altered while carbon-intensive transportation is still encouraged as many second homes require car travel, and some dense ski destinations even justify investments for new airports – which themselves may be subject to the tertiary impacts of climate change with carbon policies making air travel more expensive. Last but not least, it should be recalled that this study was limited to detached houses only, leaving room for research on alternative forms of second 'homes' such as caravans, RVs, and other camping modes, which may bring in increased adaptive capacities to their users, if not the destinations, with their non-fixed spatial locations.

References

Abegg, B., & Steiger, R. (2011). Will Alpine summer tourism benefit from climate change? A review. *Instituts für Interdisziplinäre Gebirgsforschung (IGF)*, *4*, 268–277.

Adamiak, C., Hall, C. M., Hiltunen, M. J., & Pitkaenen, K. (2016). Substitute or addition to hypermobile lifestyles? Second home mobility and Finnish CO_2 emissions. *Tourism Geographies*, *18*(2), 129–151. https://doi.org/10.1080/14616688.2016.1145250

Adamiak, C., Pitkänen, K., & Lehtonen, O. (2017). Seasonal residence and counterurbanization: The role of second homes in population redistribution in Finland. *GeoJournal*, *82*(5), 1035–1050. https://doi.org/10.1007/s10708-016-9727-x

Adie, B. A. (2020). Place attachment and post-disaster decision-making in a second home context: A conceptual framework. *Current Issues in Tourism*, *23*(10), 1205–1215. https://doi.org/10.1080/13683500.2019.1600475

Adie, B. A., & de Bernardi, C. (2020). 'Oh my god what is happening?': Historic second home communities and post-disaster nostalgia. *Journal of Heritage Tourism*. https://doi.org/10.1080/1743873X.2020.1828429

Amelung, B. & Moreno, A. (2009). *Impacts of climate change in tourism in Europe. PESETA-Tourism study*. JRC Working Papers JRC55392, Joint Research Centre (Seville site). Publications office of the European Union.

Ashley, R. M., Balmforth, D. J., Saul, A. J., & Blanskby, J. D. (2005). Flooding in the future – predicting climate change, risks and responses in urban areas. *Water Science and Technology*, *52*(5), 265–273. https://doi.org/10.2166/wst.2005.0142

Back, A. (2020). Temporary resident evil? Managing diverse impacts of second-home tourism. *Current Issues in Tourism*, *23*(11), 1328–1342. https://doi.org/10.1080/13683500.2019.1622656

Back, A., & Marjavaara, R. (2017). Mapping an invisible population: The uneven geography of second-home tourism. *Tourism Geographies*, *19*(4), 595–611. https://doi.org/10.1080/14616688.2017.1331260

Barke, M. (1991). The growth and changing pattern of second homes in Spain in the 1970s. *Scottish Geographical Magazine*, *107*(1), 12–21. https://doi.org/10.1080/00369229118736802

Barke, M. (2007). Second homes in Spain: An analysis of change at the provincial level, 1981–2001. *Geography*, *92*(3), 195–207. https://doi.org/10.1080/00167487.2007.12 094200

Brida, J. G., Osti, L., & Santifaller, E. (2009). Second homes and the need for policy planning. *Tourismos*, *6*(1), 141–163.

Butsic, V., Hanak, E., & Valletta, R. G. (2011). Climate change and housing prices: Hedonic estimates for ski resorts in Western North America. *Land Economics*, *87*(1), 75–91. http://doi.org/10.3368/le.87.1.75

Ciscar, J. C., Soria, A., Goodess, C. M., Christensen, O. B., Iglesias, A., Garrote, L., Moneo, M., Quiroga, S., Feyen, L., Dankers, R., Nicholls, R., Richards, J., Bosello, F., Roson, R., Amelung, B., Moreno, A., Watkiss, P., Hunt, A., Pye, S., . . . van Regemorter, D. (2009). *Climate change impacts in Europe. Final report of the PESETA research project.* JRC Working Papers JRC55391, Joint Research Centre (Seville site).

Czarnecki, A., & Frenkel, I. (2015). Counting the "invisible": Second homes in Polish statistical data collections. *Journal of Policy Research in Tourism, Leisure and Events*, *7*(1), 15–31. https://doi.org/10.1080/19407963.2014.935784

Demiroglu, O. C., Dannevig, H., & Aall, C. (2013). The multidisciplinary literature of ski tourism and climate change. In M. Kozak & N. Kozak (Eds.), *Tourism research: An interdisciplinary perspective* (pp. 223–237). Cambridge Scholars.

Demiroglu, O. C., Saygili-Araci, F. S., Pacal, A., Hall, C. M., & Kurnaz, M. L. (2020a). Future Holiday Climate Index (HCI) performance of urban and beach destinations in the Mediterranean. *Atmosphere*, *11*(9), 911. https://doi.org/10.3390/atmos11090911

Demiroglu, O. C., Turp, M. T., Kurnaz, M. L., & Abegg, B. (2020b). The Ski Climate Index (SCI): Fuzzification and a regional climate modeling application for Turkey. *International Journal Biometeorology*, *65*, 763–777. https://doi.org/10.1007/s00484-020-01991-0

Esri. (2021a). *Network analysis coverage.* https://doc.arcgis.com/en/arcgis-online/reference/network-coverage.htm

Esri. (2021b). *Configure travel modes.* https://doc.arcgis.com/en/arcgis-online/reference/travel-modes.htm

European Centre for Medium-ranged Weather Forecasts (ECMWF). (2019a). *CAMS monitors unprecedented wildfires in the Arctic.* https://atmosphere.copernicus.eu/cams-monitors-unprecedented-wildfires-arctic

European Centre for Medium-ranged Weather Forecasts (ECMWF). (2019b). *Arctic wildfires continue to blaze.* https://atmosphere.copernicus.eu/arctic-wildfires-continue-blaze

European Environment Agency (EEA). (2020). *Corine Land Cover (CLC) 2018, Version 2020_20u1.* https://land.copernicus.eu/pan-european/corine-land-cover/clc2018?tab=metadata

Flognfeldt, T., & Tjørve, E. (2013). The shift from hotels and lodges to second-home villages in mountain-resort accommodation. *Scandinavian Journal of Hospitality and Tourism*, *13*(4), 332–352. https://doi.org/10.1080/15022250.2013.862440

Førland, E. J., Jacobsen, J. K. S., Denstadli, J. M., Lohmann, M., Hanssen-Bauer, I., Hygen, H. O., & Tømmervik, H. (2013). Cool weather tourism under global warming: Comparing Arctic summer tourists' weather preferences with regional climate statistics and projections. *Tourism Management*, *36*, 567–579. https://doi.org/10.1016/j.tourman.2012.09.002

Frost, W. (2004). A hidden giant: Second homes and coastal tourism in south-eastern Australia. In C. M. Hall & D. K. Müller (Eds.), *Tourism, mobility, and second homes: Between elite landscape and common ground* (pp. 162–173). Channel View Publications.

Galinato, G. I., & Tantihkarnchana, P. (2018). The amenity value of climate change across different regions in the United States. *Applied Economics*, *50*(37), 4024–4039. https://doi.org/10.1080/00036846.2018.1441507

Goble, B. J., Lewis, M., Hill, T. R., & Phillips, M. R. (2014). Coastal management in South Africa: Historical perspectives and setting the stage of a new era. *Ocean and Coastal Management*, *91*, 32–40. https://doi.org/10.1016/j.ocecoaman.2014.01.013

Hall, C. M. (2015). Second homes planning, policy and governance. *Journal of Policy Research in Tourism, Leisure and Events*, *7*(1), 1–14. https://doi.org/10.1080/19407963.2014.964251

Hall, C. M., & Müller, D. K. (2004). Introduction: Second homes, curse or blessing? Revisited. In C. M. Hall & D. K. Müller (Eds.), *Tourism, mobility, and second homes: Between elite landscape and common ground* (pp. 3–14). Channel View Publications.

Halverson, J. B., & Rabenhorst, T. (2013). Hurricane Sandy: The science and impacts of a superstorm. *Weatherwise*, *66*(2), 14–23. https://doi.org/10.1080/00431672.2013.762838

Hiltunen, M. J. (2007). Environmental impacts of rural second home tourism – case Lake District in Finland. *Scandinavian Journal of Hospitality and Tourism*, *7*(3), 243–265. https://doi.org/10.1080/15022250701312335

Hiltunen, M. J., Pitkänen, K., & Halseth, G. (2016). Environmental perceptions of second home tourism impacts in Finland. *Local Environment*, *21*(10), 1198–1214. https://doi.org/10.1080/13549839.2015.1079701

Hiltunen, M. J., Pitkänen, K., Vepsäläinen, M., & Hall, C. M. (2013). Second home tourism in Finland: Current trends and eco-social impacts. In Z. Roca (Ed.), *Second home tourism in Europe: Lifestyle issues and policy responses* (pp. 165–198). Ashgate.

Hoogendoorn, G., & Fitchett, J. M. (2018). Perspectives on second homes, climate change and tourism in South Africa. *African Journal of Hospitality, Tourism and Leisure*, *7*(2), 1–18.

Huhtala, A., & Lankia, T. (2012). Valuation of trips to second homes: Do environmental attributes matter? *Journal of Environmental Planning and Management*, *55*(6), 733–752. https://doi.org/10.1080/09640568.2011.626523

Kaltenborn, B. P., Andersen, O., & Nellemann, C. (2007). Second home development in the Norwegian mountains: Is it outgrowing the planning capability? *The International Journal of Biodiversity Science and Management*, *3*(1), 1–11. https://doi.org/10.1080/17451590709618158

Kaltenborn, B. P., Andersen, O., & Nellemann, C. (2009). Amenity development in the Norwegian mountains: Effects of second home owner environmental attitudes on preferences for alternative development options. *Landscape and Urban Planning*, *91*(4), 195–201. https://doi.org/10.1016/j.landurbplan.2009.01.001

Kaltenborn, B. P., Andersen, O., Nellemann, C., Bjerke, T., & Thrane, C. (2008). Resident attitudes towards mountain second-home tourism development in Norway: The effects of environmental attitudes. *Journal of Sustainable Tourism*, *16*(6), 664–680.

Karim, F. (2019). *How do second homes and coastal short-term rentals affect municipal planning and decision making in the context of climate change* [Master's thesis, Dalhousie University]. http://hdl.handle.net/10222/76776

Kondo, M. C., Rivera, R., & Rullman Jr, S. (2012). Protecting the idyll but not the environment: Second homes, amenity migration and rural exclusion in Washington State. *Landscape and Urban Planning*, *106*(2), 174–182. https://doi.org/10.1016/j.landurbplan.2012.03.003

Krikken, F., Lehner, F., Haustein, K., Drobyshev, I., & van Oldenborgh, G. J. (2019). Attribution of the role of climate change in the forest fires in Sweden 2018. *Natural Hazards and Earth System Sciences*, *21*(7), 2169–2179. https://doi.org/10.5194/nhess-21-2169-2021

Łabuz, T. A. (2015). Environmental impacts – coastal erosion and coastline changes. In The BACC II Author Team (Eds.), *Second assessment of climate change for the Baltic Sea Basin* (pp. 381–396). Springer Open.

Langdalen, E. (1980). Second homes in Norway – a controversial planning problem. *Norsk Geografisk Tidsskrift*, *34*(3), 139–144. https://doi.org/10.1080/00291958008552059

Liu, J., Hertel, T. W., Diffenbaugh, N. S., Delgado, M. S., & Ashfaq, M. (2015). Future property damage from flooding: Sensitivities to economy and climate change. *Climatic Change*, *132*(4), 741–749. https://doi.org/10.1007/s10584-015-1478-z

The Local. (2018). *Swedish wines achieve record year thanks to summer heat.* www.thelocal.se/20181102/swedish-wines-achieve-record-year-thanks-to-summer-heat/

The Local. (2019). *Record number of new Swedish wines expected this year.* www.thelocal.se/20190516/a-record-number-of-new-swedish-wines-are-expected-this-year/

Long, D. P., & Hoogendoorn, G. (2013). Second home owners' perceptions of a polluted environment: The case of Hartbeespoort. *South African Geographical Journal*, *95*(1), 91–104.

Lundmark, L., & Marjavaara, R. (2005). Second home localizations in the Swedish mountain range. *Tourism*, *53*(1), 3–16.

Marjavaara, R., & Müller, D. K. (2007). The development of second homes' assessed property values in Sweden 1991–2001. *Scandinavian Journal of Hospitality and Tourism*, *7*(3), 202–222. https://doi.org/10.1080/15022250601160305

Marjavaara, R., Müller, D. K., & Back, A. (2019). Från sommarnöje till Airbnb: En översikt av svensk fritidshusforskning. *Ymer*, *2019*, 53–77.

Müller, D. K. (2002). Second home ownership and sustainable development in Northern Sweden. *Tourism and Hospitality Research*, *3*(4), 343–355. https://doi.org/10.1177/146735840200300406

Müller, D. K. (2004). Second homes in Sweden: Patterns and issues. In C. M. Hall & D. K. Müller (Eds.), *Tourism, mobility and second homes: Between elite landscape and common ground* (pp. 244–258). Channel View.

Müller, D. K. (2005). Second home tourism in the Swedish mountain range. In C. M. Hall & S. Boyd (Eds.), *Nature-based tourism in peripheral areas: Development or disaster* (pp. 133–148). Channel View.

Müller, D. K. (2006). The attractiveness of second home areas in Sweden: A quantitative analysis. *Current Issues in Tourism*, *9*(4–5), 335–350. https://doi.org/10.2167/cit269.0

Müller, D. K. (2007). Second homes in the Nordic countries: Between common heritage and exclusive commodity. *Scandinavian Journal of Hospitality and Tourism*, *7*(3), 193–201. https://doi.org/10.1080/15022250701300272

Müller, D. K. (2011). The internationalization of rural municipalities: Norwegian second home owners in Northern Bohuslän, Sweden. *Tourism Planning & Development*, *8*(4), 433–445. https://doi.org/10.1080/21568316.2011.605384

Müller, D. K. (2013). Second homes and outdoor recreation: A Swedish perspective on second homes use and complementary spaces. In Z. Roca (Ed.), *Second home tourism in Europe: Lifestyle issues and policy responses* (pp. 121–140). Ashgate.

Müller, D. K., & Hall, C. M. (2003). Second homes and regional population distribution: On administrative practices and failures in Sweden. *Espace Populations Sociétés*, *21*(2), 251–261.

Müller, D. K., Hall, C. M., & Keen, D. (2004). Second home tourism impact, planning and management. In C. M. Hall & D. K. Müller (Eds.), *Tourism, mobility and second homes: Between elite landscape and common ground* (pp. 15–32). Channel View Publications.

Nellemann, C., Vistnes, I., Jordhøy, P., Støen, O. G., Kaltenborn, B. P., Hanssen, F., & Helgesen, R. (2010). Effects of recreational cabins, trails and their removal for restoration of reindeer winter ranges. *Restoration Ecology*, *18*(6), 873–881. https://doi.org/10.1111/j.1526-100X.2009.00517.x

Nepal, S. K., & Jamal, T. B. (2011). Resort-induced changes in small mountain communities in British Columbia, Canada. *Mountain Research and Development*, *31*(2), 89–101. https://doi.org/10.1659/MRD-JOURNAL-D-10-00095.1

Opačić, V. T., & Koderman, M. (2018). Second home development in Croatia and Slovenia. In C. M. Hall & D. K. Müller (Eds.), *The Routledge handbook of second home tourism and mobilities* (pp. 167–178). Routledge.

Persson, I. (2015). Second homes, legal framework and planning practice according to environmental sustainability in coastal areas: The Swedish setting. *Journal of Policy Research in Tourism, Leisure and Events*, *7*(1), 48–61. https://doi.org/10.1080/19407963.2014.933228

Pintaldi, E., Hudek, C., Stanchi, S., Spiegelberger, T., Rivella, E., & Freppaz, M. (2017). Sustainable soil management in ski areas: Threats and challenges. *Sustainability*, *9*(11), 2150. https://doi.org/10.3390/su9112150

Ragatz, R. L. (1970). Vacation homes in the northeastern United States: Seasonality in population distribution. *Annals of the Association of American Geographers*, *60*(3), 447–455. https://doi.org/10.1111/j.1467-8306.1970.tb00734.x

Rey-Valette, H., Rulleau, B., Hellequin, A. P., Meur-Ferec, C., & Flanquart, H. (2015). Second-home owners and sea-level rise: The case of the Languedoc-Roussillon region (France). *Journal of Policy Research in Tourism, Leisure and Events*, *7*(1), 32–47. https://doi.org/10.1080/19407963.2014.942734

Rhys, P. (2021, January 20). *Sweden is turning into a wine hotspot because of climate change*. Business Insider. www.businessinsider.com/sweden-wine-industry-climate-change-2021-1?r=US&IR=T

Rutty, M., & Scott, D. (2010). Will the Mediterranean become "too hot" for tourism? A reassessment. *Tourism and Hospitality Planning and Development*, *7*(3), 267–281. https://doi.org/10.1080/1479053X.2010.502386

Rutty, M., Scott, D., Matthews, L., Burrowes, R., Trotman, A., Mahon, R., & Charles, A. (2020). An inter-comparison of the Holiday Climate Index (HCI:Beach) and the Tourism Climate Index (TCI) to explain Canadian tourism arrivals to the Caribbean. *Atmosphere*, *11*(4), 412. https://doi.org/10.3390/atmos11040412

Shellito, B. A. (2006). Second-home distributions in the USA's Upper Great Lakes states: Analysis and implications. In N. McIntyre, D. Williams, & K. McHugh (Eds.), *Multiple dwelling and tourism: Negotiating place, home and identity* (pp. 194–206). Cabi.

Sjökvist, E., Mårtensson, J. A., Dahné, J., Köplin, N., Björck, E., Nylén, L., Berglöv, G., Brunell, J. T., Nordborg, D., Hallberg, K., Södling, J., & Berggreen Clausen, S. (2015). *Klimatscenarier för Sverige: Bearbetning av RCP-scenarier för meteorologiska och hydrologiska effektstudier.* SMHI.

Swedish Meteorological and Hydrological Institute (SMHI). (2020). *Swedish portal for climate change adaptation.* www.klimatanpassning.se/en

Steiger, R., Scott, D., Abegg, B., Pons, M., & Aall, C. (2019). A critical review of climate change risk for ski tourism. *Current Issues in Tourism*, *22*(11), 1343–1379. https://doi.org/10.1080/13683500.2017.1410110

van Vuuren, D. P., Edmonds, J., Kainuma, M., Riahi, K., Thomson, A., Hibbard, K., Hurtt, G. C., Kram, T., Krey, V., Lamarque, J. F., Masui, T., Meinshausen, M., Nakicenovic, N., Smith, S. J., & Ros, S. K. (2011). The representative concentration pathways: An overview. *Climatic Change*, *109*(5), 5–31. https://doi.org/10.1007/s10584-011-0148-z

Vestøl, O., Ågren, J., Steffen, H., Kierulf, H., & Tarasov, L. (2019). NKG2016LU: A new land uplift model for Fennoscandia and the Baltic Region. *Journal of Geodesy*, *93*, 1759–1779. https://doi.org/10.1007/s00190-019-01280-8

Wilcke, R. A. I., Kjellström, E., Lin, C., Matei, D., Moberg, A., & Tyrlis, E. (2020). The extremely warm summer of 2018 in Sweden – Set in a historical context. *Earth System Dynamics*, *11*(4), 1107–1121. https://doi.org/10.5194/esd-11-1107-2020.

Willberg, E., Järv, O., Väisänen, T., & Toivonen, T. (2021). Escaping from cities during the COVID-19 crisis: Using mobile phone data to trace mobility in Finland. *ISPRS International Journal of Geo-Information*, *10*(2), 103. https://doi.org/10.3390/ijgi10020103

Wolfe, R. I. (1951). Summer cottagers in Ontario. *Economic Geography*, *27*(1), 10–32.

4 Climate-wise second home tourism: policy and media discourses on the climate impacts of second homes in Finland

Kati Pitkänen and Manu Rantanen

Introduction

The very first second home climate change programme was launched in Finland in 2019. Initiated by the Finnish second home owner association (Vapaa-ajan asukkaiden Liitto (VAAL)), the programme aims to promote "climate-wise second home tourism" but also enhance the capacity of second home owners to counter the rising criticism targeted towards the climate impacts of second homes in Finland (VAAL, 2019). The programme states that since second homes are a major element of mobility and time use in Finland, it is expected that the public discourse will eventually pay attention to and turn critical towards the climate impacts of second homes caused by, for instance, travelling to second homes by private cars.

The climate change programme highlights especially second home related mobility, the qualities of the second home buildings, and ways of using second homes as the three main potential threats for climate. The programme gives recommendations on how to combat the negative environmental impacts by, for example, preferring electric and gas cars and sustainable on-site energy solutions as well as changing the second home culture in a more sustainable direction (VAAL, 2019).

The programme is an interesting and new type of a perspective to the second home discourse in Finland. The second home public discourse in Finland has been dominated by the myth of rural idyll, and second homes represent close-to-nature getaways from the urban life (Vepsäläinen & Pitkänen, 2010; Pitkänen, 2011). In the images of the second home tourists, the potential harmful environmental impacts are downplayed by the tourists' own experiences and importance of nature as a part of the second home practices (Hiltunen et al., 2016). The initiative of VAAL, however, indicates that these discourses of stability and environmental stewardship may become increasingly challenged by the climate change debates. Climate change has become the most vigorously debated environmental topic over the past decades politically, but also with a penetrating presence in the media (Kangas & Lyytimäki, 2020).

In this chapter, we look at how the relationship between second homes and climate change is understood in the current public discourse. We will answer the following questions:

- How are the climate impacts of second homes or impacts of climate change to second home tourism acknowledged in the policy and media discourses?

DOI: 10.4324/9781003091295-4

- How has the public discourse changed over the years?
- Is the sustainability of the second home culture challenged or criticised?
- How does the public discourse reflect the scientific evidence of second homes' climate impacts and the carbon footprint of second homes?

We will analyse the media accounts of some of the leading Finnish newspapers during past decades as well as the key national policy documents and strategies aimed at developing rural second home tourism in Finland. Besides that, the policy documents of the province South Savo and one of its newspapers will be analysed in order to understand the perspective of an area where second home owners are economically and socially highly important. Based on the results, we will critically discuss how climate-wise second home tourism is understood in the public discourse and outline possible gaps in the current second home research.

What is climate-wise second home tourism?

The climate impacts of second homes has been a relatively under-researched topic both in Finland and globally. There is a growing interest and literature in climate change vulnerability adaption and resilience with case studies around the world (e.g., Cheong, 2018; Hoogendoorn & Fitchett, 2018; Adie, 2020), but less is known about the potential contribution of second homes to climate change or the carbon footprint of second homes.

The carbon emissions of second homes have mainly been addressed in studies on second home travel modes and mobility (Adamiak et al., 2016; Næss et al., 2019). According to Hiltunen (2007), a significant and growing share of the negative environmental impacts in the Nordic countries is caused by the motorized mobility between the first and the second home as almost all second home mobility is carried out using private cars. Næss et al. (2019) have estimated that the carbon emissions of travel to second homes in Norway amount to approximately 240 kg per person for domestic second homes and nearly 1650 kg for second homes located outside of Norway. In Finland, Adamiak et al. (2016) have estimated that the total CO_2 emission from trips to second homes amounts to 0.4 Mt a year. This amounts to 495.9 kg per one second home owner or user household and is equivalent to one person's round-trip flight from Finland to Central Europe.

In Finland, the carbon emissions of second homes have also been assessed in relation to energy use of the second home building stock. Second home energy use has been estimated to range between 1500 kWh for second homes used only in the summer to 8000 kWh for second homes with low electric heating also during the winter (Rytkönen & Kirkkari, 2010, p. 22; see also Salo et al., 2017). The annual overall energy consumption of second homes was calculated to be 1100 GWh annually in 2010. This was predicted to grow up to 1400–1650 GWh in 2020 along with the increasing equipment rate and electric heating of second home stock as well as the second home stock. This equals approximately 0.3–0.37 Mt of CO_2 annually (Rytkönen & Kirkkari, 2010, p. 17).

The broader second home environment nexus has been studied from various perspectives. The direct and indirect impacts of second homes on environment have been studied by, for example, Hiltunen (2007) and Hiltunen et al. (2013) who have analysed the environmental impacts of second homes and current trends in second home development in Finland. They conclude that the environmental impacts of second homes in Finland are caused by housing and living, shoreline building, and physical mobility related to second home travelling. Also, the environmental perceptions of second home tourists have been studied in many countries (e.g., Kaltenborn et al., 2009; Long & Hoogendoorn, 2013). Researchers have pointed out a disjuncture between the second home tourists' actions and the conceptualization of second homes as a sustainable and environmentally conscious activity (Pitkänen, 2011; Hiltunen et al., 2016; Lait, 2018). Hiltunen et al. (2016) have shown that second home owners themselves are much less concerned about the potential harmful environmental impacts than non-users or random visitors to second homes. Researchers have also shown that although sometimes implied, second home mobility does not directly substitute long-haul air travel, but second home owners' overall travel and consumption patterns place them among the highly mobile groups of society with potential for high environmental impacts (Hiltunen, 2007; Adamiak et al., 2016).

Calculating the carbon footprint of second homes in Finland

Climate impacts of consumption of households are often measured and visualised by the carbon footprint. A carbon footprint is the total amount of greenhouse gases that are generated by our actions and is measured by a carbon dioxide equivalent (CO_2e) that converts the warming potential of all gases to an equivalent amount of carbon dioxide. The annual carbon footprint of Finns ranges between 10.1–12.6 tons of CO_2e per capita (60.1 Mt Finland total), being among the highest in the world. Roughly one third of the footprint is caused by transport, another third by housing and energy use, and the rest by the consumption of food, beverages, and other products and services (Nissinen & Savolainen, 2019). The overall carbon footprint has increased in the 2000s along with increasing overall consumption.

Second homes are not only a major form of domestic leisure but also comprise approximately a quarter of all residential buildings in Finland (a third of all detached houses) (Statistics Finland, 2020a, 2020b). There are over half a million second homes in Finland (Statistics Finland, 2020b). The overall carbon footprint of second homes has recently been estimated by Tuominen (2019, see also Koivula et al., 2019) in the South Savo region. According to the study, the main components of the second home carbon footprint are similar to the overall carbon footprint of households. Thirty-five percent of the second home carbon footprint in the South region is caused by travelling, 34% is caused by energy use (electricity), and the rest by the purchases of products, equipment, and services. Tuominen (2019, p. 69) estimates that the carbon footprint of a single South Savo second home is, on average, 2 tons of CO_2e (an average 427 kg CO_2e per second home tourist).

If the results of South Savo are generalised to other regions, the overall carbon footprint of second homes in Finland is roughly 1 Mt of CO_2e annually, thus 1–2% of the total carbon footprint of Finland. In comparison to the emissions from some of the other key consumption related sectors such as waste management (1.8 Mt) or traffic (11.3 Mt), this is less but still significant. Per capita second home use would comprise under 5% of an average Finn's carbon footprint. The climate impacts of second homes can be assumed also to differ significantly depending on the type of a second home, travel distance, and patterns of use.

Second homes and climate change in the Finnish public discourse The media and policy document analysis

We performed a qualitative content analysis (Sarajärvi & Tuomi, 2017) focusing on newspapers and key political documents. Data was collected both nationally and regionally. South Savo region was included in order to understand the regional perspective. South Savo is the second biggest second home province in Finland with about 50000 second homes in 2019. In South Savo, the percentage of second home population of the total residential population was the highest of all provinces, 42% (Statistics Finland, 2020b). The majority of the second home owners that live outside the region come from the metropolitan area of Helsinki.

Three of the newspapers that we chose for the media analysis were owned by Sanoma Corporation, the largest media group in Finland. They are published in Helsinki, the capital of Finland, but have a national perspective: *Helsingin Sanomat* (the largest newspaper in Finland, published daily), *Ilta-Sanomat* (an evening newspaper and second largest newspaper), and *Taloussanomat* (the largest business online daily newspaper). The fourth newspaper that we studied was *Länsi-Savo*. It is a regional newspaper, which is published in Mikkeli, South Savo. We used the digitized archives of Sanoma Corporation and the digital collection of the National library of Finland for *Länsi-Savo*. The first search terms that we used included the most common synonyms of second homes and second homers. The second search terms were climate change and greenhouse effect. (The search terms: vapaa-ajan asunto (with different spellings), mök*, kesämök*, loma-asu*, kakkosasu*, monipaikkai*, huvil*, kesäasun*, kesäasuk* and ilmasto*, kasvihuone*). The studied period was from 1990 to 2019 (*Länsi-Savo* from 1990 to 2018).

The result of the search was 1856 articles, out of which 189 were relevant. After removing the duplicates, the data comprised of 96 articles for further inspection (see Table 4.1). The number of articles was low until a peak between 2007–2011. Few articles dealing with second homes and climate change were published in the 2010s. In 2019, the theme was again under discussion more (Figure 4.1).

In parallel to the newspapers, we also looked at the key policy documents and strategies aimed at guiding the development of rural second home tourism in Finland (see Table 4.1). These include rural policy and regional development strategies and programmes as well as climate change strategies. Besides national level policies, we looked at the policies and strategies of South Savo. Similar to the newspaper data, the programmes were searched for all mentions of second homes

Table 4.1 Media and policy document analysis

Newspaper data	Policy documents
Helsingin Sanomat (72 articles) *Taloussanomat* (1 article) *Ilta-Sanomat* (2 articles) *Länsi-Savo* (21 articles)	Rural Policy Programme 2014–2020 Island Development Programme 2017–2019 Energy and climate strategies 2001, 2005, 2008, 2013, 2014, 2015, 2016 (total seven pieces) South Savo Regional Programme 2018–2021 Savo Climate Programme 2025
Total: 96 articles	Total: 11 mentions in policy documents

Mentions of second homes and climate change in articles by years

1996	5	2004	1	2012	5
1997	0	2005	4	2013	5
1998	0	2006	2	2014	0
1999	2	2007	14	2015	2
2000	2	2008	14	2016	0
2001	3	2009	12	2017	5
2002	2	2010	12	2018	7
2003	1	2011	3	2019	15

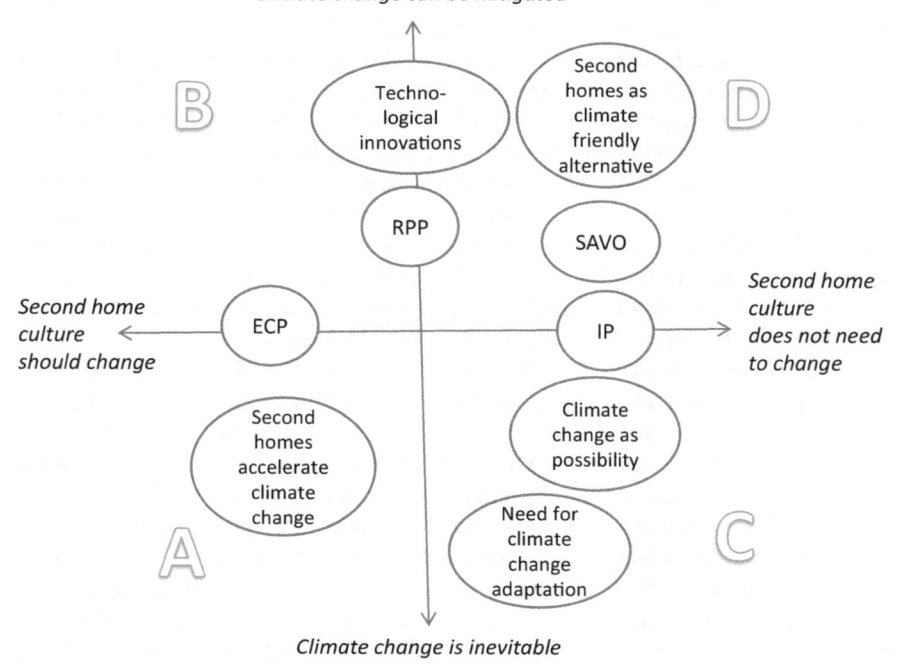

Figure 4.1 Second home discourses (ECP = Energy and Climate Program, RPP = Rural Policy Program, IP = Island Programme, SAVO = South Savo Programme and Savo Climate Programme)

and climate change and/or the greenhouse effect. The programmes and strategies included very few explicit mentions of the relationship between second homes and climate change.

Changing press coverage

As presented in Table 4.1, there have been two stages when more articles were published about the relationship between climate change and second homes, the years between 2006 and 2011, and the end of the 2010s. The first peak is in line with the overall development of climate change related press coverage in Finland. According to Lyytimäki and Tapio (2009), climate press coverage increased notably in the period 2007–2009. This was due to exceptionally mild winters and lack of snow cover in Southern Finland, climate policy statements of some of the key political and economic figures in Finland, international climate change negotiations, and the increase of the visibility of climate change related research such as from the IPCC (Lyytimäki & Tapio, 2009; Kangas & Lyytimäki, 2020).

Besides the overall increase in climate change related press coverage, the public discussion on nuclear power is also reflected in the result. At the time of the first peak, one nuclear reactor was being built, and a government resolution was adopted for the next reactor. Energy consumption and efficiency were topical themes, and studies were published on the energy consumption and efficiency of second homes (Rytkönen & Kirkkari, 2010). These were also visible in the media as a discussion against the energy-consuming patterns of use of second homes. In general, from 2000 to 2010, there was a rise of more diverse discourses regarding rurality in the media than there had been previously (Alasuutari & Alasuutari, 2011). The number of articles that emphasized the rural policy perspective of rural areas declined, and the number of articles that dealt with environmental issues increased.

The overall press coverage of climate change decreased in the 2010s, but the theme has remained more prominent than in the 1990s (Kangas & Lyytimäki, 2020). Similar development can also be distinguished in relation to our data. The discussion about climate change has increased again during the past years, boosted by the increasing prominence of the theme in international and national political agendas and research efforts but also through social media, celebrities, and the tangibility of the effects of climate change in everyday life (Kangas & Lyytimäki, 2020).

Besides frequencies, terminologies have also varied through the past decades. Whereas in the 1990s it was more typical to refer to the greenhouse effect, this has been replaced by climate change in the 2000s (also Kangas & Lyytimäki, 2020). The discussion on second homes and climate change has had some recurring contexts, such as waste management, recycling, and protection of the environment. These articles usually defend second homes. The articles related to energy consumption, however, are more critical towards second homes and often describe second home culture as a luxurious way of life, causing a waste of energy. Many of the articles (26 pcs.) were letters to the editor, written in a somewhat provocative style:

> A bit of a two-faced politics is the rant of the Greens as their woman candidate is travelling with her whole family to the other side of the globe and polluting the climate, even though the party even forbids grandpa and grandma

from heating their cottage and sauna with firewood because it pollutes the air too much.

(Länsi-Savo, 27 November 2018)

Considering the differences between newspapers that were published in the capital region and in the Lakeland area, *Länsi-Savo* treated second homes generally more positively than the newspapers of the Sanoma Corporation.

In contrast to the newspapers, the Finnish policy programmes rarely connect the dots between second homes and climate change. However, the increasing energy consumption of second homes was mentioned especially in the early 2000s reports attached to the national energy and climate strategies.

Five discourses of second homes and climate change

We used two dimensions to scrutinise how the newspapers and policy documents considered the second home–climate nexus. On one hand, we looked at whether the articles and documents acknowledged that second homes may contribute to climate change and second home culture should change to prevent harmful impacts. On the other hand, we paid attention to if the documents saw that climate change could be mitigated or was it considered practically inevitable. Consequently, four possible and opposite approaches emerge. From a critical perspective, second home use is considered bad for the environment and should be restricted (A) or second home culture needs to change in order to mitigate climate change (B). From a less critical perspective, second homes can be approached through the need for climate change adaptation (C) or as technological platforms for innovations targeted at climate change mitigation (D).

We found five different types of discourses in the newspaper articles. These and the main discourses of the policy documents are presented in Figure 4.1 in relation to the four dimensions described previously.

Although only a few articles belonged to the *climate change is a possibility for second home development* category, in the early stage of the studied period, this kind of attitude to climate change could be found in the context of the country's subarctic climate. It was assumed that longer and warmer summer periods could increase the demand for Finnish second home plots from abroad and create new possibilities in the future:

However, there would be no significant change in terms of land use planning and the use of the shorelines. On the other hand, plots on the shoreline by the Lake Saimaa could be considerably more in demand abroad as the summer season lengthens.

(Länsi-Savo, 24 April 1996)

A more common discourse was to refer to the *need for adaptation* as climate change with its consequences threatens the possibilities of carrying on second home life as before. The articles did not question the ways second homes are used nowadays but stated that climate change causes various threats for their future use. The mentioned threats included, for example, floods, droughts or other extreme weather phenomena, weakening of the quality of water, and alien invasive species.

> In the summer, hot days and droughts become more common. Boating, swimming, and second home seasons lengthen, but algal blooms can increase in the warming waters.
>
> (Helsingin Sanomat, 2 November 2009)

> Climate change increases heat waves, which together with the nutrient load of the water system are causing toxic cyanobacterial blooms. They damage aquatic ecosystems and collapse their recreational value. Residents of the hot coastal towns will not be delighted by the swimming restrictions. The health risks of extreme heat waves are worsened by the lack of relief provided by the natural waters.
>
> (Helsingin Sanomat, 27 July 2018)

Climate change adaptation was also mentioned in the Island Programme and both Savo Programmes. The programmes mentioned especially the need to prepare for power outages caused by increasing extreme weather and storms. Besides distributed or on-site energy production, the Island Programme also demanded taking the increasing extreme weather changes into consideration in the land use planning, building regulations, and mobility needs.

In the newspaper articles, second homes were often portrayed as an *environmentally friendly activity and option* for other more damaging alternatives, such as flying abroad. It was emphasised that the attitude of second home owners is positive for protecting the environment and prevention of climate change. Second home culture was seen to be fundamentally connected to a positive attitude towards environmental issues such as recycling, waste management, and nature protection, and that is why second home owners feel positive about the actions for preventing climate change:

> Cottage life is basically ecological. It is based on the idea of a simple, organic and healthy lifestyle. The cottages are characterized by the use of renewable wood as a building material and energy source, the use of natural products, perhaps growing of food as food prices rise, recycling and living in harmony with other species of nature.
>
> (Helsingin Sanomat, 15 September 2008)

> Pesonen believes that the climate change debate is already beginning to influence Finns' travel choices. "I believe that domestic tourism will be boosted by a bolder recognition that it will be a climate-friendly alternative to travelling abroad." Second homes still hold on as a way of holidaying for Finns, as their popularity has remained stable between 2002 and 2017.
>
> (Helsingin Sanomat, 15 July 2019)

The possibilities of technical innovations, digitalization, and multi-locality were often highlighted by the newspapers and policy documents. In this discourse, the approach to second homes is relatively neutral, although admitting that there are ways to diminish the climate change effects of second homes. In the newspapers, the focus has been on individual and home level technical innovations such as air-source heat pumps, electric cars, and photovoltaic cells:

> "My wife and I have decided not to travel on vacation by plane. . . . On vacation we go to see domestic natural attractions – but we don't drive around the country." The family thus has a car. "We drive calmly to the cottage. It takes 3.6 litres per 100 km and minimizes emissions." "I will buy the first electric car for consumers."
>
> (Helsingin Sanomat, 15 October 2009).

> Finns could have the greatest impact on their carbon footprint by making their leisure trips by public transport instead of a car. This raises the question whether a visit to a second home would be possible without a car or whether second homes should be visited less often. Travelling by car is a good example of how the political debate on climate change can easily turn against itself. Climate change requires swift solutions, but at the same time, it should be possible to show the possible and realistic timetable for switching to electric cars, for example. Instead of intimidation and threats, attractive paths towards a low-carbon lifestyle should be provided.
>
> (Helsingin Sanomat, 19 May 2019)

In the policy documents, both individual and system-level changes are suggested or foreseen. The Savo Climate Programme lists the development of eco-efficiency of second homes as one of the measures to respond to climate change in the region. A concrete tool, 'Ekopassi', is presented as a tool to evaluate and assess the eco-efficiency of individual second homes in terms of their accessibility, material consumption/carbon footprint (kg/m^2), energy consumption (kWh/m^2), share of renewable energy (%), water supply and sewerage, and waste management. The national Rural Policy Programme also implicitly refers to the negative impacts of the rural dispersed community structure to the traffic emissions, energy efficiency, and climate impacts. Digitalisation and increasing opportunities in place-independent work such as teleworking are mentioned as potential factors that will alleviate the negative impacts through reducing traffic. The Island Programme, in turn, mentioned that second homes increase the consumption and traffic emissions, but these can be alleviated by converting second homes into permanent residences.

In the most critical discourse, second home culture was seen to *accelerate climate change*. In the newspapers, the modern and well-equipped second homes that represent elitism were especially condemned. Energy inefficiency, private cars, and burning of wood were also seen as problematic:

> It feels like we are in a deep sleep. We are buying bigger and bigger muscle cars regardless of emissions, building ever-bigger electrically heated detached houses and more winter-warm second homes.
>
> (Helsingin Sanomat, 4 October 2007)

> It is pointless to talk about very nature-friendly summer cottage life if you need flat screen TVs, broadband and other gadgets.
>
> (Länsi-Savo, 4 August 2008)

> Second homes and apartment saunas belong mainly only to the Finnish culture. Both are actual sources of emission . . . Every builder of a second home should be required to plant trees at least the amount that are logged out of the way of second homes and roads leading to them. Of course, the whole second home culture can be questioned. Other European countries get along well without them and saunas.
>
> (Helsingin Sanomat, 30 December 2018)

The national Energy and Climate strategies have been critical especially to the increasing energy consumption at second homes. The background reports for the 2001 and 2005 strategies included a table estimating the future energy consumption at second homes as a consequence to the increasing standard of equipment and number of second homes. In both years, the energy consumption was estimated to increase by over 20% during the next 20 years, although in the 2001 report, it was also hoped for that the increasing energy efficiency of electric equipment and energy taxation would decrease the energy consumption at second homes. In the 2008 background report, in backcasting to the 2005 report, it was noted that as the general standards of living have improved, the size and equipment rate of second homes have also continued to increase, and many second homes have been converted into residences that can be used year-round. This has increased traffic and demands for services in the dispersed rural settlements. In the later climate strategies and their background reports, the mentions of second homes have been more random. The 2013 background report mentions that second homes are a source of black carbon emissions originating from burning wood for heating and saunas (Hildén et al., 2013). In the 2016 report, second homes are seen to slow down the energy efficiency development since "old [less energy efficient] appliances are re-used at second homes" (Ministry of the Employment and the Economy, 2017, p. 21).

Discussion and conclusions

Climate change has become the most prominent environmental problem in the mass media during the past decades in Finland. In this article, we have analysed how and if climate change is discussed in the context of second homes. According to the results, two peaks in the press coverage can be distinguished. Alike to the broader climate change press coverage (Lyytimäki & Tapio, 2009), the first peak dates in the turn of the 2010s as a reflection to the mild and snowless winters and global political agendas. In the context of second homes, the increasing need for the adaptation of consequences of climate change and the increasing energy consumption especially raised concern both in the media and in the political strategies.

The second peak we are living right now. Besides the overall increasing publicity and interest in climate change, the main cause for the recent discussion in relation to second homes seems to stem from the effects of climate change in everyday life. These effects are evident not only as visible changes in the environment or weather conditions but also through various new technologies and solutions for more sustainable lifestyles. In recent years, there have been more writing than before where second homes are defended by arguing that they could be used in more ecological ways because of the technical innovations in heating of second homes and travelling by car.

The discussion about the relationship of second homes and climate change seems to have continued relatively neutrally until recently. The critical arguments were the most common between the years 2007 and 2010 and were related to criticism of the increasing energy consumption of better equipped and increasingly luxurious second homes. Contrary to the fears of VAAL (2019), the public discourse has not turned critically towards second homes. Instead of directly criticising second home lifestyles and consumption, the recent public discourse focuses more on presenting solutions and technological innovations designed to make second home living (even) more sustainable. The 2010s seems to have been a relatively calm period in the second press coverage. This can be a reflection of the overall slowing down of building of new second homes and decrease of second home property prices during the past decade (Statistics Finland, 2020b; Yle, 2020).

Considering the differences between newspapers that were published in the capital region and in the Lakeland area, *Länsi-Savo* treated second homes generally more positively than the newspapers of the Sanoma Corporation. That is understandable in light of the importance of second homes for the regional development of South Savo. That led to the dominance of writings where second homes were not questioned in *Länsi-Savo*. In the early period, the main question was the adaptation to climate change, whereas later, the articles about possibilities to use technical innovations for mitigating climate change had been more common. Similar difference can be noticed also between the policy documents so that those strategies targeted at rural development (Rural Policy Programme, Island Programme, South Savo Programmes) are more positive to second home culture than the climate programmes that take a more neutral stand. However, none of the analysed political documents criticise or question the sustainability of Finnish second home culture, which is surprising considering the importance of second homes as a part of the Finnish way of life.

The public discourses are not always aligned with the scientific understanding of what constitutes the climate impacts of second homes. The carbon footprint is the sum of the emissions caused by travelling between the first and the second home, building and energy use, as well as consumption related to second homes (Koivula et al., 2019). These themes are invariably present in the Finnish media and policy discourse which seem to struggle to concretise the climate impacts of second homes.

The most noticeable concrete theme in the Finnish public discourse has been energy use. Since the 1990s, second homes were increasingly equipped and electrified, and the second home culture started to change from modest summer cottages into bigger and better-equipped second homes that could be used year-round (Pitkänen, 2011). These changes were reflected in the media discourse in the early 2000s, and the energy efficiency of second homes and the second home way of life in general was questioned. In the turn of the 2010s, the Finnish Ministry of Environment commissioned a large study of the second homes' potential for enhancing sustainable consumption and eco-efficiency (Rytkönen & Kirkkari, 2010). The study concluded that heating of and travelling to second homes are the main reasons for energy consumption at second homes and forecasted that increasing income levels and wealth will increase the emissions of second homes if no major eco-efficiency measures are taken. During the 2010s, the energy efficiency or increasing standard of equipment of second homes has not been heavily criticised, but the focus has been on the eco-efficiency measures and technological innovations such as solar panels, heat pumps, and geothermal energy. Meanwhile, second home culture has continued changing, and the modern second homes are bigger and better equipped than ever before. According to the main energy service provider of South Savo, second homes are the main source of the increasing energy consumption in the region.

Similar to the energy use, the consumption related to second homes was also questioned from the 2000s as a response to the changes in second home culture. Against the discourse that emphasized the ideals of the modesty and simplicity of cottage life (Vepsäläinen & Pitkänen, 2010), the consumption-centred second home discourse was boosted by national rural and island policy from the 1990s (Rantanen, 2021). Luxurious second homes were launched annually in national second home fairs from the year 2000, which raised the media publicity of the consumption-centred second home culture even more. This discourse collided with rising environmental awareness, raising also critical voices of the acceptability of the direction into which the second home culture was changing.

The environmental impacts of travelling between the first and second home has received less attention. Traffic emissions are acknowledged in the rural policy documents that, however, see that the potential increase in the emissions will be combatted by the decreasing need for mobility when second homes are converted into year-round use or permanent residences. As, for example, Vepsäläinen et al. (2015) have noted, similar expectations and hopes have been set by the rural developers and policy makers for decades. However, instead of a permanent move to rural areas, second home tourists have opted for a multi-local lifestyle combining flexibly the rural and urban lifestyles (Vepsäläinen et al., 2015). Instead of decreasing mobility, such multi-local lifestyles embed an increasing mobility between the urban and rural. Second home tourists are also more mobile than ever in their everyday life at the second home. A rainy day is no longer spent inside reading a book but driving to a nearby city for shopping and attractions (Rantanen, 2014).

The patterns of travel and second home use have been revised during the year 2020. Due to the Covid-19 pandemic, second home mobility was restricted for a while, and when the restrictions were lifted, the second home rentals and sales have peaked to an all-time high as people have been investing their time and money into a safe place (Pitkänen et al., 2020). Furthermore, the patterns of mobility have changed as people have been forced to stay put in one place at a time and avoid social contact. Teleworking has enabled place-independent work, and many have shifted their home office to their second home. For the first time, the cities have not been the only winners in the amount of migration, but also some second home rural municipalities have witnessed positive migration (Yle, 2020). It remains to be seen how these new developments affect the public discourses and how climate change and other environmental issues are approached in the context of second homes in the 2020s.

There is limited research on the second home vs. climate change nexus not only in Finland but also internationally. In the few existing studies, the focus is more on climate change vulnerability and adaptation than the potential harmful contribution of second homes. One explanation could be that second homes have seldom attracted the attention of environmental researchers as well as the falling of second homes in between different fields of study such as tourism and housing. The Finnish second home climate change programme demands more research on the potential climate risks of second homes but also better understanding of the climate impacts of the individual choices of second home owners (VAAL, 2019). Our study ends in a similar notion. According to our study, a theme that seems to be prominent in the public discourse but not touched upon at all in research is the potential of technical innovations and solutions to help mitigate the climate impacts of second homes. More research is needed not only on how these solutions can help to mitigate climate impacts but also how acceptable and desired such solutions are and how the second home culture could adapt to a more sustainable normal.

References

Adamiak, C., Hall, C. M., Hiltunen, M. J., & Pitkaenen, K. (2016). Substitute or addition to hypermobile lifestyles? Second home mobility and Finnish CO2 emissions. *Tourism Geographies*, *18*(2), 129–151. https://doi.org/10.1080/14616688.2016.1145250

Adie, B. A. (2020). Place attachment and post-disaster decision-making in a second home context: A conceptual framework. *Current Issues in Tourism*, *23*(10), 1205–1215. https://doi.org/10.1080/13683500.2019.1600475

Alasuutari, P., & Alasuutari, E. (2011). Maaseudun merkitykset suomalaisessa julkisessa keskustelussa. Diskurssianalyyttinen tarkastelu (Sitran selvityksiä 50). *The Finnish Innovation Fund Sitra*. https://media.sitra.fi/2017/02/24050617/SelvityksiC3A42050.pdf

Cheong, S. M. (2018). Second homes and vulnerability after Superstorm Sandy in Ortley Beach, New Jersey. *The Professional Geographer*, *70*(4), 583–592. https://doi.org/10.1080/00330124.2018.1432369

Hildén, M., Karvosenoja, N., Koskela, S., Kupiainen, K., Liski, J., Manninen, K., Paunu, V.-V., Repo, A., & Savonlahti, M. (2013). *Kansallisen energia- ja ilmastostrategian päivityksen ympäristövaikutusten arviointi*. Suomen ympäristökeskus 19.3.2013. https://tem.fi/documents/1410877/2626968/SYKE_strategian_arviointi.pdf/74aef6c7-431e-4ab6-9e12-0989f5b4f6c3/SYKE_strategian_arviointi.pdf

Hiltunen, M. J. (2007). Environmental impacts of rural second home tourism – Case lake district in Finland. *Scandinavian Journal of Hospitality and Tourism, 7*(3), 243–265. https://doi.org/10.1080/15022250701312335

Hiltunen, M. J., Pitkänen, K., & Halseth, G. (2016). Environmental perceptions of second home tourism impacts in Finland. *Local Environment, 21*(10), 1198–1214. https://doi.org/10.1080/13549839.2015.1079701

Hiltunen, M. J., Pitkänen, K., Vepsäläinen, M., & Hall, C. M. (2013). Second home tourism in Finland: Current trends and eco-social impacts. In Z. Roca (Eds.), *Second homes in Europe: Lifestyle issues and policy responses* (pp. 165–200). Ashgate.

Hoogendoorn, G., & Fitchett, J. M. (2018). Perspectives on second homes, climate change and tourism in South Africa. *African Journal of Hospitality, Tourism and Leisure, 7*(2), 1–18.

Kaltenborn, B. P., Andersen, O., & Nellemann, C. (2009). Amenity development in the Norwegian mountains: Effects of second home owner environmental attitudes on preferences for alternative development options. *Landscape and Urban Planning, 91*(4), 195–201. https://doi.org/10.1016/j.landurbplan.2009.01.001

Kangas, H.-L., & Lyytimäki, J. (2020). Luontoa vaivaa viestintävaje. In H. Mattila (Ed.), *Elämän verkko. Luonnon monimuotoisuutta edistämässä* (pp. 233–247). Gaudeamus.

Koivula, E., Tuominen, R., Lahtinen, M., Poutamo, S., & Saloranta, M. (2019). *Etelä-Savon matkailun hiilijalanjälki. Kohti vastuullista matkailua* (XAMK kehittää 76). Kaakkois-Suomen Ammattikorkeakoulu XAMK. www.theseus.fi/handle/10024/170534

Lait, M. (2018). The paradox of nature and elite second homes: Examining the eco-social impacts of Meech Lake cottagers in Gatineau Park, Québec. *Annals of Leisure Research, 21*(3), 302–323. https://doi.org/10.1080/11745398.2018.1426366

Long, D., & Hoogendoorn, G. (2013). Second home owner perceptions of their environmental impacts: The case of Hartbeespoort. *Urban Forum, 25*(4), 517–530. https://doi.org/10.1007/s12132-013-9208-y

Lyytimäki, J., & Tapio, P. (2009). Climate change as reported in the press of Finland: From screaming headlines to penetrating background noise. *International Journal of Environmental Studies, 66*(6), 723–735.

Ministry of the Employment and the Economy. (2017). *Taustaraportti kansalliselle energia- ja ilmastostrategialle vuoteen 2030*. Työ- ja elinkeinoministeriö, 1.2.2017 (päivitetty 2.2.2017). https://tem.fi/documents/1410877/3570111/Energia+ja+ilmastostrategian+TA USTARAPORTTI_1.2.+2017.pdf/d745fe78-02ad-49ab-8fb7-7251107981f7/Energia+ja +ilmastostrategian+TAUSTARAPORTTI_1.2.+2017.pdf?t=1486100831000

Næss, P., Xue, J., Stefansdottir, H., Steffansen, R., & Richardson, T. (2019). Second home mobility, climate impacts and travel modes: Can sustainability obstacles be overcome? *Journal of Transport Geography, 79*, 102468. https://doi.org/10.1016/j.jtrangeo.2019.102468

Nissinen, A., & Savolainen, H. (2019). *Julkisten hankintojen ja kotitalouksien kulutuksen hiilijalanjälki ja luonnonvarojen käyttö-ENVIMAT-mallinnuksen tuloksia* (Suomen ympäristökeskuksen raportteja 15/2019). Finnish Environment Institute. http://hdl.handle.net/10138/300737

Pitkänen, K. (2011). *Mökkimaisema muutoksessa: Kulttuurimaantieteellinen näkökulma mökkeilyyn* [Doctoral dissertation, University of Eastern Finland]. UEF/EREPOSITORY. https://erepo.uef.fi/handle/123456789/10452

Pitkänen, K., Hannonen, O., Toso, S., Gallent, N., Hamiduddin, I., Halseth, G., Hall, C. M., Müller, D. K., Treivish, A., & Nefedova, T. (2020). Second homes during corona – safe or unsafe haven and for whom? Reflections from researchers around the world. *Matkailututkimus, 16*(2), 20–39. https://doi.org/10.33351/mt.97559

Rantanen, M. (Ed.). (2014). *Modernisoituvat mökkeilytyylit. Paikallisten palveluympäristöjen muutosvoima. (Ruralia-instituutin raportteja 123)*. University of Helsinki. https://helda.helsinki.fi/bitstream/handle/10138/229344/Raportteja123.pdf?sequence=1&isAllowed=y

Rantanen, M. (2021). Monipaikkaisten asukkaiden toimijuuden representaatiot yhteiskunnallisen muutoksen välineenä. *Finnish Journal of Rural Studies, 29*, 131–163. https://doi.org/10.51807/maaseututkimus.112890

Rytkönen, A., & Kirkkari, A.-M. (Eds.). (2010). *Vapaa-ajan asumisen ekotehokkuus* (Suomen ympäristö 6/2010). Ministry of Environment. https://helda.helsinki.fi/handle/10138/37982

Salo, M., Nissinen, A., Mattinen, M., & Manninen, K. (2017). Ilmastodieetti – mihin sen antamat ilmastopainot perustuvat? *Finnish Environment Institute*. https://beta.ilmastodieetti.fi/pdf/Ilmastodieetti_dokumentaatio_2017-10-13.pdf

Sarajärvi, A., & Tuomi, J. (2017). *Laadullinen tutkimus ja sisällön analyysi*. Tammi.

Statistics Finland. (2020a). *Building stock 2019*. www.stat.fi/til/rakke/2019/rakke_2019_2020-05-27_kat_002_en.html

Statistics Finland. (2020b). *Most free-time residences were built in Kuusamo in the 2000s*. www.stat.fi/til/rakke/2019/rakke_2019_2020-05-27_tie_001_en.html

Tuominen, R. (2019). *Etelä-Savon matkailun alueellinen hiilijalanjälkilaskenta, raportti. Kaakkois-Suomen ammattikorkeakoulu XAMK*. www.xamk.fi/wp-content/uploads/2017/03/Etela-Savon-matkailun-alueellinen-hiilijalanjalkilaskenta_raportti_27052019_netti.pdf

Vapaa-ajan asukkaiden Liitto (VAAL) ry. (2019). *Vapaa-ajan asukkaiden liiton ilmastonmuutosohjelma*. https://asiakas.kotisivukone.com/files/valli.kotisivukone.com/Uutiset_2019/Vaal_ryn_ilmastomuutosohjelma.pdf

Vepsäläinen, M., & Pitkänen, K. (2010). Second home countryside. Representations of the rural in Finnish popular discourses. *Journal of Rural Studies, 26*(2), 194–204. https://doi.org/10.1016/j.jrurstud.2009.07.002

Vepsäläinen, M., Strandell, A., & Pitkänen, K. (2015). Muuttuvan vapaa-ajan asumisen hallinnan haasteet kunnissa. *Yhdyskuntasuunnittelu, 2*, 13–38. www.yss.fi/journal/muuttuvan-vapaa-ajan-asumisen-hallinnan-haasteet-kunnissa/

Yle. (2020). *Koronakriisi sai suomalaiset muuttamaan suurista kaupungeista maaseutumaisiin kuntiin – "Ilmiö on poikkeuksellinen", sanoo muuttoliiketutkija*. https://yle.fi/uutiset/3-11494111

Appendix 1: Analysed policy programmes

Finnish Government. (2001). Kansallinen ilmastostrategia. Valtioneuvoston selonteko eduskunnalle. Valtioneuvoston selonteko eduskunnalle 27.3.2001 (VNS 1/2001 vp). https://tem.fi/documents/1410877/2628005/Selonteko.pdf/a0b41756-6f0f-4007-9f0a-3ee350d4a266/Selonteko.pdf

Finnish Government. (2005a). Lähiajan energia- ja ilmastopolitiikan linjauksia – kansallinen strategia Kioton pöytäkirjan toimeenpanemiseksi. Valtioneuvoston selonteko eduskunnalle 24. päivänä marraskuuta 2005. https://tem.fi/documents/1410877/2627974/Strategia+2005/e1fde1d6-4019-42e8-b05d-0125b21d809a/Strategia+2005.pdf

Finnish Government. (2005b). Lähiajan energia- ja ilmastopolitiikan linjauksia – kansallinen strategia Kioton pöytäkirjan toimeenpanemiseksi. Taustaraportti. https://tem.fi/documents/1410877/2627974/Strategia+2005/e1fde1d6-4019-42e8-b05d-0125b21d809a/Strategia+2005.pdf

Finnish Government. (2008). Pitkän aikavälin ilmasto- ja energiastrategia Valtioneuvoston selonteko eduskunnalle 6. päivänä marraskuuta 2008. https://tem.fi/documents/1410877/2627938/Selonteko+2008.pdf/f9b30f57-e51f-464c-ae7f-956b070a0f88/Selonteko+2008.pdf

FinnishGovernment.(2016).Valtioneuvostonselontekokansallisestaenergia-jailmastostrategiasta vuoteen 2030. https://tem.fi/documents/1410877/3570111/Kansallinen+energia-+ja+ilmastos trategia+vuoteen+2030+24+11+2016+lopull.pdf/a07ba219-f4ef-47f7-ba39-70c9261d2a63/Kansallinen+energia-+ja+ilmastostrategia+vuoteen+2030+24+11+2016+lopull.pdf

Hildén, M., Karvosenoja, N., Koskela, S., Kupiainen, K., Laine, A., Rinne, J., Seppälä, J., Savolahti, M., & Sokka, L. (2008). Pitkän aikavälin ilmasto- ja energiastrategian ympäristöarviointi. Suomen ympäristökeskus.

Hildén, M., Karvosenoja, N., Koskela, S., Kupiainen, K., Liski, J., Manninen, K., Paunu, V-V., Repo, A., & Savolahti, M. (2013). Kansallisen energia- ja ilmastostrategian päivityksen ympäristövaikutusten arviointi. Suomen ympäristökeskus. https://tem.fi/documents/1410877/2626968/SYKE_strategian_arviointi.pdf/74aef6c7-431e-4ab6-9e12-0989f5b4f6c3/SYKE_strategian_arviointi.pdf

Ministry of Agriculture and Forestry. (2017). *Saaristo-ohjelma 2017–2019: Saaret, meri, järvet, joet ja rantavyöhyke aluekehitystekijöinä.* (Maa- ja metsätalousministeriön julkaisuja 6/2017). https://julkaisut.valtioneuvosto.fi/handle/10024/80070

Ministry of Employment and the Economy. (2001). Kasvihuonekaasujen vähentämistarpeet ja mahdollisuudet Suomessa. (Kansallisen ilmastostrategian taustaselvitys. Kauppa- ja teollisuusministeriön julkaisuja 4/2001). https://tem.fi/documents/1410877/2628005/Taustaraportti.pdf/79ff5765-4789-4b32-9227-6af8019d3243/Taustaraportti.pdf

Ministry of Employment and the Economy. (2013). Kansallinen energia- ja ilmastostrategia Valtioneuvoston selonteko eduskunnalle 20. päivänä maaliskuuta 2013 (VNS 2/2013 vp). (Työ-jaelinkeinoministeriönjulkaisuja8/2013).https://tem.fi/documents/1410877/2626968/Energia-_ja_ilmastostrategia_2013.pdf/ce0e9b73-f907-454b-b52b-87fa9fa481d2/Energia-_ja_ilmastostrategia_2013.pdf

Ministry of Employment and the Economy. (2014). Mahdollisuuksien maaseutu. Maaseutupoliittinen kokonaisohjelma 2014–2020 (Työ- ja elinkeinoministeriön julkaisuja 9/2014). www.maaseutupolitiikka.fi/uploads/MANE-raportit/Mahdollisuuksien_maaseutu_25022014.pdf

Ministry of Employment and the Economy. (2014). Energia- ja ilmastotiekartta 2050. Parlamentaarisen energia- ja ilmastokomitean mietintö 16. päivänä lokakuuta 2014. (Työ- ja elinkeinoministeriön julkaisuja 31/2014). https://tem.fi/documents/1410877/2628105/Energia-+ja+ilmastotiekartta+2050.pdf/1584025f-c5c7-456c-a912-aba0ee3e5052/Energia-+ja+ilmastotiekartta+2050.pdf

Ministry of Employment and the Economy. (2015). Selvitys energiapolitiikan vaihtoehdoista. (Työ- ja elinkeinoministeriön julkaisuja 25/2015). https://tem.fi/documents/1410877/2628109/Virkamiesselvitys+energiapolitiikan+vaihtoehdoista.

pdf/2202f950-da88-4d90-a3b5-9d4fbdb3c7c7/Virkamiesselvitys+energiapolitiikan+vaih toehdoista.pdf

Ministry of Employment and the Economy. (2017). Taustaraportti kansalliselle energia- ja ilmastostrategialle vuoteen 2030 1.2.2017 (päivitetty 2.2.2017). https://tem. fi/documents/1410877/3570111/Energia-+ja+ilmastostrategian+TAUSTARAPOR TTI_1.2.+2017.pdf/d745fe78-02ad-49ab-8fb7-7251107981f7/Energia-+ja+ilmastostrate gian+TAUSTARAPORTTI_1.2.+2017.pdf

Mörsky, S. K., Panula-Ontto-Suuronen, A., & Saari, A. (2013). *Uudistava, ekovastuullinen Savo. Savon ilmasto-ohjelma 2025, Etelä-Savo ja Pohjois-Savo.* (Elinvoimaa alueille 3/2013). Etelä-Savon elinkeino-, liikenne- ja ympäristökeskus. www.doria.fi/ handle/10024/90378

Regional Council of South Savo. (2018). *Etelä-Savon maakuntaohjelma 2018–2021.* http://es2017.kixit.fi/resources/public//Maakuntaliitto/Maakuntaohjelma/Maakunt-aohjelma_2018-2021.pdf

5 Fighting Mother Nature

Second home owners, risk awareness, and post-disaster planning on Fire Island, New York

Bailey Ashton Adie

Introduction

According to the IPCC (2014), anthropogenic climate change poses a significant threat to humanity. This threat is heightened in certain areas where changing weather patterns are steadily increasing the natural hazard risk as well as those places which are now exposed to new hazards. This is of particular importance in the context of second homes as these are often located in areas of natural beauty, such as coastlines and mountainous areas, which are themselves more highly prone to natural hazard risks (Adie, 2020). Examples of common hazards confronted by second home owners are volcanic activity (Ruiz & Hernández, 2014), landslides (Amore, 2023), hurricanes (Adie, 2023), and drought (Hoogendoorn & Fitchett, 2018). However, regardless of the heightened risk levels faced by second home owners, there has been relatively little research undertaken in order to ascertain either their awareness of or their responses to this risk. This is partly due to the fact that most research into disasters and homeownership has predominantly focused on primary homeowners, with few discussions of second home owners as their own unique community. It is this gap which this chapter seeks to fill. Building on the findings of Adie (2023), this chapter discusses the risk awareness and risk mitigation undertaken by second home owners in Ocean Beach, Fire Island, New York, USA following Hurricane Sandy.

Second homes, place attachment, and risk awareness

Second homes are complex entities whose definition alone is often very context specific (Hall & Müller, 2004), and there a variety of motivations for their ownership. While motivations are often very personal, there are some observed common reasons why an individual may purchase a second home. Both communing with nature (Bjerke et al., 2006; Dias & Domingues, 2018; Jaakson, 1986; Müller, 2002; Tuulentie, 2006) and escape (Chaplin, 1999; Nouza et al., 2018; Perkins & Thorns, 2006; Stedman, 2006a; Williams & Van Patten, 2006) have been highlighted as common motivating factors. Additionally, some individuals purchase a second home to be a locus of family gatherings or to hand down to children and grandchildren (Blondy et al., 2018; Jansson & Müller, 2004; Williams & Van Patten, 2006).

DOI: 10.4324/9781003091295-5

Unsurprisingly then, second homes may also be inherited properties, although some inherited properties may have previously been primary family homes (McIntyre et al., 2006; Svels & Åkerlund, 2018; Williams & Van Patten, 2006). Furthermore, while this chapter will be dealing solely with second homes purchased or retained for personal use, it must be noted that some second homes are purchased solely as investment properties (Norris & Winston, 2010; Paris, 2018).

Understandably, as the motivation between second home ownership is so diverse, the rationale behind the development and levels of place attachment related to the second home are equally varied. Place attachment in the context of second homes is defined as "the sense of place or sets of meaning associated with the recreation homes and the surrounding settings [which] are intertwined with natural, social, historical, and cultural processes" (Kaltenborn, 1997, p. 186), emphasizing the importance of personal experience and memory (Nouza et al., 2018; Tuulentie, 2007). Previous research has shown that levels of place attachment can vary significantly when compared with permanent residents. Various studies have shown that second home owners are more place attached (Stedman, 2006a, 2006b), less place attached (Nielsen-Pincus et al., 2010), or equally so, albeit for a different reason than primary homeowners (McIntyre & Pavlovich, 2006). In McIntyre and Pavlovich's (2006) research, coastal second home owners in New Zealand drew their place attachment from their physical setting, whereas the permanent residents cited the community as more important, although they too appreciated their home's setting.

In comparison, other studies have emphasized the importance of community elements in the development of place attachment in second home owners (Adie, 2023; Kelly & Hosking, 2008; Selwood & Tonts, 2006). In Adie (2023), interpersonal relationships were key elements of place attachment among coastal second home owners in the US, but in this case, there was, along with community ties, an emphasis on the importance of the second home as a locus for both family memories and intergenerational interaction. In the case of Selwood and Tonts (2006), place attachment was strongly tied to personal history with the second home destination, with those who had owned their homes longer exhibiting higher levels of place attachment. These individuals were especially invested in the preservation of the local community, particularly the built environment, highlighting an element of nostalgia. This is echoed in the findings of Adie and de Bernardi (2020) where one group of second home owners also lamented the changing landscape, in particular the construction of more modern and larger properties. The other group, instead, had nostalgia driven by their families' longer history in the location and a feeling of intergenerational community connection, which is more akin to the place attachment observed in permanent residents (McIntyre & Pavlovich, 2006; Stedman, 2006a, 2006b). Thus, as can be seen, place attachment among second home owners can be driven by a variety of factors but may very well be significantly high either due to emotional attachment as a result of personal history in the location or due to the self-selection of appealing physical environments (Anton & Lawrence, 2014).

Understanding second home owners' place attachment becomes of greater importance in the face of increased hazard risk, particularly as there has been a noted interaction between place attachment levels and risk awareness. Previous research on primary homeowners has highlighted that risk awareness can trigger recognition of a homeowners' place attachment (Anton & Lawrence, 2014) or even have a detrimental impact on place attachment levels (Peng et al., 2017; Ruiz & Hernández, 2014). However, and perhaps more importantly in hazard prone areas, place attachment can have an indirect impact on risk mitigation strategies. This is due to the fact that risk awareness has a direct influence on eventual adoption of mitigation measures (Brenkert-Smith et al., 2012; Palm & Hodgson, 1992), with emotional responses having a significant impact on the level of response (Miceli et al., 2008). Place attachment has been noted as having two distinct impacts on risk awareness: risk minimization or risk mitigation.

Risk minimization has been highlighted by multiple authors (Bonaiuto et al., 2016; De Dominicis et al., 2015; Domingues et al., 2021; Domingues et al., 2018). The literature review on place attachment and natural hazard risk performed by Bonaiuto et al. (2016, p. 48) noted "a tendency for highly attached people to both deny the existence of, and not properly avoid, natural environmental risks." However, this risk denial or minimization can cause significant issues, particularly in the development of safer and more resilient built environments and communities and can actually increase the personal risk faced by residents (Bonaiuto et al., 2016). In contrast, place attachment in other studies has been found to increase a property owner's desire to enact mitigation strategies (Burley et al., 2007; Ghasemi et al., 2020; Kick et al., 2011; Mishra et al., 2010; Ratnam et al., 2016). Risk in this context is viewed as an element of place and thus accepted as something that must be confronted in order to continue habitation (Burley et al., 2007; Ratnam et al., 2016). However, not all mitigation strategies are sufficient to confront the risks faced by certain communities. For example, in the studies undertaken by Kick et al. (2011) and Lambert et al. (2021), place attachment prevents more drastic mitigation measures, such as eventual relocation. Thus, regardless of whether individuals are minimizing or mitigating the risk faced, place-attached homeowners will stay in the hazard-prone location, even suffering financial hardship to maintain their residence (Nouza et al., 2018). In most instances, only external issues such as government decision-making or high levels of financial precarity will result in relocation (Brenkert-Smith et al., 2012; Bukvic & Owen, 2017; Bukvic et al., 2015; Bukvic et al., 2018; Poussin et al., 2014).

Within the context of second homes, the impact of place attachment on risk awareness and eventual risk mitigation responses following a disaster has been discussed conceptually by Adie (2020). Based on her model (Figure 5.1), individuals who have stronger levels of place attachment have two specific risk responses should there be no extenuating external factors: return or return and adapt. Either response could indicate a risk-aware individual, but, in the case of those who do not to adapt, factors such as adaptation cost may be the cause for lack of action. In contrast, risk deniers are most likely to return without adapting, either due to a normalization of risk or to a minimization of its potential impact, as has been noted in the literature on primary homeowners. However, as has been noted, second homes are often maintained or purchased due to personal reasons as opposed to pragmatic ones seen in primary homes (i.e. a location close to work). Thus, according to Adie's (2020) model, place attachment would be the dominant factor in any response to hazard risk.

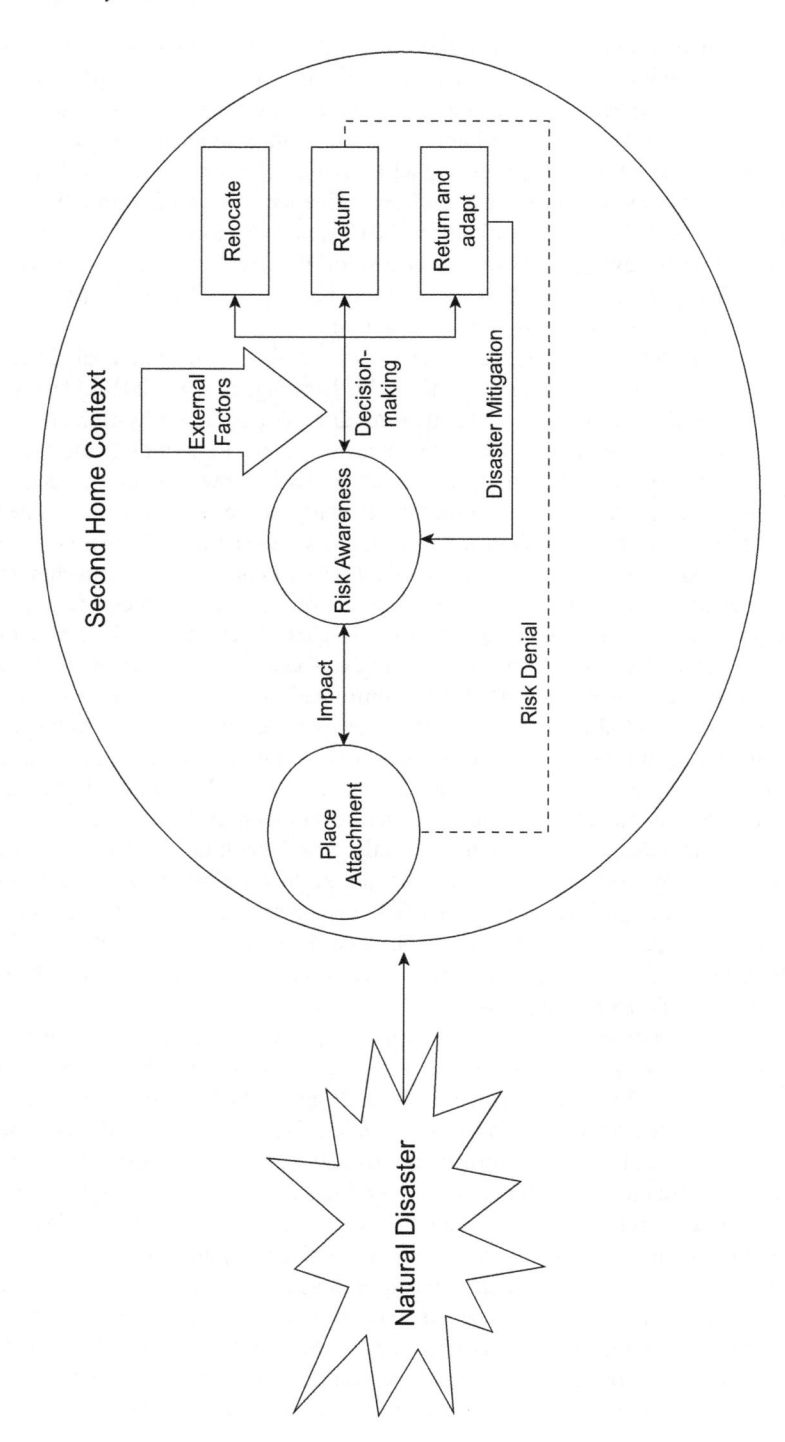

Figure 5.1 Post-disaster decision-making process of second home owners

Fire Island context

Fire Island is located off the southern coastline of Long Island, New York, USA. A narrow barrier island, it is only a quarter mile wide at its broadest point. However, it is quite long at almost 31 miles in total. The island has historically been used for a variety of activities, including whaling, but was uninhabited until the mid-19th century (Koppelman & Forman, 2008). It was at this time that the island's usage pattern changed considerably with the construction of the first beach resort, the Surf Hotel. The resort proved popular, and the island's reputation as a beach destination grew. Eventually, this led to the establishment of the first second home community, Point O'Woods, in 1894 (Koppelman & Forman, 2008). Leisure and recreation on the island continued over the years, which has resulted in what are, today, 17 communities where approximately 95% of the housing stock is second homes. Ocean Beach, the largest of these communities, with a total of 562 second homes, is one of two official villages on the island, having been incorporated in 1921, only 13 years after its founding (Koppelman & Forman, 2008).

Fire Island, as a barrier island, faces natural hazards on a regular basis, including significant dune erosion. However, one of the most immediately destructive risks is the result of the island's risks factors during Atlantic hurricane season, which occurs between June and November each year. During hurricane or tropical storm events, wind damage, storm surges, and post-storm flooding are common, and longer-term residents will have significant experience with these types of hazards. However, while residents have experience with storm-related damage, the strength of Hurricane Sandy was unlike any hurricane in most residents' living memory as the last extremely destructive hurricane to make landfall was the Long Island Express in 1938.

Hurricane Sandy made landfall on Fire Island on 29 October 2012 and left a raft of damage in its wake. The damage was significant, with 200 homes completely destroyed and 2,200 damaged (U.S. Army Corps of Engineers, n.d.). The island's natural defense also took on substantial damage with the large protective sand dunes having been entirely destroyed (Blake et al., 2013), with approximately 54.4% of total beach volume lost (Hapke et al., 2013). According to the U.S. Geological Survey (Hapke et al., 2013, p. 1), the storm "profoundly impacted the morphology of Fire Island . . . that has left the barrier island vulnerable to future storms." Thus, the associated risks of natural hazards are significantly higher for second home owners, which is reflected in the increased insurance costs and housing regulations implemented post-disaster.

Methodology

The interview data that informs this study was collected over the holiday weekend of 4 July 2017 as part of a wider body of work on second home owners and post-disaster decision-making. This was determined to be a period with high owner occupancy based on the researcher's own knowledge of the study area as well as the findings of previous research (Stewart & Stynes, 2006). Interviews were initially drawn from within the researcher's own network due to their position as a community insider, and further participants were reached through snowball sampling (Robinson, 2014). This insider status allowed for the unhindered discussion of the topics under study (Dwyer & Buckle, 2009), which allowed for more detail and emotional openness than may be expected when discussing with an outsider. The interviews were semi-structured, further providing space for freedom of expression, which resulted in a total of 14 interview sessions. These lasted anywhere from seven to 35 minutes, with most second home owners being located in Ocean Beach or the neighbouring community of Seaview. The demographic profile of these participants was predominantly over the age of 65, retired, and highly educated. The interviewee pool also skewed marginally more female. In terms of history of ownership, a little fewer than half of the interviewees had inherited their second home.

Findings

All 14 of the interviewees had chosen to return to Fire Island following the Hurricane Sandy and subsequent storm damage, and all showed high levels of place attachment, as reported in a previous work (Adie, 2023). Interestingly, while none chose to sell their main second home, one of the respondents owned another house in Ocean Beach which they did sell as it had become too expensive to maintain. This is a clear example of an investment property whose ownership was purely utilitarian, and its post disaster sale is in line with previous research on non-place-attached responses to known risk, and this was in direct contrast to their treatment of the property they considered their second home. It should also be noted that two interviewees spoke of their past experiences with hurricanes and associated natural hazards, but they did not discuss future risks during their interview.

As has been highlighted in the literature, there are two main risk responses observed in place-attached individuals, barring the influence of external extenuating factors. The first of these, return and rebuild, was the most common response as observed in three-quarter of all interviews that discussed risk. Of these respondents, only Respondents 1, 2, and 13 experienced damage, with the rest having minor to no damage to their homes. Additionally, most of the respondents who chose to return and rebuild were clearly aware of the risk but chose to accept it as an element of the place that they loved. Both Respondents 8 and 2 had fixed the damage to their homes, which was minimal in the case of Respondent 8, but they also didn't express worry over another Hurricane Sandy level event. In particular, Respondent 2 noted that their insurance would cover damage, so it wasn't an issue. Respondent 3 not only expressed their acceptance of the risk but also related it to other hazard risks faced by primary homeowners in the US.

> Actually, the things that have caused more damage in Ocean Beach than hurricanes have been the famous nor'easters around Halloween. The Halloween storm of whatever year it was caused much more flooding and much more damage here than Hurricane Sandy, and it's not our first hurricane. So, you know it's, it's a way of life here. It's like, you know, people in California have to be used to fires.

Respondent 7 also related the risk faced by the island's second home owners to primary homeowners in other parts of the US. In particular, they noted that it was unfair to demonize the second home owners for living in a risk-prone area as there were hazards no matter where you lived. They also emphasized that another big storm was inevitable and had a very fatalistic view of the outcome of future events of this magnitude: "If we got hit here, this whole island would be gone." They were not alone in their view that another large storm would happen at some point, as can be seen in the response of Respondent 14.

> You know you look at it on a July day where it's beautiful blue sky, no clouds – you don't think about it.

In this case, their acceptance of what they viewed as an unavoidable event allowed them to put the risk at the back of their mind. Respondent 1, who admitted that they were less place attached to their home than their family and who experienced moderate damage, took a more pragmatic and humanist approach to the next big storm. "Houses you can rebuild. Lives you can't." (Respondent 1). For them, risk to property was not a major concern so long as people were not hurt. In contrast, Respondent 6 expressed risk denial in relation to another large hurricane event while simultaneously illustrating risk awareness to natural hazards: "We're here to deal with what the environment hurls at us, and hopefully that won't ever happen again."

While all of the previous respondents acknowledged the risks associated with their continued homeownership, the risk was often minimized, predominantly due to its being an element of place that had always been there. In comparison, both Respondent 10 and 13 expressed significant concern for the future of their homes. Respondent 10 noted that they had previously viewed storm damage as a normal element of owning their coastal home, but Sandy changed that.

> This one changed how I think now. Now I'm like, you know what, we are very vulnerable. I'm very nervous about the bay coming up more than the ocean coming down.

They were also keenly aware of the impact of coastal erosion and highlighted the need for high dunes as a protective measure for homeowners. Their responses indicated an expectation that mitigation measures should be undertaken by the government in the form of coastal engineering. Respondent 13 also indicated the need for government assistance, but, in their case, it was in relation to financial aid to assist in mitigation activities. In particular, Respondent 13 had experienced extensive flooding, and, while they had fixed much of the damage, they expressed a desire to undertake further mitigation such as lifting their house up on stilts, a common flood mitigation action on the island. However, they noted that this was very expensive and that they would only be able to engage in this type of mitigation if they had financial assistance from the government.

In line with the need for mitigation expressed by Respondent 13, those who chose to return, rebuild, and adapt in order to mitigate risks had invariably experienced moderate to significant damage as a result of Sandy and successive hazard events. However, the level of mitigation was highly dependent on individual circumstances. For example, Respondent 12 had flooding throughout their house and damage to many of their household goods. They acknowledge the risks faced at their home but also stated that "you can't control the weather and the bay." They had the most minimal mitigation response to future risk, namely the purchasing of flood insurance, as the repairs were noted as being too expensive to repeat in the event of more storm damage at a later date. In comparison, Respondent 5, who experiences repeated heavy flood due to their proximity to the bay, rebuilt using different building materials which had proven to be more resistance to damage during Sandy, but they were not able to mitigate to the extent that they wished.

> I mean, I'm hoping that I can raise it, but it's very expensive. So, after the hurricane I built it back so that everything's hard wood, and so hopefully . . . I had put an addition on the house before the hurricane, and the little bathroom in the back was hardwood and ceramic floor. And, of course, you know the toilet and the shower, and that was the only room that I only had to wash out. It wasn't damaged at all. So, I built everything back with hardwood instead of, you know, instead of drywall and instead of insulation . . . I built it back with hardwood so that, if we get flooded again, I'll just have to replace the couch and the beds and the washer and dryer and things.

As can be seen, Respondent 5 is keenly aware of the potential damage to their property from repeated flooding, but, as with Respondent 13, raising their house on stilts is currently financially unfeasible. In the long term, raising a house is better financially as residents in immediate flood risk zones risk extremely high flood insurance premiums if they do not raise their property. However, the costs to raise a property are high, and many cannot afford the upfront costs.

In some instances, though, this choice is taken away from homeowners. For example, Respondent 11 found themselves forced to raise their home on stilts due to external regulations. They acknowledged the high risk involved in staying, calling the hurricane "a reality check that so many things are out of your control." However, while their house had experienced some damage, they had originally only planned to rebuild due to the cost involved in mitigation, as was the case of Respondent 13. The decision to mitigate was as a result of the discovery that their foundation was unsound. They indicated that laying a new foundation was akin to building new, and thus the house had to be lifted.

Discussion

Hurricane Sandy was the most damaging natural hazard event to hit Fire Island since 1938, with a substantial impact on both the natural and built infrastructure. Given the place attachment of the homeowners discussed in a previous work (Adie, 2023), it is clear that there is a continuing impact of second home owners' place attachment on risk awareness and risk mitigation following a major hazard event and the ensuing disaster, supporting the model proposed by Adie (2020). As can be seen in the findings, the majority of respondents chose to return and rebuild. In line with previous research (De Dominicis et al., 2015; Domingues et al., 2021; Domingues et al., 2018), most minimized the impact of the natural hazard risk that they faced by retaining their second home. However, this group of second home owners were clearly highly risk aware, with many viewing another massively damaging storm as an inevitability due to their location. While this contrasts with the aforementioned works as well as Bonaiuto et al. (2016), it appears to support the work by Lambert et al. (2021) whose primary homeowners often were disinclined to undertake personal mitigating adaptations and instead expected government action and support to address the issue. This emphasis on the need for government intervention was also reflected in the return-and-rebuild homeowners, albeit only in two instances.

For those who chose instead to return, rebuild, and adapt, the adaptation was, for most of the respondents, an accepted necessity in the face of increasing risk, predominantly from flooding. However, this group was significantly more constrained by personal finances, as has been emphasized in previous works (Bukvic & Owen, 2017; Bukvic et al., 2015; Bukvic et al., 2018; Poussin et al., 2014). This led to a variety of mitigation strategies, including the use of more traditional building techniques in the rebuilding process, raising their house above the flood line, or even the simple act of purchasing flood insurance. The most expensive measure, raising the house, also lowers the homeowners' risk the most, whereas the purchasing of flood insurance merely lowers the potential financial risk, whereas the physical property will remain highly vulnerable to future natural hazards. In all three cases, the cost of physically lifting a house was highlighted as a barrier to true risk reduction, with the only respondent who lifted their house having done so due legal requirements. However, the eventual cost of mitigating was viewed as justified even though it was financially difficult for some of the respondents, supporting Nouza et al.'s (2018, p. 239) finding that "the value assigned to second home ownership is, taken as a whole, outweighs the stress connected with financing it".

What is interesting to note in the findings is that almost all of the respondents have clear high levels of risk awareness and significant experience of natural hazards. However, the majority did not choose to mitigate these potential risks. This can perhaps be explained by the experiences of the two groups. Whereas those who chose to adapt their homes had experienced significant damage, the majority of those who chose merely to return and rebuild had minimal damage. In the few instances where there was more substantial damage, the decision to only rebuild was purely financial, with two individuals having the financial stability to afford repairs without concern and the other being constrained by costs required to do anything beyond repair the damage. This supports Kick et al.'s (2011) findings that note that those who face repeat flood loss are more likely to enact risk mitigations. More specifically, because the majority of the homeowners did not and do not experience repeat flood damage, they are less inclined to alter their current behaviour.

Conclusion

As coastal second home properties will inevitably face increasing natural hazard risks, it becomes essential to understand not only second home owners' awareness but also their response to this risk. This chapter has sought to address this issue through the use of a post-disaster second home context in the USA and building on previous work highlighting the high place attachment levels of this group of home-owners. Based on the findings and discussion, it becomes clear that this group of second home owners is highly risk aware, but this risk awareness, which is mediated through their place attachment, resulted in two diverse responses to the risk, namely whether or not to undertake any adaptations to mitigate the risk, which is in line with previous research. The decision to mitigate was, interestingly, not tied to perceived future risk but instead past personal experiences of hazard impacts at their own property. Thus, in order to create more resilient second home communities, the risk of natural hazard impacts needs to be stressed to homeowners, with an emphasis on the types of damage they may face and post-impact costs to fix this damage. Furthermore, assumptions around the financial stability of second home owners need to be adjusted, particularly as those who inherit their property may not be as well off as previous generations or whose property may now be in a much more affluent area than when it was first purchased. In order to address this issue, there should also be an easing of access to mitigation activities, particularly in regard to financial cost.

One of the limitations of this research is the relatively small number of interviews collected. It is acknowledged that it would be beneficial to have a much broader array of responses, particularly from other communities on the island. Furthermore, Fire Island, as a long-standing second home enclave, may prove to be unique when compared to other second home locations that have a mix of primary and second home owners. Future research should engage with second home owners in these areas as well. Additionally, it would be of interest to assess the same process of place attachment's impact on risk awareness and risk mitigation in a less hazard prone environment where the risk is less consistent and/or damage as a result of natural hazards is much rarer. This would provide a greater understanding of the phenomenon and also be useful in clarifying the applicability proposed by Adie (2020) more generally.

References

Adie, B. A. (2020). Place attachment and post-disaster decision-making in a second home context: A conceptual framework. *Current Issues in Tourism*, *23*(10), 1205–1215. https://doi.org/10.1080/13683500.2019.1600475

Adie, B. A. (2023). Should I stay or should I go? Hurricane Sandy and second home tourism on Fire Island, New York. In C. M. Hall & G. Prayag (Eds.), *Tourism, cyclones, hurricanes, and flooding*. Channel View Publications.

Adie, B. A., & de Bernardi, C. (2020). 'Oh my god what is happening?': Historic second home communities and post-disaster nostalgia. *Journal of Heritage Tourism*. https://doi.org/10.1080/1743873X.2020.1828429.

Amore, A. (2023). Reframing sustainability and resilience in the recovery of the Cinque Terre following the 2011 floods. In C. M. Hall & G. Prayag (Eds.), *Tourism and flooding*. Channel View Publications.

Anton, C. E., & Lawrence, C. (2014). Home is where the heart is: The effect of place of residence on place attachment and community participation. *Journal of Environmental Psychology, 40*, 451–461. https://doi.org/10.1016/j.jenvp.2014.10.007

Bjerke, T., Kaltenborn, B. P., & Vittersø, J. (2006). Cabin life: Restorative and affective aspects. In N. McIntyre, D. R. Williams, & K. E. McHugh (Eds.), *Multiple dwelling and tourism: Negotiating place, home and identity* (pp. 87–102). CABI.

Blake, E. S., Kimberlain, T. B., Berg, R. J., Cangialosi, J. P., & Beven, J. L. (2013). *Tropical cyclone report: Hurricane Sandy (AL182012) 22–29 October 2012*. National Hurricane Center. www.nhc.noaa.gov/data/tcr/AL182012_Sandy.pdf

Blondy, C., Plumejeaud, C., Vacher, L., Vye, D., & Bontet, C. (2018). Do second home owners only play a secondary role in coastal territories? A case study in Charente-Maritime (France). In C. M. Hall & D. K. Müller (Eds.), *The Routledge handbook of second home tourism and mobilities* (pp. 233–244). Routledge.

Bonaiuto, M., Alves, S., De Dominicis, S., & Petruccelli, I. (2016). Place attachment and natural hazard risk: Research review and agenda. *Journal of Environmental Psychology, 48*, 33–53. https://doi.org/10.1016/j.jenvp.2016.07.007

Brenkert-Smith, H., Champ, P. A., & Flores, N. (2012). Trying not to get burned: Understanding homeowners' wildfire risk-mitigation behaviors. *Environmental Management, 50*, 1139–1151. https://doi.org/10.1007/s00267-012-9949-8

Bukvic, A., & Owen, G. (2017). Attitudes towards relocation following Hurricane Sandy: Should we stay or should we go? *Disasters, 41*(1), 101–123. https://doi.org/10.1111/disa.12186

Bukvic, A., Smith, A., & Zhang, A. (2015). Evaluating drivers of coastal relocation in Hurricane Sandy affected communities. *International Journal of Disaster Risk Reduction, 13*, 215–228. https://doi.org/10.1016/j.ijdrr.2015.06.008

Bukvic, A., Zhu, H., Lavoie, R., & Becker, A. (2018). The role of proximity to waterfront in residents' relocation decision-making post-Hurricane Sandy. *Ocean and Coastal Management, 154*, 8–19. https://doi.org/10.1016/j.ocecoaman.2018.01.002

Burley, D., Jenkins, P., Laska, S., & Davis, T. (2007). Place attachment and environmental change in coastal Louisiana. *Organization & Environment, 20*(3), 347–366. https://doi.org/10.1177/1086026607305739

Chaplin, D. (1999). Consuming work/productive leisure: The consumption patterns of second home environments. *Leisure Studies, 18*(1), 41–55. https://doi.org/10.1080/026143699375041

De Dominicis, S., Fornara, F., Cancellieri, U. G., Twigger-Ross, C., & Bonaiuto, M. (2015). We are at risk, and so what? Place attachment, environmental risk perceptions and preventive coping behaviours. *Journal of Environmental Psychology, 43*, 66–78. https://doi.org/10.1016/j.jenvp.2015.05.010

Dias, J. A., & Domingues, A. (2018). Follow the sun: Retirees motorhomes' movements, meanings and practices during the winter season in the Algarve. In C. M. Hall & D. K. Müller (Eds.), *The Routledge handbook of second home tourism and mobilities* (pp. 338–352). Routledge.

Domingues, R. B., de Jesus, S. N., & Ferreira, O. (2021). Place attachment, risk perception, and preparedness in a population exposed to coastal hazards: A case study in Faro Beach, southern Portugal. *International Journal of Disaster Risk Reduction, 60*, 102288. https://doi.org/10.1016/j.ijdrr.2021.102288

Domingues, R. B., Santos, M. C., de Jesus, S. N., & Ferreira, O. (2018). How a coastal community looks at coastal hazards and risks in a vulnerable barrier island system (Faro beach, southern Portugal). *Ocean and Coastal Management*, *157*, 248–256. https://doi.org/10.1016/j.ocecoaman.2018.03.015

Dwyer, S. C., & Buckle, J. L. (2009). The space between: On being an insider-outsider in qualitative research. *International Journal of Qualitative Methods*, *8*(1), 54–63. https://doi.org/10.1177/160940690900800105

Ghasemi, B., Kyle, G. T., & Absher, J. D. (2020). An examination of the social-psychological drivers of homeowner wildfire mitigation. *Journal of Environmental Psychology*, *70*, 101442. https://doi.org/10.1016/j.jenvp.2020.101442

Hall, C. M., & Müller, D. K. (2004). Introduction: Second homes, curse or blessing? Revisited. In C. M. Hall & D. K. Müller (Eds.), *Tourism, mobility and second homes: Between elite landscape and common ground* (pp. 3–14). Channel View Publications.

Hapke, C. J., Brenner, O., Hehre, R., & Reynolds, B. J. (2013). *Coastal Change from Hurricane Sandy and the 2012–13 winter storm season – Fire Island, New York*. U.S. Geological Survey Open-File Report 2013–1231, 37p. https://pubs.usgs.gov/of/2013/1231/pdf/ofr2013-1231.pdf

Hoogendoorn, G., & Fitchett, J. M. (2018). Perspectives on second homes, climate change and tourism in South Africa. *African Journal of Hospitality, Tourism, and Leisure*, *7*(2). www.ajhtl.com/uploads/7/1/6/3/7163688/artricle_46_vol7_2__2018.pdf

IPCC. (2014). *Climate change 2014: Impacts, adaptation, and vulnerability. Part A: Global and sectoral aspects. Working group II contribution to the fifth assessment report of the intergovernmental panel on climate change*. Cambridge University Press.

Jaakson, R. (1986). Second-home domestic tourism. *Annals of Tourism Research*, *13*, 367–391. https://doi.org/10.1016/0160-7383(86)90026-5

Jansson, B., & Müller, D. K. (2004). Second home plans among second home owners in Northern Europe's periphery. In C. M. Hall & D. K. Müller (Eds.), *Tourism, mobility and second homes: Between elite landscape and common ground* (pp. 261–272). Channel View Publications.

Kaltenborn, B. P. (1997). Nature of place attachment: A study among recreation homeowners in Southern Norway. *Leisure Sciences*, *19*(3), 175–189. https://doi.org/10.1080/01490409709512248

Kelly, G., & Hosking, K. (2008). Nonpermanent residents, place attachment, and "sea change" communities. *Environment and Behavior*, *40*(4), 575–594. https://doi.org/10.1177/0013916507302246

Kick, E. L., Fraser, J. C., Fulkerson, G. M., McKinney, L. A., & De Vries, D. H. (2011). Repetitive flood victims and acceptance of FEMA mitigation offers: An analysis with community-system policy implications. *Disasters*, *35*(3), 510–539. https://doi.org/10.1111/j.1467-7717.2011.01226.x

Koppelman, L. E., & Forman, S. (2008). *The fire island national seashore: A history*. State University of New York Press.

Lambert, C. E., Holley, J. R., McComas, K. A., Snider, N. P., & Tucker, G. K. (2021). Eroding land and erasing place: A qualitative study of place attachment, risk perception, and coastal land loss in Southern Louisiana. *Sustainability*, *13*, 6269. https://doi.org/10.3390/su13116269

McIntyre, N., & Pavlovich, K. (2006). Changing places: Amenity coastal communities in transition. In N. McIntyre, D. R. Williams, & K. E. McHugh (Eds.), *Multiple dwelling and tourism: Negotiating place, home and identity* (pp. 239–261). CABI.

McIntyre, N., Roggenbuck, J. W., & Williams, D. R. (2006). Home and away: Revisiting "escape" in the context of second homes. In N. McIntyre, D. R. Williams, & K. E.

McHugh (Eds.), *Multiple dwelling and tourism: Negotiating place, home and identity* (pp. 114–128). CABI.

Miceli, R., Sotgiu, I., & Settanni, M. (2008). Disaster preparedness and perception of flood risk: A study of the alpine valley in Italy. *Journal of Environmental Psychology*, *28*, 164–173. https://doi.org/10.1016/j.jenvp.2007.10.006

Mishra, S., Mazumdar, S., & Suar, D. (2010). Place attachment and flood preparedness. *Journal of Environmental Psychology*, *30*, 187–197. https://doi.org/10.1016/j.jenvp.2009.11.005

Müller, D. K. (2002). Reinventing the countryside: German second-home owners in Southern Sweden. *Current Issues in Tourism*, *5*(5), 426–446. https://doi.org/10.1080/13683500208667933

Nielsen-Pincus, M., Hall, T., Force, J. E., & Wulfhorst, J. D. (2010). Sociodemographic effects on place bonding. *Journal of Environmental Psychology*, *30*(4), 443–454. https://doi.org/10.1016/j.jenvp.2010.01.007

Norris, M., & Winston, N. (2010). Second-home owners: Escaping, investing or retiring? *Tourism Geographies*, *12*(4), 546–567. https://doi.org/10.1080/14616688.2010.516401

Nouza, M., Ólafsdóttir, R., & Sæþórsdóttir, A. D. (2018). Motives and behaviour of second home owners in Iceland reflected by place attachment. *Current Issues in Tourism*, *21*(2), 225–242. https://doi.org/10.1080/13683500.2015.1072139

Palm, R., & Hodgson, M. (1992). Earthquake insurance: Mandated disclosure and home-owner response in California. *Annals of the Association of American Geographers*, *82*(2), 207–222. www.jstor.org/stable/2563894

Paris, C. (2018). Australian holiday homes: Places of escape and sites of investment. In C. M. Hall & D. K. Müller (Eds.), *The Routledge handbook of second home tourism and mobilities* (pp. 152–166). Routledge.

Peng, L., Lin, L., Liu, S., & Xu, D. (2017). Interaction between risk perception and sense of place in disaster-prone mountain areas: A case study in China's three gorges reservoir area. *Natural Hazards*, *85*, 777–792. https://doi.org/10.1007/s11069-016-2604-6

Perkins, H. C., & Thorns, D. C. (2006). Home away from home: The primary/secondary-home relationship. In N. McIntyre, D. R. Williams, & K. E. McHugh (Eds.), *Multiple dwelling and tourism: Negotiating place, home and identity* (pp. 67–81). CABI.

Poussin, J. K., Botzen, W. J. W., & Aerts, J. C. J. H. (2014). Factors of influence on flood damage mitigation behaviour by households. *Environmental Science & Policy*, *40*, 69–77. https://doi.org/10.1016/j.envsci.2014.01.013

Ratnam, C., Drozdzewski, D., & Chapple, R. (2016). Can place attachment mediate perceptions of bushfire risk? A case study of the Blue Mountains, NSW. *Australian Journal of Emergency Management*, *31*(4), 62–66. https://knowledge.aidr.org.au/resources/ajem-oct-2016-can-place-attachment-mediate-perceptions-of-bushfire-risk-a-case-study-of-the-blue-mountains-nsw/

Robinson, O. C. (2014). Sampling in interview-based qualitative research: A theoretical and practical guide. *Qualitative Research in Psychology*, *11*(1), 25–41. https://doi.org/10.1080/14780887.2013.801543

Ruiz, C., & Hernández, B. (2014). Emotions and coping strategies during an episode of volcanic activity and their relations to place attachment. *Journal of Environmental Psychology*, *38*, 279–287. https://doi.org/10.1016/j.jenvp.2014.03.008

Selwood, J., & Tonts, M. (2006). Seeking serenity: Homes away from home in Western Australia. In N. McIntyre, D. R. Williams, & K. E. McHugh (Eds.), *Multiple dwelling and tourism: Negotiating place, home and identity* (pp. 161–179). CABI.

Stedman, R. C. (2006a). Places of escape: Second-home meanings in Northern Wisconsin, USA. In N. McIntyre, D. R. Williams, & K. E. McHugh (Eds.), *Multiple dwelling and tourism: Negotiating place, home and identity* (pp. 129–144). CABI.

Stedman, R. C. (2006b) Understanding place attachment among second home owners. *American Behavioral Scientist, 50*(2), 187–205. https://doi.org/10.1177/0002764206290633

Stewart, S. I., & Stynes, D. J. (2006). Second homes in the Upper Midwest. In N. McIntyre, D. R. Williams, & K. E. McHugh (Eds.), *Multiple dwelling and tourism: Negotiating place, home and identity* (pp. 180–193). CABI.

Svels, K., & Åkerlund, U. (2018). Second homes and the commons: Terms for second home leaseholds and collective action in Kvarken Archipelago, Finland. In C. M. Hall & D. K. Müller (Eds.), *The Routledge handbook of second home tourism and mobilities* (pp. 39–51). Routledge.

Tuulentie, S. (2006). Tourists making themselves at home: Second homes as a part of tourist careers. In N. McIntyre, D. R. Williams, & K. E. McHugh (Eds.), *Multiple dwelling and tourism: Negotiating place, home and identity* (pp. 145–157). CABI.

Tuulentie, S. (2007). Settled tourists: Second homes as a part of tourist life stories. *Scandinavian Journal of Hospitality and Tourism, 7*(3), 281–300. https://doi.org/10.1080/15022250701300249

U.S. Army Corps of Engineers. (n.d.). *Fact sheet – Fire Island Hurricane Sandy debris removal*. Retrieved March 13, 2018, from www.nan.usace.army.mil/Media/Fact-Sheets/Fact-Sheet-Article-View/Article/487616/fact-sheet-fire-island-hurricane-sandy-debris-removal/

Williams, D. R., & Van Patten, S. R. (2006). Home *and* away? Creating identities and sustaining places in a multi-centred world. In N. McIntyre, D. R. Williams, & K. E. McHugh (Eds.), *Multiple dwelling and tourism: Negotiating place, home and identity* (pp. 32–50). CABI.

6 How plastic talks

Second home owners as entrepreneurs and climate change in Tulum, Mexico

Mario A. Velázquez García

Introduction

Emergent recent research has focused on mobilities from the global North to the global South and how these flows of people, ideas and materials shape and are shaped by the places in which second home owners settle. The second home owners arriving from Europe, the US or Canada who decide to stay in Mexico and other Latin American countries often not only have different ways of mobilising resources but also different interests, norms and values; this generates controversies regarding resources and materials that shape and are reshaped by the place (Clausen & Velázquez, 2018; Hall & Müller, 2018). This chapter seeks to draw connections between second home owners and entrepreneurship because the group of second home owners in Tulum in this case study have settled for a time in this specific place, setting up enterprises. This research explores how these actors negotiate their position among the different actors in the Mexican context by using and localising the global and national narrative on climate change.

The chapter applies a spatial perspective to identify the sociocultural processes and underlying controversies and struggles over place disguised as sustainable transitions. The paper positions plastic waste, specifically plastic bottles, in the fore and analyses how the Italian second home owners with entrepreneurial enterprises interact with the wide range of actors involved in resolving the plastic waste challenges in Tulum in Caribbean Mexico. Climate change has exposed inequalities across the world, and the global discourse surrounding it has generated a vacuum of power, inviting renegotiations and adjustments at a local level (IPCC, 2018). This has raised questions concerning how climate change facilitates, promotes or constrains some projects and identities compared to others, in this case in Tulum. In line with Harris et al. (2018), adaptation is understood as a process that requires engagement and negotiation between different actors with diverse needs, interests and aspirations. Exploring these questions can contribute to the emerging debate about how global and national climate agendas are internalised and reconfigured by different actors as they implement their projects and strategies at a local level. Specifically, this chapter focuses on how the second home owners' particular position and their efforts to navigate it affects the implementation of the climate change agenda in Tulum. Debate continues over whether participatory processes

DOI: 10.4324/9781003091295-6

can be a sustainable process that translates into equitable development (Higgins-Desbiolles, 2018). We that attention must be applied to the ways in which actors actively engage, navigate and oppose participatory practices to pursue their livelihood interests and thereby reshape climate implementation strategies. The relevance of uncovering such different positionings is that they can serve as alternative frames to mediate discussions, as will be further illustrated in this paper. Thereby, the chapter seeks to establish a progressive space for discussion and to provide new insights regarding the sustainability agenda in which the Sustainable Development Goal #17 (SDG 17) about multi-stakeholder collaboration and participation is central (Wahl et al., 2020). Moreover, it seeks to close the gap in the scarce literature about second home owners as entrepreneurs who are significant actors in the (re)shaping of climate change adaptation processes and outcomes at a local level. The focus is, as noted, on the Italian second home owners as entrepreneurs; therefore, other actors' agency will be discussed in relation to these actors.

Second home owners and entrepreneurship

Second home owners perceived as transnational entrepreneurs have been scarcely researched in a Latin American context. The entrepreneurship literature has mainly focused on the Western context, but an emerging body of scholarly literature is examining entrepreneurship in Latin America (Dana et al., 2020). The mobilities approach in the entrepreneurial literature concerning second home owners is often neglected. By linking second home owners and transnational entrepreneurship, the chapter seeks to not only contribute to understanding why and how second home owners settle and become entrepreneurs in this specific place but also to provide knowledge about the social, spatial and institutional contexts. Contextualising in that manner allows for the unfolding of historical and lived experiences, as well as how and why the actors pursue their livelihood interests and mobilise their resources in shaping the locality (Dana et al., 2020).

Second home owners are often perceived as exploiting existing resources, causing an increase in living costs for the residents, for instance, a rise in real estate (among others), (Persson, 2018) and being less engaged in solving challenges in the communities. However, in terms of understanding second home owners within an entrepreneurial framework, due to them setting up tourism-related entrepreneurial businesses, it becomes apparent that second home owners engage with the community's challenges. These second home owners can be identified as entrepreneurs because they introduce new standards or innovative ideas as well as competitiveness and preferences in the tourist location they settle in for a period of time (Velázquez & Clausen, 2021). They are recognised as significant drivers of economic development due to their impact on poverty alleviation and job creation (Acs et al., 2008). Moreover, they know the socio-political context and local resources and integrate and position themselves in local networks; they can also provide access to global networks. Whereas the entrepreneur is perceived as an individual and often as a 'heroic' actor (Johannisson, 1990) providing and operating within networks and providing access to global or regional markets (Clausen,

2017), this chapter also seeks to inform entrepreneurship literature by addressing the concept as a collective actor rather than an individual. From a sociological perspective, this group of entrepreneurs within specific assets is an important player and has a significant policy impact on the communities not only in economic terms but also in sociocultural and political terms if we direct the attention to Mexico and Latin America (Velázquez & Clausen, 2021). Moreover, this perspective invites us to consider these actors' 'strong' and 'weak' ties to understand how they participate in climate governance processes in the community.

Governing climate change

Climate change is a global debate which is often framed around either international or national policies, whereas everyday micro-practices are marginalised in people's understanding of how the implementation of these strategies should take place and their outcomes on a local level (Huitema et al., 2018). Because climate change strategies often concern basic aspects of human livelihoods, production and resource access, these strategies represent struggles and are open to some degree of negotiation on a local level. There is no universal definition of governance, and as suggested by Hall and Müller (2018), it can be defined as "the act of governing" (Hall & Müller, 2018, p. 17). However, a core concept in climate governance is participation, and this paper participatory governance is understood in line with Huitema's et al. (2018) argument that there is a need to know about the informal way of how the subnational actor influence and (re)shape climate agendas and their outcomes at a local level. The climate debate is at the centre of politics, and the difficulties involved in prioritising the different political agendas often become struggles over resources, facilitating some narratives and struggles while constraining others. Climate change governance entails a search for generating transparent actions in public institutions and private companies as well as for citizens (Hall, 2016; Funder & Mweemba, 2018). This is intimately linked to yet another important aspect of governance: accountability and responsiveness. The climate governance perspective recognises that no one sole actor has the responsibility, tools or capacity to tackle complex unjust systemic issues related to climate change. In Tulum, the nearby Mayan heritage and rich biodiversity in the Sian Ka'an Nature Reserve (UNESCO, 2021) are primary attractions for tourism, and scholarly literature suggests that tourism can play a major role in sustainable development in fragile zones; it can do this not only by conserving and preserving biodiversity but also by generating revenue as an alternative livelihood to local communities and by reducing inequalities if tourist actors engage in the local communities. However, this case study demonstrates that within governing climate change, a variety of meanings are embedded which are reactivated and articulated within pre-existing meanings in the specific contexts. The different actors actively engage in the act of climate governance through their practices, which influence the use of the public and private spaces and are rooted in their positioning in the community or region.

Tulum and the Riviera Maya

Tourism in the Caribbean is booming; the southern Mexican states of Yucatan and Quintana Roo have experienced a vast expansion since 2012. Tulum is situated in the state of Quintana Roo and is considered an emerging tourist destination. This region is known as Zona Maya and forms part of the Sian Ka'an (which means 'origin of the sky'); it is a Biosphere Reserve and a UNESCO Heritage Site and is the largest protected area in the Mexican Caribbean (UNESCO, 2021). Among millennials, Tulum is a top destination, and the town became Mexico's first sustainable tourism zone, nominated in 2018 (Interview, José Tourism Secretary, municipality). Opposed to Cancún's exclusive and expensive high-end tourism, Tulum is recognised for being a relaxed and spiritual tourist destination. Beneath the sustainable image of Tulum promoted by its advertising, residents and second home owners and entrepreneurs in Tulum have increasingly questioned several activities due to an overwhelming growth in tourism.

Methodological approaches

Aligned with methodological approaches employing a plurality of world views, cultural differences and research praxis (Pritchard et al., 2011), this study is based on fieldwork conducted in March 2019. Moreover, both authors possess significant contextual knowledge substantiated over a period of 20 years. This has allowed unique insight due to the trust already established with local groups and communities, and local and regional authorities, and has facilitated the exchange of knowledge and ideas as well as invitations to participate in meetings, events and informal gatherings with various actors. While the field had different connotations for the different actors involved, there were commonalities at the level of reasoning but also important distinctions to maintain or even to defend. Discussing different meanings and narratives is a basic anthropological asset and a model for interdisciplinarity and innovative exploration. As Bosman and Dredge (2014) also suggested, professionals, in their case within tourism planning, must be able to cope in highly different circumstances addressing numerous issues: "the education of future professionals who have responsibility for managing complex, dynamic landscapes must extend beyond narrow fields and disciplinary divides" (Bosman & Dredge, 2014, p. 266).

For this study, interviews were conducted during March 2019 with key actors within the NGO world, with local and regional governmental representatives occupying key positions in relation to tourism and environmental issues, Mayan residents, local grassroots movements and tourists. We conducted focus groups interviews with the NGOs and grassroots movements, and we engaged in hours of informal conversations with all the actors in different settings and participated in meetings whenever they organised activities or interventions relevant to the plastic project. The interviews and informal conversations were conducted both in English and Spanish, and we encouraged the respondents to drive the conversations to gain valuable insights about the negotiations and underlying assumptions. A significant insight was the strong identity and cultural relations between the different groups of expats (Italians, Germans and the US group of second home owners) as well as the support in creating common proposals related to environmental issues in the community. Moreover, some of the entrepreneurs clearly were brokers, not only between the group of second home owners to the local authorities but also between the NGOs, Mayan residents and the local authorities. Video clips, photos and road and mind mapping have been used.

Italian second home owners' governance strategies

Tulum has several expat groups from the US, Italy, Germany and Canada. However, the Italians identify themselves significantly differently from American and Canadian second home owners. Based on the interviews and observing the group in meetings with the local authorities and their narratives about them as a group, it becomes clear that they identify as being particularly concerned about the environment: "rather than only caring for the environment in Tulum, we actually care for the planet" (Interview, María, Italian entrepreneur, 19 March 2019). Whereas the Canadian and US group rarely participate in events related to the climate debate and generally only discuss the pollution of plastic bottles because "it is a mess when you want to enjoy the sand" (Interview, John, US second home owner, 22 March 2019), they engage in social events organised by the North American second home owners, such as 'Thank God it is Friday'.

The second home owners from Canada and the US stated that their preferred way of engaging in environmental issues in the area is to donate to US-based environmental NGOs to ensure "something happens" (Interview, James, Canada, 20 March 2019). The Italian enterprises are related to the tourism industry and aligned with the image of Tulum as a spiritual and yoga destination. The majority of the Italian second home owners have an educational background within the arts and share the same interest in strengthening events within the arts; they typically prefer not to refer to plastic bottles as waste if they can be perceived as art. For instance, in recent years, they have created art installations in collaboration with the local authorities and Mexican artists from Central Mexico, namely 'Art with Me' (Dobson, 2018), which has attracted hundreds of international tourists (Interview, Carlos, 'Art with Me', 3 March 2019). The local initiatives led by the Italian entrepreneurs, art-based organisations and environmental NGOs have held campaigns at the cenotes (sinkholes) to generate sensitivity between residents and tourists. Struggles over access to resources and space is contested and subject to continuing social and political struggles (Velázquez & Clausen, 2021; Wahl et al., 2020). In particular, the group of Italian second home owners and environmental NGOs exert significant influence on the emergence of the climate debate. One way of creating awareness is by building art installations that are attractive to tourists as well as residents (Dobson, 2018; Guy, 2018). The Italian second home owners support and facilitate services to the tourists who participate in the festival 'Art with Me' (Guy, 2018; Heslin, 2018). The installations are found in the jungle around Tulum and do cause conflicts with the Mayan communities and local Mexican residents who question the sustainability of this approach to climate change. The festival takes place once per year and has attracted visitors from more than 50 countries in the last couple of years. One of the organisers states the following:

> My hope is that Art with Me will become a reference point for tourism and lifestyle travel in Tulum, where people don't just travel to Tulum for vacation, but also play an active role in protecting it, now and for future generations.
>
> (Interview, Maria, 15 March 2019)

The festival identifies the initiative as follows:

> A community-driven arts and culture festival centered around the celebration of art in all its forms, with an intention to enrich the local community, preserve the natural environment, and strengthen the artistic development of Tulum thorough conscious and sustainable practices. A portion of all ticket sales will be donated to support our environmental commitment to Tulum.
>
> (Art with Me, 2020)

Consequently, 'Art with Me' uses tourism not only to provide a platform to the Italian entrepreneurs' voices in the climate debate staging their global network but with this increasing interest from tourists and environmental NGOs, the local authorities are also put under pressure to either contest or align with the framed meaning of climate change. The festival provides its guests an incentive to take a sustainability pledge that includes using cloth bags over plastic, bringing a portable water bottle and promising not to throw cigarette butts any other place than the trash can. In return, they give guests a discounted price on festival tickets. The initiative also hosts a range of what they refer to as 'art experiences', talks and activities to create awareness around environmental issues as well as facilitating meetings between stakeholders. Thus, the Italian entrepreneurs strengthen their positioning by exposing their global networks. Maria states that the last couple of years, the group has frequently set up installations with 'waste-art' in expensive tourist shops to create awareness and mobilise tourists to participate also by donations.

According to Maria, "the increasing plastic bottle pollution is an environmental nightmare". This crisis narrative is used to justify the interest of the Italians who need to protect their segment of the tourism industry apart from being concerned about the environmental degradation. Acting upon the global climate discourse regarding plastic pollution in a local context reconfigures the meaning of sustainability and turns it into a political issue which implicates a power relationship. According to the Italians, the waste management in the present governmental administration is neglected. In general, the Mexican government is perceived as corrupt and inefficient and as not providing the necessary support when the civil society or organisations initiate activities.

> We love our Mexican hosts . . . it could be nice with a government that pay attention to all the initiatives taken by us . . . they are too focused on money.

The tourism representative in the municipality is not even from Tulum, he doesn't know anything . . . it never benefits the Mexicans.

(Interview, Veronica, 15 March 2019)

Thus, the narrative about the corrupt Mexican government is reproduced at a local level and reconfirmed when there is a lack of commitment and engagement.

There exists a top-down, money-based power structure in this country that discourages people from putting energy into long-term projects . . . The first art festival is an example of this.

(Interview, Maria, 12 March 2019)

These excerpts explicitly manifest some of the symbolic and concrete boundaries between the Italian entrepreneurs and the other actors. While art-based events that Italian second home owners organise in Tulum gain international attention and create enthusiasm and engage the expat communities and tourists in Tulum, the residents (including Mayans) declined to participate; only a few Mayan people showed up or participated in the organising meetings. Several Mayan informants explicitly expressed their frustrations with the Italian entrepreneurs due to their attitudes towards the Mayans' lifestyle and lack of understanding of other ways of perceiving environmental costs and uses of resources, which this quote describes clearly:

It is poor Mayan families and they don't have the same idea as we [the Italian entrepreneurs] do (. . .) they use bottles but it is not sustainable for nature to use bottles for bananas for instance or other plants . . . but they are poor.

(Interview, Maria, 13 March 2019)

In general, the Italian entrepreneurs' perceptions about Mayan communities are illustrated in this quote:

While you may well afford to pay your way even on a modest income the unhappy fact is that many indigenous people, the Mayans living here are very poor and they use plastic because they think it is better . . . they do not know . . . even though they are guides and know about nature.

(Interview, Julia, 23 March 2019)

The tourists play a key role in the Italian entrepreneurs' strategy because Tulum is recognised for its focus on the spiritual and yoga tourism, mostly due to the sacred Mayan ruins just at the outskirts of Tulum. This segment is generally attentive to the environmental footprint and donates to the local NGOs or participates in the organised 'clean-up' days on the beach. Furthermore, they engage in the crisis narrative and tap into the discourse about rethinking plastic bottles as a resource and not as waste. However, this quote encapsulates what several tourists expressed: "I try, you know. But you don't think "no I will not buy this beer" because it creates the trash. You just want to drink the beer and eat your taco, you know. Don't want to think about the trash all the time, you know? It's too difficult. Too much worry! It's no good for you" (Personal communication, Robert, Italian tourist, 28 March 2019). This illustrates excellently the discrepancies between tourists' intentions and their actions.

The local authorities' governance strategies

Despite the existence of a national climate agenda which has led the Mexican capital of Mexico City, and several states such as the state of Hidalgo, to ban plastic bags and require separating plastic bottles in the waste management system, the local authorities in Tulum are hesitant to implement these strategies. The former local administration implemented in Plan Municipal de Desarrollo 2016–2018 a waste strategy (Plan Municipal de Desarrollo, 2016–2018) wherein plastic bottles were separated in the outskirts of Tulum and recycled in a nearby town. However, with the entrance of a new administration and political party, namely Partido Acción Nacional (PAN), 2018–2021, the priorities changed, and the authorities were keen on environmental issues related to how to prevent further growth within the town (Plan Municipal de Desarrollo, Tulum, 2019–2021) and shift the focus away from waste. In Mexico, each political administration changes after each election, and the new administration is interested in suggesting and implementing their own political agenda to distinguish themselves from former administrations. Despite the Italian second home owners' frustrations at this development from the local authorities, they had to accept it to prevent further controversy. However, in reality, it is not so straightforward. The local authorities depend on the community actors with whom such arrangements are made; this leaves room for community members to act differently. According to the local authorities, their waste strategies are not being implemented adequately due to a lack of knowledge (among the tourists, residents, business owners and developers) and infrastructure. However, as one of several tourists noted, there are trash cans in public spaces that are separated into organic and inorganic, yet it all ends up in the same hole. As they noted, "what is the point then . . . " (Personal communication, Rosa, 12 March 2019). While the local government recognises that Tulum is facing challenges with waste in general, the authorities question the fact that plastic bottles are such a serious problem in the area, and according to José, the secretary of the municipality, "it is of course an issue in Tulum with waste and might also be with plastic, however, this group (Italians) does not have any other data to support their complaints than some photos, and without presenting facts, it becomes very arbitrary" (Municipality, José, 16 March 2019).

While the local authorities have made moves to enforce regulations and control of where and how waste is a challenge in the municipality for biodiversity, the weak enforcement generates a governance gap between taxation and control. The plastic bottle waste in particular is yet to be considered a "crisis or even close to an environmental nightmare", according to José from the municipality. He emphasises that the bottles also serve a socioeconomic purpose for the bottle collectors, who mainly are Mayans or poor migrants who settle for some months in search of work in the tourism sector. Though it is not a governmental strategy, "it is worth taking into consideration in Tulum that face harsh socioeconomic challenges", according to José (Personal communication, José, 12 March 2019). Thus, the 'crisis narrative' set into play by the Italian entrepreneurs is countered with optimism from the authorities, and governmental resources are converted into transparent and visible (accountable) actions such as bins in the main streets with containers separating *orgánico* and *no-orgánico*, as well as spots with innovative playgrounds where bottles are thrown from a distance into large baskets (Plan Municipal de Desarrollo, Tulum, 2019–2021). That way, the government demonstrates accountability to its citizens. It becomes obvious that the government is concerned that the 'crisis narrative' in the climate debate generates a decrease in tourism or jeopardises the main income driver for Tulum, which is tourism. The local authorities do seek to counteract the 'crisis narrative' and show an interest in dialogue by supporting and facilitating infrastructure in relation to the art events that the Italians apply for when they organise installations with the NGO 'Art with Me'. Nonetheless, José also emphasises that the main challenge in Tulum is not plastic as such but rather that 62% of the tourism-related business are informal, and the average livelihood conditions in the town are below the poverty line. This refers to the largest community in Tulum, the Mayan population, who occupies the low-paid jobs mainly within the tourism sector and suffers from marginalisation, poor working conditions and lack of access to education. The inequalities in Tulum have only increased during the COVID-19 pandemic, during which tourism has suffered severely.

Mayan communities and cenotes enterprises

Although the Mayans accept that there is some concern about the environmental degradation, it cannot be considered a crisis or even critical, which clearly echoes deeper concerns for poor livelihood conditions and subsistence challenges related to this marginalised segment of Tulum experience. Several Mayan communities that generally are subject to discriminatory practices directly explained in informal talks that they felt marginalised despite being invited to art events or organising meetings. Aligned with the findings in Funder and Mweemba's (2018) study, this case study also demonstrates that the Mayans did not have the knowledge and vocabulary that the Italians or NGOs have. They joined the conversations only when it directly concerned or impacted the cenotes or their neighbourhoods because then they have experiences to share. However, their experiences rarely become relevant, as they live in areas where the Italians never pass by nor realise there are art events in their neighbourhoods. They feel that they share opinions but that they do not have any voice; they also reuse the bottles in their gardens as flowerpots or small containers instead of throwing them out. In general, the Mayans expressed indifference to the Italian art installations as their approach to, for instance, plastic bottles was pragmatic, they saw more benefits for reusing the bottles in flowerpots than art installations. Yet, according to the Mayans, it was useless to join the conversations because the Italians and other second home owner groups would never understand nor agree with their ideas.

Increased tourism in the area has provided diversification of livelihood income for the Mayan community due to more open access to cenotes (sinkholes) that the Mayans own; cenotes have become one of the main attractions in the area. The cenotes are interconnected underground rivers, and the river system extends to all the Yucatán peninsula; a major challenge, however, is the excessive and unregulated use of the cenotes and that tourists throw plastic bottles in the cenotes which pollute the whole river system of cenotes. Despite being identified as one group, the Mayans are not a homogenous group (Balslev & Andersson, 2020), and the cenote enterprises reflect this by not having a strong voice in local politics, which is intimately related to the Mayans' historical and political marginalisation. This also generates a lack of support from the authorities to facilitate infrastructure and to communicate guidelines concerning pollution to the tourists. This lack of knowledge regarding the carrying capacity causes considerable anxieties in the Italian second home owner group. Despite several attempts, the Italian entrepreneurs have had no success in convincing the Mayans to change the way they use the cenotes for tourism purposes:

> We tried to engage them and talked about our events . . . Art with Me and the small exhibitions with different installations . . . but they never really seemed to bother . . . they also live outside Tulum or in the outskirts . . . they don't really care, I think (Interview, Donato, 18 March 2019) and we have never received any suggestion from them how they cope with the plastic bottles in their cenotes . . . I am not sure they know how much damage plastic does to our environment.
> (Personal communication, Nicolas, 19 March 2019)

The Mayan community's lack of response and engagements generate an ongoing headache for the Italian second home owners. Overall, the Italians are less aware of, or do not intervene in, the internal boundaries between the authorities and the Mayan communities nor seek to bridge some of these fragmented communities:

> They (Mayan groups and authorities) will never really work together. Too much competition for scarce access to resources and historical issues that has nothing to do with us.
> (Personal communication, Maria, 24 March 2019)

The Mayans are not directly affected by the overuse of cenotes and cumulative impacts on the resource system, and the key barriers are mistrust of the authorities and Europeans, as well as the existing asymmetrical power relations which constrain knowledge exchange and trust. Overall, the cenote owners prioritise having a diversified household income, and the main interest is to benefit from a resource which is now valued within tourism, and as several owners clearly expressed:

> Why is everybody so keen on telling us what to do and not to do? They (government and Italian second home owners) have never showed any interest in us and our living conditions until now – we do it our way.
> (Personal communication, Juan, 15 March 2019)

Plastic talks: controversies over space and resources

Clearly, the local authorities enter dialogue with the Italian entrepreneurs, yet they also describe the group as disregarding local practices and as being overly concerned with their own business interests rather than the interests of residents and the community. As explained by one council member of the government:

> They are only promoting their own interest – they believe art is everything but it does not solve any problems. Look at the streets all the Mayan women selling souvenirs to low prices, they should buy that or set up businesses to support these women instead of only thinking about plastic bottles – they have a lifestyle we do not have . . . It (plastic bottle) is not a problem. It might be a problem in Europe not here.
> (Personal communication, Juan, administration Tulum, 13 March 2019)

This quote aptly demonstrates the power asymmetries and uneven economic conditions which are crucial in this context and immensely impact local politics and social realities. Thus, the constantly changing interplay between the global and the local impacts how waste issues and, in this case, plastic bottles are displayed, conceived of and managed. Therefore, global and national contexts as well as specific local politics, representation strategies and social conditions have set the stage for a climate debate and need to be taken into consideration. The president of the NGO is *Cambio – No al Plástico*, an Italian second home owner and entrepreneur who has been living in Tulum for five years. She owns a bed and breakfast and engages in various activities related to environmental issues. The NGO consists of 12 core persons, all Italian second home owners and entrepreneurs in Tulum, and seeks to give voice to the climate through interventions such as cleaning the streets or beaches; it actively proposes actions to the local authorities to reduce plastic use. Apart from supporting NGOs that work with climate issues, the Italian entrepreneurs also claim to care about the community:

> It's as paying back [to the community and its indigenous people] (. . .) we owe it to this unique place and the planet.
> (Personal communication, Juana, 12 March 2019)

However, as demonstrated in the analysis, it is only within certain groups of the population the climate change debate and interventions are considered relevant and necessary. Reconfiguring the global climate change debate in the local communities, the Italian entrepreneurs position climate change as a crisis narrative as a means to differentiate and distinguish them from the 'others'. This also emphasises and clearly demonstrates the asymmetrical power relations, as the Italian entrepreneurs have access to resources and are different than the Mexican authorities with transparent practices when organising the 'Art with Me' festival and inviting everybody to the art installations in the streets (not to the festival events though). Although art and other events and initiatives resulted in greater appreciation of what the different groups represent, the ongoing negotiations and exploitations in a town such as Tulum embedded in historical and socio-political power asymmetries still uphold fragmentations.

Conclusions

Global climate strategies have become a tool for the Italian entrepreneurs to gain access to resources and to create a space for the Italian second home owners as an entrepreneurial group to (re)negotiate their position in the community towards the range of different actors: the local authorities, the different Mayan entrepreneurs and communities, the residents, NGOs, art communities and tourists. Rather than the global climate change focus on plastic, deforestation and biodiversity, the meaning of climate represented in plastic is reconfigured in the micro-sociocultural, economic and political processes of implementation in which the Italian entrepreneurs pave the way to promote their economic and cultural (art-based) projects. Climate change at a local level thus intervenes in struggles over resources and rights to space, as inspired by Laclau and Mouffe (1985); it becomes a 'battlefield' for competing visions of the future in Tulum.

The case illustrates how climate change's contingent meanings vary depending on the inclusion and exclusion of actors and how it is contextualised and used and implemented in the existing local and regional power asymmetries. This generates a flexibility that is directed towards multiple directions and levels which entail the specific interests, values and norms of a group or individuals. Overall, the case study is exemplary because it provides insights into how people engage with governance of their communities; they seize the space for dialogue and to reposition their interests, values and norms. Though the study also effectively pays attention to the difficulties and barriers to how to mediate for the common good to create socioeconomic and environmental change. Despite the significance of international climate governance system, the role of the subnational governance and local government is increasingly important for implementation of climate strategies in which the inclusiveness of a range of actors and their interests, capabilities and values need to be taken into consideration.

References

Acs, Z., Desai, S., & Hessels, J. (2008). Entrepreneurship, economic development and institutions. *Small Business Economics, 31*, 219–234. https://doi.org/10.1007/s11187-008-9135-9

Art with Me. (2020). *Tulum event partner hotels*. Retrieved January 3, 2021, from https://artwithme.org/hotel-partners/

Balslev, H., & Andersson, V. (2020). Linking action research and PBL. A Mexican case of co-creation. In *Educate for the future: PBL, sustainability and digitalisation 2020* (pp. 510–521). Aalborg University.

Bosman, C., & Dredge, D. (2014). Teaching about tourism in a post-disciplinary planning context. In D. Dredge, D. Airey, & M. J. Gross (Eds.), *The Routledge handbook of tourism and hospitality education* (pp. 265–278). Routledge.

Clausen, H. B. (2017). Social entrepreneurship and tourism development in Mexico: A case study of North American social entrepreneurs in a Mexican town. In P. J. Sheldon & R. Daniele (Eds.), *Social entrepreneurship and tourism. Philosophy and practice* (pp. 195–207). Springer.

Clausen, H. B., & Velázquez, M. A. G. (2018). National Mexican tourism policy and North American second home owners in Mexico: Local tourism development and Mexican identity. In C. M. Hall & D. K. Müller (Eds.), *The Routledge handbook of second home tourism and mobilities* (pp. 64–74). Routledge.

Dana, L.-P., Ratten, R., & Honyenuga, B. Q. (Eds.). (2020). *African entrepreneurship: Challenges and opportunities for doing business*. Palgrave Macmillan.

Dobson, J. (2018, June 3). Tulum's Art with Me festival instantly becomes a world class event. *Forbes*. www.forbes.com/sites/jimdobson/2018/06/03/tulums-art-with-me-festival-instantly-becomes-a-world-class-event/?sh=42acb1f514d5

Funder, M., & Mweemba, C. E. (2018). Interface bureaucrats and the everyday remaking of climate interventions: Evidence from climate change adaptation in Zambia. *Global Environmental Change, 55*, 130–138. https://doi.org/10.1016/j.gloenvcha.2019.02.007

Guy, J. (2018, January 18). Uncontrolled development turns Mexican tourist paradise into an environmental time bomb. *Equal Times*. www.equaltimes.org/uncontrolled-development-turns?lang=en

Hall, C. M. (2016). Heritage, heritage tourism and climate change. *Journal of Heritage Tourism, 11*(1), 1–9. https://doi.org/10.1080/1743873X.2015.1082576

Hall, C. M., & Müller, D. K. (2018). Governing and planning for second homes. In C. M. Hall & D. K. Müller (Eds.), *The Routledge handbook of second home tourism and mobilities* (pp. 17–26). Routledge.

Harris, L. M., Chu, E. K., & Ziervogel, G. (2018). Negotiated resilience. *Resilience 6*(3), 196–214. https://doi.org/10.1080/21693293.2017.1353196

Heslin, M. (2018). *This 'forest' in Mexico is made from recycled plastic* (2nd ed.). Lonely Planet.

Higgins-Desbiolles, F. (2018). Sustainable tourism: Sustaining tourism or something more? *Tourism Management Perspectives, 25*, 157–160. https://doi.org/10.1016/j.tmp.2017.11.017

Huitema, D., Boasson, E. L., & Beunen, R. (2018). Entrepreneurship in climate governance at the local and regional levels: Concepts, methods, patterns and effects. *Regional Environmental Change, 18*, 1247–1257. https://doi.org/10.1007/s10113-018-1351-5

IPCC. (2018). *Special report. Global warming of 1.5°C*. www.ipcc.ch/report/sr15/

Johannisson, B. (1990). Community entrepreneurship – cases and conceptualization. *Entrepreneurship and Regional Development, 2*(1), 71–88. https://doi.org/10.1080/08985629000000006

Laclau, E., & Mouffe, C. (1985). *Hegemony and socialist strategy: Towards a radical democratic politics*. Verso.

Persson, I. (2018). The rise and fall of the houses of Attefall: Effects of reduced building regulation in coastal municipalities with large numbers of second homes. In C. M. Hall & D. K. Müller (Eds.), *The Routledge handbook of second home tourism and mobilities* (pp. 86–97). Routledge.

Plan Municipal de Desarrollo, Tulum, 2016–2018, Municipio de Tulum, Quintana Roo, México.

Plan Municipal de Desarrollo, Tulum. (2019–2021). Municipio de Tulum, Quintana Roo, México.

Pritchard, A., Morgan, N., & Ateljevic, I. (2011). Hopeful tourism: A new transformative perspective. *Annals of Tourism Research, 38*(3), 941–963. https://doi.org/10.1016/j. annals.2011.01.004

UNESCO. (2021). *Sian Ka'an Biosphere Reserve, Mexico*. https://en.unesco.org/biosphere/lac/sian-ka_an

Velázquez, M. A. G., & Clausen, H. B. (2021). *La politíca pública del Turismo en México. Laconstrucción de nuestra identidad*. Benémerita Universidad Autónoma de Puebla (BUAP), México.

Wahl, J., Lee, S., & Jamal, T. (2020). Indigenous heritage tourism development in a (post-)COVID world: Towards social justice at Little Bighorn Battlefield National Monument, USA. *Sustainability, 12*(22). https://doi.org/10.3390/su12229484

7 Extreme weather event risk awareness among second home owners and their economic and non-economic response strategies

Evidence from the Beskids Mountains in Poland

Adam Czarnecki, Aneta Dacko, and Mariusz Dacko

Introduction

Over twenty years ago Faulkner's (2001) study highlighted the ever-increasing frequency, scale and, consequently, severity of natural and human-induced disasters and crises impacting the tourism sector itself, and also the entire communities dependent on it. However, at that time Faulkner (2001) concluded that, despite the clearly unfavourable and worsening trend, there was insufficient relevant research addressing both risk and impact assessment as well as the community's demand for preventive and mitigating responses to disasters. Rather than an answer to Faulkner's (2001) opinion, the considerable increase in the number and scope of studies dealing with this issue over the past two decades can be attributed to societal concerns resulting from the rapidly changing world and communities' genuine need for protection and support (Bhattamishra & Barrett, 2010).

Without doubt, global climate change has had noticeable and increasingly drastic consequences for local geographies (Pyhälä et al., 2016), including frequent and recurring extreme weather events such as heavy rainfall, hurricanes and cloudbursts resulting in flooding and landslides. Much research has therefore been done at the micro-scale (small areas) on the local footprint of climate change (Schneider & Root, 1996), and specifically on the origins, consequences, awareness, risk assessment and the intervention strategies for natural disasters with regard to tourism and the tourism-dependent communities (Scott et al., 2019). These relate, for instance, to geological disasters such as landslides (Dhakal et al., 2020) or earthquakes (Chan et al., 2020), as well as hydrological and meteorological hazards such as floods (Atanga, 2020) and hurricanes (Granvorka & Strobl, 2013).

Due to nature of the experience of (often local) events and the resulting microcrises, it may be that they could also be simpler to tackle due to the possible financial and institutional support from the major part of the society not affected by the disaster (Coles & Buckle, 2004). However, besides previous experience and greater or lesser opportunities to receive aid in preparing for (ex-ante) and tackling the effects

DOI: 10.4324/9781003091295-7

of extreme weather events (post-factum), people's risk awareness and assessment are considered as key issues, which determine prevention, preparedness, response and recovery within the community as well as measures, resource allocation and effectiveness of such actions of adaptation and resilience (Bronfman et al., 2019).

It is clear that all members of tourism-based communities, including permanent and seasonal residents (second home owners) are exposed to these events and their after-effects. However, as Hoogendoorn and Fitchett (2018) have argued, second home owners are particularly vulnerable to natural hazards which, in general, is a joint effect of the considerable capital allocated through owning a home and the immanent and value-creation features of the property, the natural amenities and landscape that are at risk due to climate change. Most second homes in Poland are located in renowned tourism regions, for instance in the mountains (Adamiak, 2014). Given the specificity of the natural environment and the scattered settlement pattern in mountainous areas, they are particularly vulnerable, not just to extreme weather events but also in the way residents can deal with them and their consequences (due to distant and inaccessible neighbours or rescue services). Hence, the question arises as to whether second home owners are aware of the natural hazards and the increasing number of extreme weather events that occur in their holiday area as well as the related seasonal housing and living risks. As a consequence, another question arises about the types of action they undertake to be warned in a timely way as well as to protect, deal with and ameliorate the actual sudden weather events, and thus how they adapt to climate change in economic and non-economic terms. That is through:

- property investment (purchases of security and surveillance systems, relevant renovation and maintenance services); and
- community self-organisation (involvement in the neighbourhood self-help groups, formal and informal local community cooperation).

The geographical setting of the study is the tourism sub-region of the Żywiec Valley in the Western Beskids mountain range of Southern Poland, a holiday and second home hot spot and, at the same time, an area particularly vulnerable to various climate change effects, mainly shallow landslides due to high relative altitudes and the highly permeable type of soil on predominantly deforested slopes, potentially causing floods in the immediate area of several local artificial reservoirs.

Theoretical background

Vulnerability of second home owners

Seemingly, "those who can afford a second home are not generally perceived as vulnerable" (Cheong, 2018, p. 583). However, there is a variety of distinct and intrinsic characteristics of second homes which make the owners much more vulnerable to extreme weather events than expected. First, like traditional tourists, second home owners long for contact with nature, and hence their properties are often located in natural amenity-rich areas (Pitkänen et al., 2011) which are at risk of deterioration due to climate change and the related extreme weather phenomena (Hoogendoorn & Fitchett, 2018). Second, by coming into possession of the property they have incurred a significant one-off cost, capital investment, which somewhat creates inflexibility in changing location in the case of a fall in property values due to a disaster (Hoogendoorn & Fitchett, 2018). Third, insufficient infrastructure and weak institutional support to provide the community with relevant preventative knowledge and formal structures such as warning systems or good quality and accessible emergency services can be experienced in remote communities where natural amenities and, consequently, second homes tend to concentrate (Hunter et al., 2005). Fourth, the irregular and intermittent presence of second home owners at their seasonal residences raises the question of security, making second home owners seek someone local to rely on (Barnett, 2014). Fifth, related to the previous question, the low level of integration with the host community and the lack of political representation in the community, insufficient familiarity with local authorities and institutions (Cheong, 2018), as well as limited knowledge of the local context, make things unnecessarily difficult and thus lead individuals to undertake ineffective or misjudged actions.

To the best of our knowledge there has not so far been much empirical research dealing with second home owners' risk perceptions and their strategies towards extreme weather events (some exceptions are studies on second home owners' vulnerability after Superstorm Sandy in the US by Cheong (2018) and risk perception of the sea-level rise among this social group in France by Rey-Valette et al. (2014), as well as other chapters in this volume). Hence the theoretical framework is constructed by applying findings from previous studies in the field based on the experience of local (mostly permanent) communities and supplementing them with the previously mentioned existing studies on second homes.

Risk perceptions and awareness of extreme weather events

For individuals to take proper actions in terms of prevention, preparedness, and mitigation, first there must be awareness of the risk of extreme weather events (Bronfman et al., 2019) as well as the risks of potential consequences of inappropriate safety and protective measures implemented. These are both considered critical in the individual's precautionary decision-making process, also against large-scale natural hazards (Tekeli-Yeşil et al., 2011). Then, what significantly and positively influences risk perception is a direct physical personal experience of a hazard (Roder et al., 2016) (i.e. tangible aspects such as material consequences and intangible elements such loss of status, control or independence as a result of an extreme weather event and the aftermath). However, this most common view has been undermined by studies suggesting that simply experiencing a natural disaster does not influence risk perception (Bronfman et al., 2020).

As a supplementary condition, Bronfman et al. (2020) point out the severity of the event's consequences, arguing that the more acute the effects the higher is the risk perception. In addition, a previous study on second home owners' risk perceptions of sea-level rise and the related threats for their properties has proven that global climate change resulting in such gradual, 'creeping' deterioration of the local environment make second home owners less sensitive about the risks and less sceptical about the consequences (Rey-Valette et al., 2014). In this respect, the spatial dimension somewhat contributes to the level of risk perception. For this reason, Howe et al. (2014) apply the concept of 'shadow of experience' to identify the geographical area affected by the event, which psychologically alters locals' risk perception. Interestingly, the physical area covered by this concept is not necessarily directly affected by the event but rather by its indirect effects such as disruptions in public transport or emergency services.

Besides the acuteness of the event, the time factor, time elapsed since experiencing the event, plays a role in shaping individual and collective risk awareness. In relation to memory, other studies have proven certain trajectories in risk awareness, for instance with respect to flood experiences, based on which higher risk awareness peaks during and immediately after an event but rapidly dissipates afterwards (Scolobig et al., 2012).

In a more general sense, according to Berkes (2009) perceptions of environmental change (including risk awareness) thus need to be understood as part of larger systems of knowledge that have been developed locally through repeated interactions with the environment and that have been handed down over generations as well as enhanced and supplemented by the expert knowledge about the issue. And even though respondents' ratings of their knowledge about hazards significantly correlate with intention to adopt preparedness and mitigation measures (Lindell & Whitney, 2000), does it also translate into choices of prevention and mitigation strategies?

Response strategies to extreme weather events and their determinants

Making relevant responses to extreme weather events depends on various factors: 1. type of risk; 2. material and financial resources; 3. human resources (an adequate number of people and their skills); 4. institutional resources (coordination, procedures, support); and 5. social resources (social capital, knowledge, agency) (Choryński, 2019). In addition, as mentioned in the previous section, risk perception by the actors is seen as another determinant of the prevention and mitigation decision-making process. However, awareness or experience in this regard does not necessarily turn into action (Dessai & Sims, 2010). Hence the relationship "between risk awareness and preparedness [is] not at all straightforward" (Scolobig et al., 2012, p. 499). Although the assumption that preparedness is a result of risk awareness and the positive linkage between awareness and actions can be undermined, the way in which people perceive environmental changes influences how they respond to them (Spence et al., 2011), suggesting that individual and collective perceptions of risk shape choices of preparatory and coping strategies as well as the resources employed to put them into practice.

In general, one can distinguish two main types of coping strategy, material/economic (physical) and social/non-economic ones. The first encompasses purchasing insurance, constructing and renovating the house and its technical infrastructure and providing early-warning systems and as such can be seen as an anticipatory (preparedness) strategy. The second, often considered as a responsive strategy, is to deal with the effects of such events and remove the disruption in the aftermath. Some responsive strategies are formed and developed in advance; however, most of them are created as formal and informal groups (including self-organisation), ad hoc groups, neighbourly help, volunteering, mutual warning systems and other collective actions. Nonetheless, it is worth pointing out the remaining 'no action' strategy. This shows that, despite existing factors that increase preparedness, some have an opposite effect and reduce mobilisation, including the infrequency and limited severity of previous disasters, lack of trust in information providers or external (expert) knowledge as well as belief that the authorities can manage the risk effectively (Scolobig et al., 2012).

The responsive strategies involve human and social resources, including family and neighbours, which is due to the fact that reactions to natural disasters are of a collective character (Stallings, 1998). Technological adaptations, institutional support and even the changing social conditions in the communities (López-Marrero & Yarnal, 2010) appear to contribute to the weakening, if not the replacement, of social capital in this respect. In light of this, a rational response would be to complement or substitute different types of strategy in order to institute a more efficient response. Thus, it is more likely for individuals to combine and then use a mixed, multiple-action strategy.

Confidence and trust between the parties involved are also important in pursuing a non-economic coping strategy. Trusting relationships within communities and towards external actors are important to enable responses to emergencies as well as to plan future strategies (Kapucu, 2008). This socio-psychological factor is the more important in terms of effective preventive and mitigation actions, as differences in the risk perception levels between locals and second home owners have been revealed in favour of the former group (Rey-Valette et al., 2014), and the low level of integration of seasonal residents with the local community have been proven (Cheong, 2018) to some extent, moderated by contextual and personal factors. As a component of social capital, trust also shapes risk perceptions, preparedness and responses to natural hazards such as avalanches (Löfstedt, 2005). Trust constitutes a necessary component of adaptation besides sharing experiences and knowledge that build social cohesion (Duhaime et al., 2004). What is more, the reciprocity enables people to act collectively (Adger, 2003).

To pursue a physical/material preparedness strategy, the owner's personal characteristics matter. Among them, an individual's wealth measured by household income has proven to positively influence material-based risk and mitigation actions (Grothmann & Reusswig, 2006). Given that warning systems are based on technological advances and the renovation/construction services and building materials are often very costly, using them to implement adaptive measures requires a significant capital allocation. In other studies, besides gender, an individual's age has proven influential, with elderly people more likely to invest in precautionary measures and security than younger ones (Bhuiyan & Khan, 2011). Similarly, education has been found to be an important factor moderating individual's intentions to undertake preparatory actions (Paul & Bhuiyan, 2010). Although not strictly a personal characteristic, 'being an owner' rather than a tenant or leaseholder proved important in explaining material investment. In other words, the institution of ownership is considered as a determinant for owner's pragmatic motivations and the resulted improved effectiveness in managing the property (i.e. greater attention to the property and carefulness) (Kucharska-Stasiak, 2013). However, given that, according to Vorkinn and Riese (2001), individuals' attitude to the natural environment results more from a direct association with a certain location and its natural characteristics than from their socio-demographics, and it is necessary to refer to contextual factors.

This group of factors comprises a range of constituents such as the local geographical setting, the specificity of which may make some strategies more or less feasible, for example, mountainous areas, scattered settlements and inaccessible emergency services. In such areas spatial circumstances somewhat limiting social contacts and potential cooperation force individuals to deal with natural hazards by themselves, thus probably more likely pursuing the material strategy. On the other hand, long distances, inaccessibility and/or, at times, the lack of relevant services due to insufficient resource allocation by the authorities may induce shifts of responsibility and the related expected actions from the public sector to individuals or community groups (Wachinger & Renn, 2010).

In this aspect, the context factor also relates to the character of an area experienced by an event (the 'shadow of experience'). Through the resulting risk perceptions and awareness, location within a 'shadow of experience' area, although sometimes extended to the surrounding area not affected directly by it, influences the type of action taken to prevent a future event (Howe et al., 2014).

The contextual factor can also be seen at the micro-scale, the property itself, proving that the home's size, equipment and standard shape the owner's reactions, resources allocated and the strategies, at least in terms of attention and concern to secure the home (Hutter, 2016).

Methodology

Are second home owners aware of natural hazards? Do they think the extreme weather phenomena have been on an upward trend in recent years? The study attempts to answer these questions and then analyses the motives of economic (material investments to secure the home), and non-economic (self-organisation manifested in various forms of neighbourly help), strategies for anticipating the effects of extreme weather events by second home owners based on the case of the Western Beskids in Southern Poland. A classification and regression trees (C&RT) interaction classification tree model was employed and developed to accomplish this. The data was obtained using a questionnaire which, for the purposes of the model, included questions that specify:

- The dependent variable, the strategy taken by the respondent to anticipate threats;

- Independent variables, respondent's socio-demographics and their opinion on the severity of weather events and the associated risks, and second home characteristics including its location.

The study was conducted in two tourism-based municipalities (Figure 7.1) from July to November 2020. The preferred form of collecting data were face-to-face interviews with respondents when holidaying in their second homes. As a result, 94 observations were collected.

In order to explain the motives of preventing and coping strategies, an exploratory data analysis was conducted to reveal hidden patterns and relationships. Interactive classification tree makes it possible to combine advanced statistical methods with an

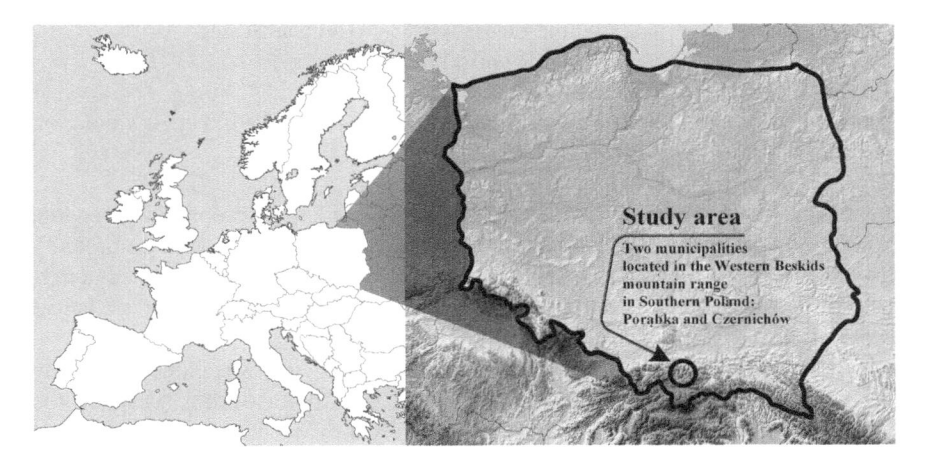

Figure 7.1 The study area
Source: Own elaboration.

Table 7.1 Description of the dependent variable

Key	Number of observations	Strategy
[H I]	41	Involvement in neighbourly help and making material investments
[_ I]	25	No involvement in neighbourly help but making material investments
[H_]	14	Involvement in neighbourly help but no material investments
[__]	14	No involvement in neighbourly help and no material investments

H – Help, I – Investment, _ – none

Source: Own study.

expert knowledge. A relatively large number of causal factors determining second home owners' coping strategies were considered, including personal traits (respondent's socio-demographics); contextual factors (second home location, social amenities in the area, home characteristics); but also some subjective factors: respondent's opinions on their community belonging; trust and collective problem-solving.

The dependent variable was created by processing and aggregating two questions: 1. involvement in neighbourly help; and 2. investments made to the property due to the extreme weather event risk). The variable was of qualitative character and comprised four alternatives/strategies.

STATISTICA software was used to develop the C&RT tree model. It was assumed that:

- the effect of misclassifications would be equal;
- the goodness-of-fit index would be assessed by Gini coefficient;
- the stop rule would be to prune for misclassification error;
- terminal nodes would consist of at least 5 observations;
- quality control of the results would be carried out using a V-fold cross validation for V=10.

The misclassification rate was 32%, and was considered acceptable given the exploratory (rather than predictive) nature of the model, as well as the complexity of human decision motives. The authors are aware that some psychological determinants of respondents' strategies have remained outside the field of statistical observation.

During the field research, valuable non-verbal knowledge was gained about the functioning of communities of second home owners in the case-study area, how the community members support each other, and how they cope with natural hazards in mountain conditions. The role of this expertise was important in the statistical procedure, specifically in correcting the somewhat automatically created tree.

Study area

The neighbouring municipalities of Czernichów and Porąbka are popular tourism-based municipalities in Southern Poland, located in the Little Beskids (*Beskid Mały*) mountain range which constitutes a physiographic unit of the Western Beskids. It is the catchment area of the Soła River and local streams which, along with the mountain steep slopes, stimulate the rapid accumulation of torrents during periods of heavy rain, posing a threat of flooding. To counteract this, a system of dams has been created on the Soła River including four dammed retention reservoirs which form the Soła Cascade. For tourists, the lakes are mainly bodies of water in the appealing natural surroundings. Because of this, the advantages for the surveyed municipalities include the excellent natural, landscape and recreational qualities. In summer, the area, known as 'Żywiec Switzerland', is crowded with tourists, and kilometre-long traffic jams form on the access roads, especially when the weekend is over, most second home owners live in the nearby Upper Silesian conurbation (a cluster of 19 adjacent cities with a total population of over two million).

Five clusters of second homes were identified for the study, designated L1, L2, L3, L4 and L5 respectively (Figure 7.2 and Table 7.2). Clusters L1-L4 are in the Czernichów municipality in the vicinity of Międzybrodzie Lake. The L5 cluster is in the forests of the Porąbka municipality in the Targanicka Pass.

These locations not only have the benefits of the unique environment (mountains, lakes, rivers and forests). Due to their mountainous character, they also pose serious challenges for second home owners, e.g. lack of access to sewage and water supply systems, difficult access in winter and, at the same time, great destructiveness from high winds (Figure 7.3), thunderstorms and torrential rain (L3's respondent: "after the landslide came down, the area was closed, there was no electricity for almost three years, we had to organise ourselves and intervene . . . extreme weather events are more intense, I saw a gale lift a sailboat and throw it down into the lake").

On the other hand, in the L5, the lack of mobile network coverage (valley surrounded by mountain peaks) is a major challenge for anticipating and warning about potential flood damage. Many second home owners from the L1 cluster were impressed by the force of the wind that destroyed the forest near their homes on the hillside (L1's respondent: "after the storm, the access road was not passable at all", "trees fell on lots and buildings"). Interestingly, apart from the damage, the storm also had its positive aspect as it has uncovered and broadened a view of the neighbouring mountains and the Międzybrodzie Lake valley.

The L3 and L5 clusters are areas which experienced extreme weather events (heavy rainfall) and their consequences (landslides and floods). Wielka Puszcza (L5) is surrounded by high mountain ridges, resulting in storm clouds remaining over the area when atmospheric fronts pass (Bodziony & Baziak, 2007). Precipitation can not only be violent, but also prolonged. Local flooding and floods are relatively common here. Wielka Puszcza has experienced as many as three floods

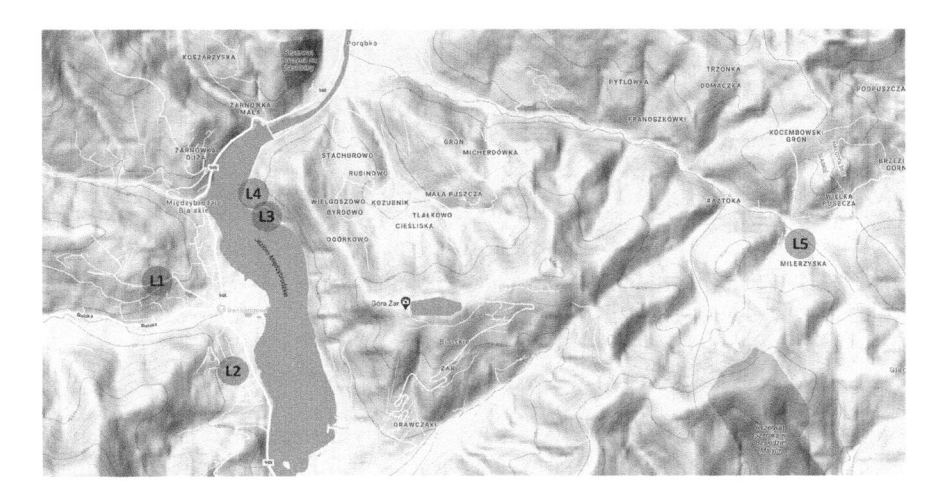

Figure 7.2 Locations of the second home clusters surveyed
Source: Own study.

Table 7.2 Characteristics of second home clusters' locations

Cluster	Descriptive characteristics
L1 (20 observations)	A cluster of over 100 second homes situated on the southern slope of a mountain at an altitude of 450–500 m AMSL; peripheral zone of Międzybrodzie Bialskie village. In December 2017, a violent gale destroyed about 30 ha of forest there.
L2 (33 observations)	Clusters of numerous second homes located around the centre of Międzybrodzie Bialskie village; good access to services and transportation. Second homes are often adjacent to the permanent homes. Generally fewer threats of natural hazards occur compared to other clusters surveyed. Some second homes are built on leased land.
L3 (21 observations)	A cluster of about 140 second homes situated by Międzybrodzie Lake on the slopes of the Little Beskids hills. The area of Łaski landslide, which became active as a result of catastrophic rainfall in May 2010. A significant number of cottages were built on leased plots.
L4 (10 observations)	A cluster of 27 second homes located on the slopes of the Little Beskids hills on the right-bank of the Soła river valley in the close proximity to the Łaski landslide. A significant number of houses were built on leased plots.
L5 (10 observations)	A cluster of over 150 second homes in the Wielka Puszcza hamlet. The settlement lies in the valley of a stream which is a right-bank tributary of the Soła River. The area is prone to landslides. It experienced floods in 1997, 2005 and 2010.

Source: Own study.

Figure 7.3 Effects of hurricane in L1 (photograph on the left taken on 19 August, 2017, photograph on the right taken on 15 April, 2019)

Source: Google Earth photographs.

in recent decades that resulted in extensive property damage and the destruction of the access road to the settlement which was cut off from the world. In L5, apart from the water itself, the destructive force is created by the debris of rocks and tree trunks carried by it. In addition, the formation time of a flood wave can be so short that it is usually practically impossible to react to prevent damage. Situations like these can cause frustration among second home owners and force them to somehow rely on neighbourly help (L5's respondent: "sluggishness, not much is being done here, damage is not being prevented, the attitude of the authorities is peculiar – this means waiting for a disaster to happen"). Lipski et al. (2006) also note that damage is particularly severe in upland catchment areas such as Wielka Puszcza, caused by torrential rains that are local but still very violent. It is not only buildings and technical infrastructure subject to the flood pressure that are destroyed. River erosion intensifies and landslides are more likely to happen.

A landslide resulting from heavy rain is a key concern of the owners from L3 (Figure 7.4). Although it has long been shown on geological maps, it used to be considered inactive. However, the landslide became active over a large area (about 18 ha) in May 2010. The movements covered almost the entire landslide area from the elevation of 510 m, down to the lake level.

Some of the houses were abandoned because they were in danger of collapsing. Other, less damaged ones are still being used, but because of the uncertain future there has been hardly any investment (L3's respondent: "as a result of the landslide, the house slid down 1.8 m . . . no permission should have been given to build massive brick houses here"; "at night, there was a violent hissing noise and bang, people came out to see what had happened, houses were cracked, many doors could not be opened or closed afterwards"). The strategy of not investing has its consequences such as stagnation, makeshift conditions, deteriorating homes and roads, local conflicts over access, and accusations of who is to blame for everything. This is noted by second home owners themselves (L3 and L4's respondents: "before the landslide, life was thriving here"; "it was only when the landslide came down and the area was closed, that I realised how much I loved coming here"; "the local authorities failed – they gave planning permissions for large houses", "the road built on the mountain undercut the slope and this contributed to the landslide during prolonged rain"). The landslide remains an unresolved problem, and poses a threat of increased activity to existing infrastructure within its boundaries. In the most pessimistic scenario, it is possible for the mountainside to entirely break

 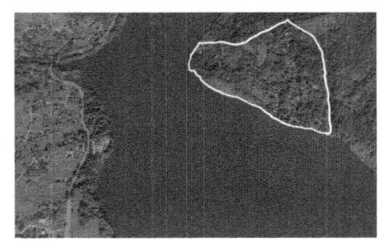

Figure 7.4 Area affected by the landslide in location L3. The photograph on the left shows the fault line marked with arrows

Source: Own photograph (on the left), Google Earth photograph (on the right).

off and slide down into the lake. Unfortunately, according to experts, there is no chance of permanent stabilisation of such an extensive landslide area.

Results

The assessment of extreme weather events intensity dynamics (i.e. violent/ extended heavy rainfall, storm and gale, long-term drought, extreme snowfall or severe frost) and the related probability and threat of damage to the secondary residences were not unequivocal according to respondents' views, although the majority of owners were inclined to the opinion that the frequency of such events was increasing and there was an actual risk of damage to property (Figure 7.5). However, it was not proven that in areas more affected by such phenomena (see: Table 7.2 for L1, L3, L5, hit by gales, floods and landslides) the threat of damage was perceived as greater than in other locations. This can be partly explained by perceptions of the long-term second home owners surveyed, who acknowledged that owning a residence in the mountains may imply certain living and housing difficulties. It should be stressed that the majority of respondents had noted an increase in the number of extreme weather events over the past few years (60%) while 70% admitted such events could damage their property. A similar proportion of respondents had declared insuring their cottage from various damages.

The question now arises of how these opinions relate to the facts? Is the view of second home owners, who spend only a portion of their time in their seasonal residences, in line with the reality? In light of the data from the local fire service in the Porąbka municipality, 655 weather-related emergency interventions were necessary to be undertaken in the last ten years. In general, the timeline data did

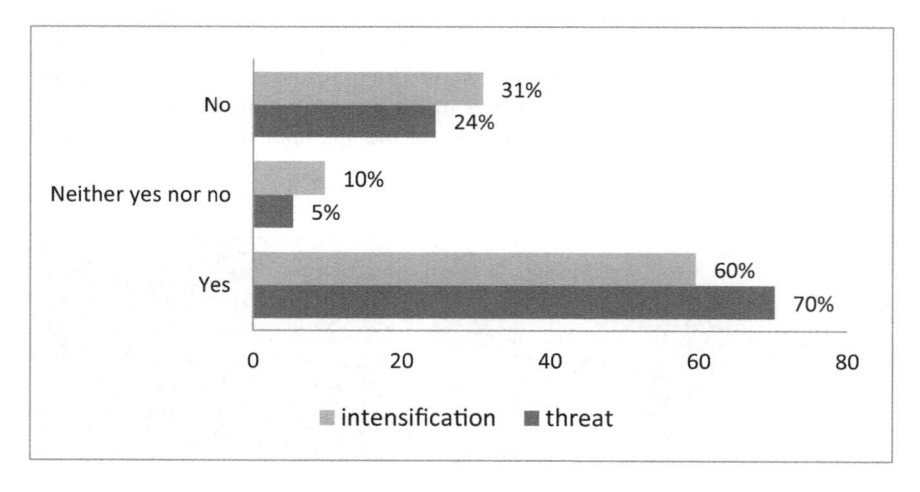

Figure 7.5 Extreme weather events and the related threats intensity assessment made by second home owners

Source: Own elaboration.

not prove a continuous upward trend but rather its irregularity, with some peaks in 2010, 2014 and 2017. It is difficult to question the destructiveness of weather events in the mountains (the damage from one of the storms is shown in Figure 7.3). As a result of rainfall in 2010, over 1,300 landslides have been activated in the entire south of Poland. There are currently 127 landslides in the Czernichów municipality covering an area of 1087 ha (over 19% of the municipality).

Second home owners' reactions to extreme weather events were uneven across the alternatives of the response strategies examined. The proportion of those who demonstrated the material/economic strategy, through the owner's investment in security and surveillance systems as well as technical improvements, renovation and maintenance services, accounted for 26%, while the proportion of followers of the social/non-economic strategy, through the owner's involvement in the neighbourhood self-help groups as well as formal and informal local community cooperation, accounted for 15%. The largest group attempted to combine the two approaches, making them complementary (44%) while only 15% remained reluctant to adopt such ideas and, in effect, did nothing in this respect. Given the varied nature of ways of experiencing the events and 'operating' to overcome the related challenges, it was relevant to understand the reasoning of an individual in choosing a response strategy.

The first identified factor influencing respondents' types of strategy to prevent and tackle extreme weather events, is the way they came into possession of a second home (Figure 7.6). This seemingly unimportant quality turned out to be critical for reasons resulting from the specificity of the case-study's geographical setting, already pointed out in the description of the research area. Accordingly, the tree's root node was split into two subsets based on this criterion. The first subset (the entire left branch of the tree) covered the relatively common way of coming into possession of the second home in the region, which is building the house on leased land (often owned by the local forest company, a former commons, e.g. in L2, L3 and L4) (Node 2).

This proves to be an influential factor in preventing users from adopting the material strategy, that is improving the property technically (unless the current and most urgent maintenance needs have to be met) and turning to neighbours and relying more on the local community for support. In other words, not surprisingly the institution of ownership (or rather lack of it) is critical to guiding the individual's effective operational practice to deal with the threat.

Among the users of second homes on leasehold land, the social factor proved crucial in differentiating the coping strategies regarding natural hazards. Respondents' very strong support for the statement that they felt a member of the local second home community was explicitly reflected in preferring neighbourly help to the material strategy (Node 4). This considered 'community belonging', aligning with the proximity of neighbours (other second home owners) resulting from the specificity of properties on leasehold land in the area, that is small plots and low separation distances, thus creating dense clusters of second homes, altogether reinforced the role of social factor in dealing with the risk (Figure 7.7). Moderate and lower 'community belonging' made the reactions and response strategies more diverse (including a mixture of the two main types of action) although the socially-dependent ones were clearly more predominant (Node 5). It also shows

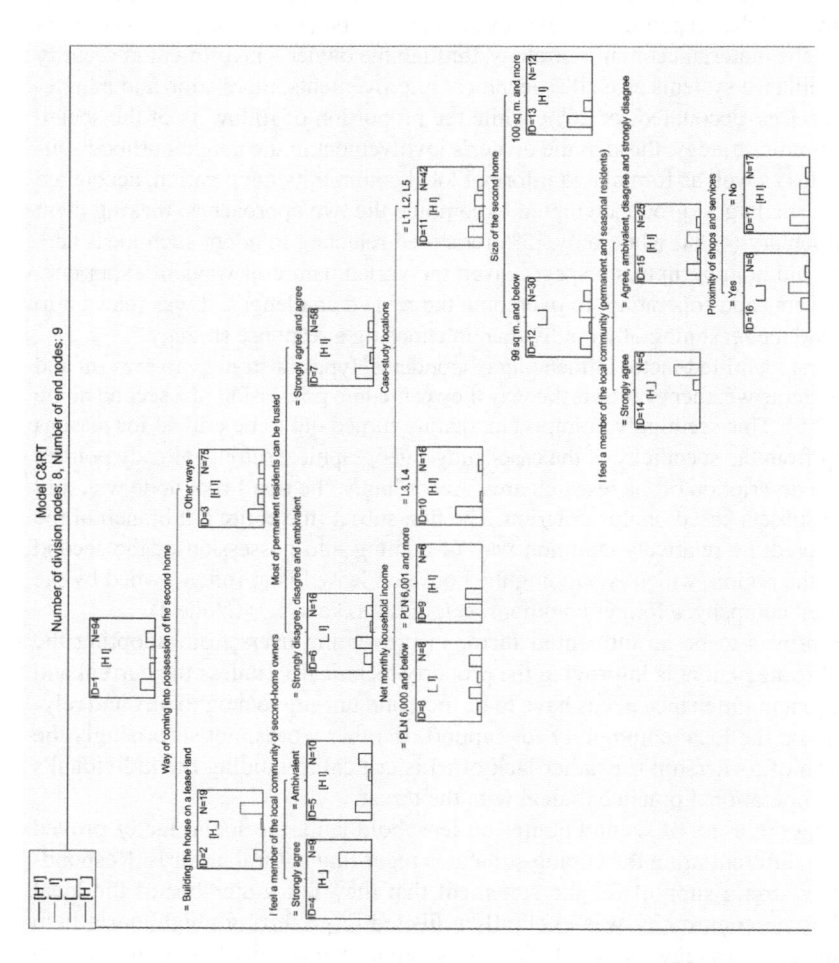

Figure 7.6 Factors behind second home owners' strategies to prevent and tackle extreme weather events and the related effects

Source: Own study.

Figure 7.7 Cottages on leasehold land in location L3 (area affected by the landslide)
Source: Own photograph.

that if one gets no support from the part of local community one has to invest and contribute financially even though the plot is leased and cannot be owned outright. On the other hand, they tend to minimise the costs of maintenance and potential improvements by engaging in the community help. All this proves that the social factor is a priority and constitutes a key component for this group of owners.

Coming back to the tree's main node, its right branch covered all the ways of coming into possession of a second home grounded in strong rights to the property (ownership, apart from the lease) which reflected a diverse range of coping strategies with a visible prevalence of the mixed (complementary) ones (Node 3). The first explanatory factor for this subset made the whole picture clearer and more understandable. For respondents who supported and strongly supported the statement on the majority of local (permanent) residents who can be trusted there was a higher propensity to fall into mixed strategy (Node 7). On the other hand, moderate and low 'community trust' made second home owners less eager to rely on a social strategy but more prone to contribute to house improvement and maintenance physically (Node 6). In the latter group, the owner's household income proved to be an important predictor, revealing that the higher the income the more likely is financial investment (at times with a combination with community help). Representatives of the lower- and middle-income groups adopted diverging strategies, either falling into the socially dependent ones or the economic ones (probably for moderate income households and/or those who are forced by an objective situation to make some investment for necessities).

To better understand strategy choices of the second home owners with the greatest declared confidence in the local community (Node 7), another predictor was identified, which is the location of a second home in one of five locations surveyed (as described in the research area section of this paper). In the second home locations affected directly and indirectly (the immediate surroundings) by the massive landslide in 2010 a mixed (complementary) coping strategy was predominant among the owners

(Node 10). They invested in necessary renovations and adjustments (after the landslide) to minimise future risks but also through the most urgent work, considered as 'sustaining'/'palliative investment', which does not increase the value of property but is needed to keep it usable. However, probably due to specificity of the situation in the aftermath of the 2010 landslide, the cooperation between permanent and seasonal residents strongly reflected in dealing with the bureaucracy, petitions, compensation, temporary safeguarding and insurance. It seems that the event strengthened community integration to some extent, as for instance second home owners had to rely on permanent residents to check and watch their property just in the aftermath of the landslide, as only locals were permitted to access the area. One should also bear in mind that, as in other locations, being socially supported minimises not just the risks and potential loss but also reduces the need to invest, at least in certain aspects. This picture is clearer than the situation defined by node 11 which includes all the other locations (also including areas affected by serious events such as flooding and hurricanes; Figure 7.8) and, at the same time, where there is a variety of almost equally distributed coping strategies.

Diversity of response strategies applied in other than landslide-affected locations can be explained first by one of the contextual factors included, which is the size of the second home (Figure 7.9).

It shows (Node 13) that the actions undertaken by owners of relatively large second homes (over 100 sq. m) are less puzzling and more focused on material investment than in the case of owners of properties smaller than 100 sq. m, for which the most prevalent strategy was 'doing nothing', meaning not demonstrating an economic, non-economic or the mixed/combined strategy (Node 12). Although the home size appeared in the tree as a predictor, it can broadly be considered as a proxy for investment itself (the money allocated and the value of the house), which is evidence that the larger the house the better the equipment and amenities as well as the fact that it is winterised (all year round), meaning there is a reason to protect it.

Figure 7.8 Cottages in the fringe of area affected by the hurricane in location L1
Source: Own photograph.

Figure 7.9 Second homes in the fringe area of the landslide in location L4
Source: Own photograph.

For the owners of smaller homes, for whom the coping strategies were again significantly differentiated, the social explanatory factor turned out to be influential in the decision-making process. Respondents who strongly supported the statement about their feeling of being a member of the local community (permanent and seasonal residents) were more prone to rely only on neighbourly help (Node 14) and did not use the material strategy at all. For the rest of respondents, a diverse mixture of strategies was still common, and among them the mixed one and the opposite, 'doing nothing', were prevalent (Node 15). The strategies demonstrated by this group of owners become more reasonably structured by employing the generally considered servicescape of the immediate surroundings of the cottage.

It can be understood in a way that one does not have to do anything, namely invest or be involved in the community/neighbouring help, if one's home is located in the vicinity of services (e.g. centre of the village), including emergency services (fire, police station, health centre) that are relevant in respect to natural hazards (Node 16). Feeling safe and secure owing to the availability and accessibility seems to somewhat remove or, at least, reduce the owner's motivation towards managing help on their own. On the other hand, the owners consider social support or rather mixed approaches in situations in which the property is far from the services, a local centre and the closest neighbours (which is common in the mountains) (Node 17).

Discussion and conclusion

The literature review has drawn attention to several key issues on extreme weather events considered as a threat to second homes, especially in theoretical reviews and desk-research studies by Fang et al. (2018) and Hoogendoorn and Fitchett (2018). However, empirical research dealing with this issue by examining second home owners' perceptions and actions (e.g. Cheong, 2018; Rey-Valette et al., 2014) has so far been quite rare.

As Hall and Müller (2004) argued, second homes are a specific segment of contemporary tourism. On a local scale they are also an important, although sometimes underrated, factor in socio-economic development. The summertime qualities of the Międzybrodzie Bialskie area surveyed were already known in the interwar period. The authorities in the Czernichów municipalities emphasize that numerous holiday homes have determined tourism and recreation as the foundation of the local economy. The authorities in the Porąbka municipality highlighted summer homes as its strength. However, the survey showed that second home owners themselves more often felt abandoned to their problems (not just the effects of extreme weather events but daily functioning) than appreciated and supported. Instead, research has provided a useful insight into how second home owners manage risk by relying on mutual trust, self-help and informal systems to anticipate and neutralise the effects of extreme weather events rather than placing their confidence in institutions. As Choryński (2019) emphasises, social self-organisation was already observed in Poland during major floods (e.g. in 1997), especially when aid and support from the authorities and services failed or proved insufficient. The model of relations examined confirmed the significant role of a sense of community and trust in other local stakeholders (e.g. permanent residents) when choosing precautionary and mitigation strategies, which was recognised in previous studies (Adger, 2003; Löfstedt, 2005). This study has also proved that the intermittent presence of owners has motivated them to search for locals to rely on with respect to property maintenance and security (Barnett, 2014).

A significant proportion of second home owners (not only affluent ones) adopted preparatory action by choosing a material investment strategy alongside or instead of neighbourly help. Investments were made in security and early-warning systems, house renovations, and, in the light of the explanatory model, the motive for such decisions was, among others, the limited trust in members of the local community. The size of the house also turned out to be an important determinant of the material strategy. The capital allocated in large, all-year-round villas was itself an additional reason to secure the house. This strategy was dependent upon strong rights to the land (the institution of ownership). It turned out that in the Czernichów municipality, a certain percentage of holiday homes were built on leased land. These were often small, non-winterised homes, usually of a light wooden construction and with lower investment. In precautionary actions, in this case, the preference was for neighbourly help. The respondents' most common strategy was to combine economic and non-economic strategies. However, a passive/reluctant strategy was also observed, not taking any measures to protect the house against the effects of extreme weather events. Such instances usually occurred when, due to the second home location, the property was somewhat secured by the close proximity of emergency services, in densely built up areas with many neighbours (permanent residents) potentially helping out in a difficult situation and thus providing the owners with a real sense of security.

Anticipating the effects of extreme weather events, the majority of respondents used a strategy of combining material property protection with social assistance (often also insuring their home). On the one hand this may prove a high awareness of natural hazards, and on the other a belief that when such an event occurs, the aid and support of local authorities, services and institutions would come too late or would be insufficient. More than a quarter of the respondents used only a material strategy. These were usually people who, for various reasons, did not integrate with the local community. Such second home owners are on their own, so they are more exposed and vulnerable to material damage when extreme weather events occur. It seems that the community/authorities should play an important role with regard to this group of second home owners by taking initiatives to integrate them with other local stakeholders. Only those whose houses are located in safe zones of the area surveyed (centres of villages, intermediate zones), in the vicinity of permanent residents, institutions and services, can afford the luxury of passivity and taking no action.

In conclusion, it should be stressed that the second home owners in the Western Beskids do not underestimate the dangers and threats of extreme weather events in the area. After direct or indirect experiences of local landslides, storms and floods, the vast majority of respondents perceived weather extremes as increasingly common and believed that they could cause serious damage to their summer homes. Based on the data on the number of interventions by local fire brigades, weather extremes are occurring not so much more frequently as irregularly. However, as the landslide has clearly shown, one extreme weather event is enough for hundreds of properties to be damaged or significantly depreciate, and for a vibrant community to stagnate.

In light of this study's findings, there is a genuine and a great need for further empirical research with regard to preventative actions and coping strategies that strengthen community robustness and resilience. As Faulkner (2001) has already pointed it out, in an era of advancing climate change, extreme weather events that first and foremost affect the local communities are considered inevitable. However, measures and strategies for adapting to these difficult challenges must first be learned and systematised and then shaped and promoted further.

References

Adamiak, C. (2014). *Drugie domy w Borach Tucholskich*. Project Report. Nicolaus Copernicus University. https://repozytorium.umk.pl/bitstream/handle/item/2595/Drugie%20 domy%20w%20Borach%20Tucholskich.pdf?sequence=1

Adger, W. N. (2003). Social capital, collective action, and adaptation to climate change. *Economic Geography*, *79*(4), 387–404. https://doi.org/10.1111/j.1944-8287.2003.tb00220.x

Atanga, R. A. (2020). The role of local community leaders in flood disaster risk management strategy making in Accra. *International Journal of Disaster Risk Reduction*, *43*. https://doi.org/10.1016/j.ijdrr.2019.101358

Barnett, J. (2014). Host community perceptions of the contributions of second homes. *Annals of Leisure Research*, *17*(1), 10–26. https://doi.org/10.1080/11745398.2014.886156

Berkes, F. (2009). Indigenous ways of knowing and the study of environmental change. *Journal of the Royal Society of New Zealand*, *39*(4), 151156. http://doi.org/10.1080/03014220909510568

Bhattamishra, R., & Barrett, C. B. (2010). Community-based risk management arrangements: A review. *World Development*, *38*(7), 923–932. https://doi.org/10.1016/j.worlddev.2009.12.017

Bhuiyan, S. H., & Khan, H. T. A. (2011). Climate change and its impacts on older adults' health in Kazakhstan. *The NISPAcee Journal of Public Administration and Policy*, *4*(1), 97–119. http://repository.uwl.ac.uk/id/eprint/3742

Bodziony, M., & Baziak, B. (2007). Skutki deszczy nawalnych na przykładzie powodzi w zlewni rzeki Wielkiej Puszczy w latach 1997 i 2005. *Czasopismo Techniczne. Środowisko*, *104*(2), 13–28.

Bronfman, N. C., Cisternas, P. C., Repetto, P. B., & Castañeda, J. V. (2019). Natural disaster preparedness in a multi-hazard environment: Characterizing the sociodemographic profile of those better (worse) prepared. *PLoS ONE*, *14*(4), 214–249. https://doi.org/10.1371/journal.pone.0214249

Bronfman, N. C., Cisternas, P. C., Repetto, P. B., Castañeda, J. V., & Guic, E. (2020). Understanding the relationship between direct experience and risk perception of natural hazards. *Risk Analysis*, *40*(10), 2057–2070. https://doi.org/10.1111/risa.13526

Chan, C.-S., Nozu, K., & Zhou, Q. (2020). Tourism stakeholder perspective for disaster-management process and resilience: The case of the 2018 Hokkaido Eastern Iburi earthquake in Japan. *Sustainability*, *12*(19). https://doi.org/10.3390/su12197882

Cheong, S.-M. (2018). Second homes and vulnerability after Superstorm Sandy in Ortley Beach, New Jersey. *The Professional Geographer*, *70*(4), 583–592. https://doi.org/10.1080/00330124.2018.1432369

Choryński, A. (2019). *Adaptacja Wielkopolskich Gmin do Ekstremalnych Zdarzeń Pogodowych w Świetle Koncepcji Elastyczności (Resilience)*. 'Adam Mickiewicz' University in Poznań. https://repozytorium.amu.edu.pl/bitstream/10593/25222/1/Rozprawa%20doktorska%20-%20Adam%20Chory%c5%84ski.pdf

Coles, E., & Buckle, P. (2004). Developing community resilience as a foundation for effective disaster recovery. *The Australian Journal of Emergency Management, 19*(4), 6–15.

Dessai, S., & Sims, C. (2010). Public perception of drought and climate change in southeast England. *Environmental Hazards, 9*(4), 340–357. https://doi.org/10.3763/ehaz.2010.0037

Dhakal, S., Cui, P., Rijal, C. P., Su, L.-J., Zou, Q., Mavrouli, O., & Wu, C.-H. (2020). Landslide characteristics and its impact on tourism for two roadside towns along the Kathmandu Kyirong Highway. *Journal of Mountain Science, 17*, 1840–1859. https://doi.org/10.1007/s11629-019-5871-3

Duhaime, G., Searles, E., Usher, P. J., Myers, H., & Fréchette, P. (2004). Social cohesion and living conditions in the Canadian Arctic: From theory to measurement. *Social Indicators Research, 66*, 295–318. https://doi.org/10.1023/B:SOCI.0000003726.35478.fc

Fang, Y., Yin, J., & Wu, B. (2018). Climate change and tourism: A scientometric analysis using CiteSpace. *Journal of Sustainable Tourism, 26*(1), 108–126. https://doi.org/10.1080/09669582.2017.1329310

Faulkner, B. (2001). Towards a framework for tourism disaster management. *Tourism Management, 22*(2), 135–147. https://doi.org/10.1016/S0261-5177(00)00048-0

Granvorka, C., & Strobl, E. (2013). The impact of hurricane strikes on tourist arrivals in the Caribbean. *Tourism Economics, 19*(6), 1401–1409. https://doi.org/10.5367/te.2013.0238

Grothmann, T., & Reusswig, F. (2006). People at risk of flooding. Why some residents take precautionary action while others do not. *Natural Hazards, 38*, 101–120. https://doi.org/10.1007/s11069-005-8604-6

Hall, C. M., & Müller, D. K. (2004). The future of second home tourism. In C. M. Hall & D. K. Müller (Eds.), *Tourism, mobility and second homes between elite landscape and common ground* (pp. 273–277). Channel View Publications.

Hoogendoorn, G., & Fitchett, J. M. (2018). Perspectives on second homes, climate change and tourism in South Africa. *African Journal of Hospitality, Tourism and Leisure, 7*(2), 1–18.

Howe, P. D., Boudet, H., Leiserowitz, A., & Maibach, E. W. (2014). Mapping the shadow of experience of extreme weather events. *Climatic Change, 127*(2), 381–389. https://doi.org/10.1007/s10584-014-1253-6

Hunter, L. M., Boardman, J. D., & Saint Onge, J. M. (2005). The association between natural amenities, rural population growth, and long-term residents' economic well-being. *Rural Sociology, 70*(4), 452–469. https://doi.org/10.1526/003601105775012714

Hutter, D. (2016, July 28). *Physical security and why it is important*. SANS Institute Reading Room. www.sans.org/reading-room/whitepapers/physical/physical-security-important-37120

Kapucu, N. (2008). Culture of preparedness: Household disaster preparedness. *Disaster Prevention and Management, 17*(4), 526–535. https://doi.org/10.1108/09653560810901773

Kucharska-Stasiak, E. (2013). Ocena kierunków i skali przekształceń własnościowych w zasobie komunalnym. In A. Nowakowska (Ed.), *Zrozumieć Terytorium: Idea i Praktyka* (pp. 285–302). University of Łódź Press.

Lindell, M. K., & Whitney, D. J. (2000). Correlates of household seismic hazard adjustment adoption. *Risk Analysis, 20*(1), 13–26. https://doi.org/10.1111/0272-4332.00002

Lipski, C., Kostuch, R., & Ryczek, M. (2006). Zniszczenia koryta potoku Wielka Puszcza poniżej zapory na skutek katastrofalnego deszczu. *Infrastruktura i Ekologia Terenów Wiejskich, 3*(2), 103–112.

Löfstedt, R. E. (2005). *Risk management in post-trust societies*. Palgrave Macmillan. https://doi.org/10.1057/9780230503946

López-Marrero, T., & Yarnal, B. (2010). Putting adaptive capacity into the context of people's lives: A case study of two flood-prone communities in Puerto Rico. *Natural Hazards, 52*, 277–297. https://doi.org/10.1007/s11069-009-9370-7

Paul, B. K., & Bhuiyan, R. H. (2010). Urban earthquake hazard: Perceived seismic risk and preparedness in Dhaka City, Bangladesh. *Disasters, 34*(2), 337–359. http://doi.org/10.1111/j.1467-7717.2009.01132.x

Pitkänen, K., Puhakka, R., & Sawatzky, M. (2011). The role of nature in the place meanings and practices of cottage owners in northern environments. *Norwegian Journal of Geography, 65*, 175–187. https://doi.org/10.1080/00291951.2011.598236

Pyhälä, A., Fernández-Llamazares, Á., Lehvävirta, H., Byg, A., Ruiz-Mallén, I., Salpeteur, M., & Thornton, T. F. (2016). Global environmental change: Local perceptions, understandings, and explanations. *Ecology and Society, 21*(3), 25. http://doi.org/10.5751/ES-08482-210325

Rey-Valette, H., Rulleau, B., Hellequin, A.-P., Meur-Férec, C., & Flanquart, H. (2014). Second-home owners and sea-level rise: The case of the Languedoc-Roussillon region (France). *Journal of Policy Research in Tourism, Leisure and Events, 7*(1), 32–47. http://doi.org/10.1080/19407963.2014.942734

Roder, G., Ruljigaljig, T., Lin, C.-H., & Tarolli, P. (2016). Natural hazards knowledge and risk perception of Wujie indigenous community in Taiwan. *Natural Hazards, 81*, 641–662. https://doi.org/10.1007/s11069-015-2100-4

Schneider, S. H., & Root, T. L. (1996). Ecological implications of climate change will include surprises. *Biodiversity and Conservation, 5*, 1109–1119. https://doi.org/10.1007/BF00052720

Scolobig, A., De Marchi, B., & Borga, M. (2012). The missing link between flood risk awareness and preparedness: Findings from case studies in an Alpine Region. *Natural Hazards, 63*, 499–520. https://doi.org/10.1007/s11069-012-0161-1

Scott, D., Hall, C. M., & Gössling, S. (2019). Global tourism vulnerability to climate change. *Annals of Tourism Research, 77*, 49–61. https://doi.org/10.1016/j.annals.2019.05.007

Spence, A., Poortinga, W., Butler, C., & Pidgeon, N. F. (2011). Perceptions of climate change and willingness to save energy related to flood experience. *Nature Climate Change, 1*, 46–49. http://doi.org/10.1038/nclimate1059

Stallings, R. A. (1998). Disaster and the theory of social order. In E. L. Quarantelli (Ed.), *What is a disaster? A dozen perspectives on the question* (pp. 127–145). Routledge.

Tekeli-Yeşil, S., Dedeoğlu, N., Braun-Fahrlaender, C., & Tanner, M. (2011). Earthquake awareness and perception of risk among the residents of Istanbul. *Natural Hazards, 59*, 427–446. https://doi.org/10.1007/s11069-011-9764-1

Vorkinn, M., & Riese, H. (2001). Environmental concern in a local context. *Environment and Behavior, 33*(2), 249–263. https://doi.org/10.1177/00139160121972972

Wachinger, G., & Renn, O. (2010). *Risk perception and natural hazards*. CapHaz-Net WP3 Report. DIALOGIK Non-Profit Institute for Communication and Cooperative Research. http://caphaz-net.org/outcomes-results/CapHaz-Net_WP3_Risk-Perception.pdf

8 Adrift among the vineyards second home owners' perceptions and reactions about climate change in the cultural landscape of the vineyards of Langhe-Roero and Monferrato, Italy

Stefania Toso

Introduction

Climate related research and international reports have already suggested how Southern European countries around the Mediterranean Sea will face major issues for their tourism destinations in the 21st century (Perry, 2005; Alcamo et al., 2007; Moreno, 2010a; Galeotti & Roson, 2012; Magnan et al., 2013; Dogru at al., 2016; Jacob et al., 2018; Demiroglu et al., 2020). In the European context, both winter and summer tourism will be affected by climate change, with different vulnerabilities and impacts dependent on the diverse subnational territories within each country (Damm et al., 2017; Koutroulis et al., 2018). In the Mediterranean basin, heat waves, heavy precipitation events, floods and water scarcity will likely undermine some of the most attractive scenery (Perry, 2005) and will cause severe economic losses (Galeotti & Roson, 2012). Specifically, Southern Europe is expected to be more vulnerable than other European regions in relation to the tourism and agriculture sectors. It has been estimated that they will be highly sensitive economic assets and among the most affected sectors as they are deeply connected to the environment and the climate (Kovats et al., 2014). Moreover, studies on climate change impacts and adaptation strategies suggest that decision-making processes in tourism are already affected by climate variations, and tourists will likely change the destination, duration and the activities of their vacation trips according to their personal perception of climate change (Nicholls, 2006; Moreno, 2010b; Gössling et al., 2012; Demiroglu et al., 2020). Likewise, second home owners are experiencing the impact of climate change, and they are actively adjusting their individual attitudes and actions towards their secondary dwellings, dealing with local inhabitants and public administrations.

According to projections, a decrease in tourist activities and agricultural yields will be significant for Italy, where the two economic sectors are deeply intertwined. In the last several decades, the creation of linkages between the agrarian sector and tourism in rural areas has generated new occupational opportunities, pivoting around the concepts of diversification and authentic experience. However, those advantages are counterbalanced by the threat of climate change impacts on agricultural products and touristic routes. In Italy, many unique agrarian landscapes that are internationally renowned as touristic destinations could face unprecedented

DOI: 10.4324/9781003091295-8

challenges linked to environmental quality maintenance and cultural identity protection. For instance, that is the case for cultural landscapes, which are the direct result of historical human activities in the natural context: both their tangible and intangible heritage is at risk as climate change is mining those processes that, decade after decade, built the local identity and community self-representation. Consequently, it can be argued that rural areas and activities performed in rural contexts, such as tourism, could face direct and indirect effects of climate variations "since they represent unique, fragile, and complex systems sustaining a multitude of functions besides agricultural production" (Hemming et al., 2013, p. 73). Explorations about the diversified and place-based linkages between tourism and agriculture have been widely researched (Torres & Momsen, 2011), but less attention has been dedicated to second home tourism and its direct and indirect mutual interaction with the agricultural sector, except for its negative effects. Therefore, the chapter seeks to examine how second home tourism and agriculture are modelling and influencing each other, which are simultaneously, and at different levels, impacted by climate change. Second home tourism and agriculture development trajectories are explored in a case study area in the Italian rural context, the cultural landscape of the vineyards of Langhe-Roero and Monferrato in the Piedmont region, Northwest Italy. The contribution is traced upon semi-structured in-depth interviews conducted in 2020 in the case study area to second home owners and rural inhabitants, aimed at investigating how second home users will respond to climate change in the next decades, according to their perception of the global issue. Quantitative data are also analyzed and mapped to better frame how modifications to viticulture and to the hydrogeological system could intersect second home geographies.

Firstly, a framework on Italian second home patterns is outlined, focusing on their vulnerabilities to climate change. Then, cultural landscapes are presented, followed by a methodology and case study introduction. After the quantitative data are examined through thematic maps, evidence from the interviews is described to express second home owners' perceptions and concerns about climate change. Lastly, final remarks are provided to support further research, suggesting a multidisciplinary approach to define successful future strategies and policies about second homes and climate change.

Italian second home patterns and climate vulnerabilities

Owning a second home in Italy is nothing unusual since it is a tradition that dates back to the Roman times, when it was not uncommon for the super-rich to own more than one extra property.

The typology of the suburban villa survived through the Middle Ages and the Renaissance, linked to the *topos* of the *locus amoenus*, becoming rooted in the collective imaginary as a dream to be pursued as an escape from urban centres. With the process of democratization after World War II and the economic boom, owning multiple houses for vacations became a family tradition, partly seen as a showcase of an urban status symbol (Hall & Müller, 2004). Due to the historically differentiated economic and political developments between the North and the South, the Italian patterns of second homes are as diverse as the landscape typologies across the whole country. From coastal areas to mountains and inner regions, the geography of second home tourism is shaped by different core features, involved actors and social, economic and cultural impacts. However, second home tourism literature related to the Italian context is scarcely understood, and the phenomenon is insufficiently monitored at the national level due to the lack of data and situated research. Even less attention has been devoted to the extent of the phenomenon in rural and marginal areas of the country, despite the clear evidence of its importance brought to light during the spread of the COVID-19 pandemic in 2020.

Although there is limited knowledge about how climate will change at the local level and how vulnerability and resilience of the tourism industry might be assessed at a local scale (Dogru et al., 2016), it is possible to outline a national framework focused on the different impacts of and vulnerabilities to climate change that correspond to the variety of second home landscapes in Italy. The national debate and academic research identify three main geographic settings characterized by holiday homes concentrated in climate sensitive contexts: coastal, mountain and rural areas.

1. Secondary homes in densely built coasts suitable for mass tourism (on the peninsula and islands)

Italian coastal areas are known to be the favoured destination of the majority of national and international summer tourists, but they are also home to 28.4% of the Italian population (17,215,609 inhabitants settled in 43,084 km²). Erosion, sea-level rise, increasing extreme weather events and threats to the marine ecosystem are among the most tangible effects of climate change, and they will affect the heavily anthropized coastline, which has been almost saturated by holiday houses since the 1980s. Local municipalities along the coasts will be forced to deal with environmental sustainability issues, hydraulic risks and tourism management (Romano & Zullo, 2014). Climate change will also cause the loss of renowned beaches and places of interest and a decrease in water resources available for tourism (Breil et al., 2007). Venice and Cinque Terre (Liguria) are recurrently in the spotlight in the international press because of the damages already occurring linked to climate change.

2. Mountain holiday homes in either neglected or renowned touristic destinations

The European Alpine Region is potentially one of most vulnerable areas to climate change and, at the same time, one of the most favoured destination for vacations in Europe after the Mediterranean region. In the Italian context, declining mountain villages are already suffering from deep depopulation and commercial desertification processes, whether as a result of past catastrophic events (e.g. earthquakes in Central Italy) or after a declining phase of their past tourist industry. In some Alpine contexts, depopulated villages have been converted into seasonal resorts and concentrated secondary dwellings that might be abandoned during non-touristic weeks of the year therefore causing a loss of cultural identity and liveability (Brida et al., 2011). On the other hand, in wealthier contexts (such as Dolomites), multilocal dwellings are also seen as part of the setting of new contemporary positive demographic trends (Perlik, 2011, 2019; Elmi & Perlik, 2014), while a negative outcome may be a process of 'Alpine gentrification' (Perlik, 2011). Moreover, mountain aesthetic features, its ecologic values and rural amenities are exploited by the global market economy, turning landscapes into commodities and fostering new inequalities among mountain regions (Perlik, 2019). In this framework, climate change will affect second home tourism in the winter season. With the reduction of the snow cover altering the snow reliability of the Alps, Alpine communities will need additional snow management tools and new touristic strategies, which are both financially and environmentally sustainable and less snow-dependent (Abegg et al., 2007).

3. Rural secondary dwellings in the countryside and in the marginal inner areas

Rural areas were affected by post-war shrinkage, associated with out-migration to cities and rural decline and deprivation. Today, Italian countryside villages host a diversity of rural second homes, old buildings rather than purpose-built homes, with their vernacular architectural elements being restored and functionally converted for leisure activities. Attracted by the landscape quality, second home owners come from metropolitan areas and beyond national borders, thus fueling a movement that boosts the local economy and seeks to preserve environmental and cultural resources. A recent study conducted by Carrosio et al. (2019) about the spreading of processes of eco-gentrification in the countryside highlights how the presence of highly mobile populations in rural areas may contribute to fighting depopulation, the same process of abandonment that generated new temporary and permanent residential spaces, leading to an increase in secondary houses starting from the 1960s. A significant portion of Italian rural territory is subject to landslides and hydraulic risks, and 91% of municipalities are involved, with more than three million households residing in highly vulnerable areas (Trigila et al., 2018). Climate change threats to rural second homes are therefore related to the territorial fragilities of rural landscapes due to the hydrogeological instability, forest management and extreme events, aggravated by land abandonment and unsustainable agricultural practices. Moreover, many rural areas in Italy are identified by distinctive landscapes, where human interaction with the natural environment has produced exceptional both aesthetic and cultural values. These so-called cultural landscapes are among the main attractive sceneries for Italian and foreign second home owners, to the extent that their modification due to climate variations and natural hazards may affect future patterns of second home tourism.

Cultural landscapes as fragile ecosystems

The term 'cultural landscape' has been challenged by scholars from various disciplines, including human geography and cultural heritage, and related narratives in both academic and administrative fields have highlighted how borderline the concept is, partly conflated with that of landscape itself (Jones, 2003) as all landscapes are at once natural and cultural (Cosgrove, 1998). Nevertheless, the adoption of such a definition by UNESCO in 1995 stimulated its use, referring to these landscapes as the result of the "interaction between people and their natural environment over space and time" (Plachter & Rossler, 1995, p. 15). The emphasis is placed on the quality and features of the mutual influence of human practices and the natural elements resulting in a distinct landscape. Thus, it is evident that climate change is already affecting cultural landscapes and the activities carried out by humans. Direct damage is expected as a result of the threats posed by extreme weather events and natural disasters on the aesthetic and physical values of cultural landscapes. Indirect, and possibly more profound, upheavals may affect the social and economic context that sustains the cultural landscape. Among the 55 cultural and natural sites inscribed on the World Heritage List in Italy, eight are listed as cultural landscapes. Those landscapes clearly identified by agriculture (such as viticulture) are particularly vulnerable to climate change as the climate is among the main elements that determines the landscape's morphology, agricultural production and the product itself, as well as all the correlated aspects of local social and cultural life. Their exceptional value resides in the results of man's interaction with the natural environment (criterion V of the UNESCO definition), a process that evolved through the ages based on human adaptation and experimentation in response to the local climate.

The vineyard landscape is a representative case in which tourism and agriculture constitute the two main economic sectors. As a driving source of income for rural inhabitants, their patterns are intertwined as wine production is also the main tourist attraction, together with the experience of the vineyard landscape. Several scholars have already discussed to what extent tourism should be considered a sector vulnerable to climate change (Dogru et al., 2016). Likewise, extensive studies have been carried out to assess the future suitability for grape production in Europe and Italy, building multiple scenarios with different climate variation simulations until 2100 (Fraga et al., 2013; Schultz & Jones, 2010; Teslić et al., 2019). The results highlight that viticulture in Southern Europe will struggle to cope with climate change, and that will endanger the wine quality and productivity, modifying the viticultural zoning. Adaptation strategies in the long term will probably include changes in vineyard geography (Fraga, 2019). This scenario would also affect the socio-cultural system with consequences to both international and domestic rural tourism connected to wine places, which includes second homes.

Methods and data

The chapter presents a preliminary discussion of the insights from a case study in a rural area in Northwest Italy, in the Piedmont Region. The data collected relates to the relationship between second home tourism, a peculiar agricultural landscape (i.e., the cultural landscape) and climate change. A qualitative approach has been adopted through the collection and analysis of in-depth semi-structured interviews, conducted in the cultural landscape the Vineyard Landscape of Piedmont: Langhe-Roero and Monferrato, which are considered the 'archetypes of European vineyards' for their aesthetic and cultural features and were listed as a World Heritage Site in 2014 (UNESCO, 2014).

Twenty-two interviews were conducted with second home owners aiming at investigating all aspects of their individual story about their second home, their engagement with the local community and their relationship with the landscape; while twenty-eight interviews were conducted with local inhabitants in order to better understand their perceptions about second home tourism in the area and the changes to the economic, social and cultural ecosystem that have occurred in the last decades. In doing so, interviewees reported individual and collective thoughts about climate change impacts on their own properties and activities as well as on the local community in the last several years. An additional six interviews were carried out among local wine producers and second home owners that started their own wine production business in the research area in order to collect qualitative data about adaptive strategies already in place or scheduled as a future response to climate change.

Due to limited local datasets about the distribution of second homes, the case study area is restricted to the municipalities in the cultural landscape site of Langhe-Roero and Monferrato within the Asti province administrative perimeter. Populated by 215,884 inhabitants with a surface of 160,000 hectares, the Asti territory is

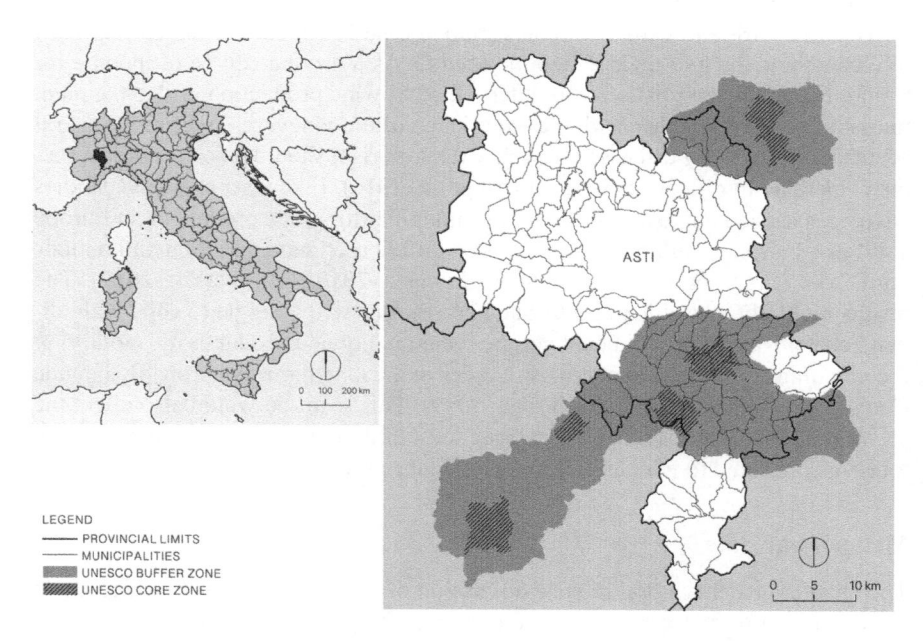

Figure 8.1 The case study area – the Asti province and the World Heritage Site of the Vineyard Landscape of Piedmont: Langhe-Roero and Monferrato

Source: Author's elaboration on Piedmont Region open data.

predominately hilly, with the town of Asti (76,164 inhabitants in 2017) as a central point, surrounded by smaller rural villages where viticulture has a predominant and historical role in the local economic, cultural and social system (Figure 8.1).

Since the Second World War, Italy has been characterized by intense building activity. Rural areas were affected by post-war shrinkage, associated with out-migration to cities and rural decline and deprivation, which created the space for holiday homes, developed from abandoned farm buildings in the countryside. During the 1970s and 1980s, new growth in population characterized the so-called 'rururban' settlements, enabled by small-scale industrial and service businesses and causing the dissemination of urban sprawl, with negative impacts on landscape. The 1990s marked a turning point where rural areas became synonymous with authenticity and traditional identity, resulting in the development of 'soft' tourism, centered on heritage and landscape (Padovani & Vettoretto, 2003), fostering a new wave of second home tourism, with international owners and users. Ferrero (1998) problematized second home tourism in the mountainous areas of Piedmont as the main cause of local transformation into a sort of extension of the urban environment.

In the province of Asti, the amount of empty and holiday dwellings increased from 1951 to 2011, from 13% of the total number of dwellings up to 24% on average, with some municipalities reaching a peak of almost 80% in 2011 (Figure 8.2). Municipalities that have accessibility issues and are considered marginal, as they are far from fundamental services, are also those that suffered the most from the processes of depopulation and commercial desertification in the past decades. This rural exodus as well as the radical transformation of the agricultural world are at the root of these phenomena (Lanzani & Curci, 2018), which has led to the availability of numerous traditional rural buildings, in many cases destined for

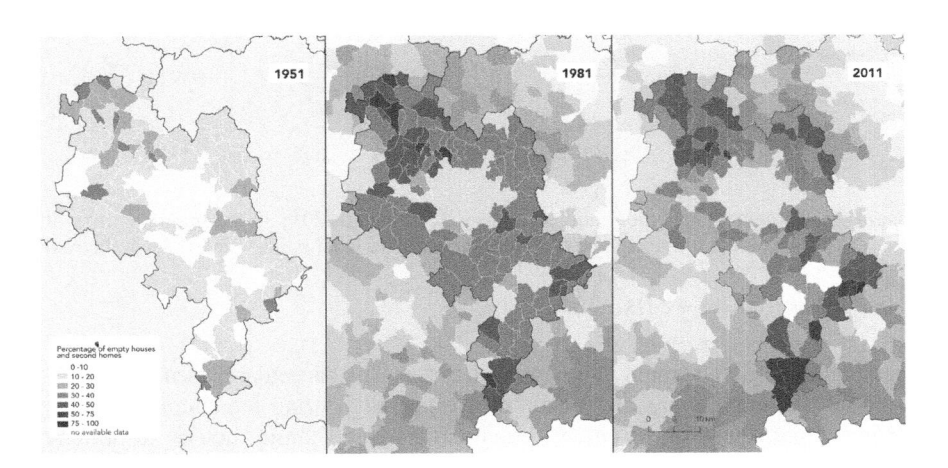

Figure 8.2 Choropleth map of the case study area about the percentage of empty and non-resident occupied dwellings from 1951 to 2011

Source: Author's elaboration on ISTAT data.

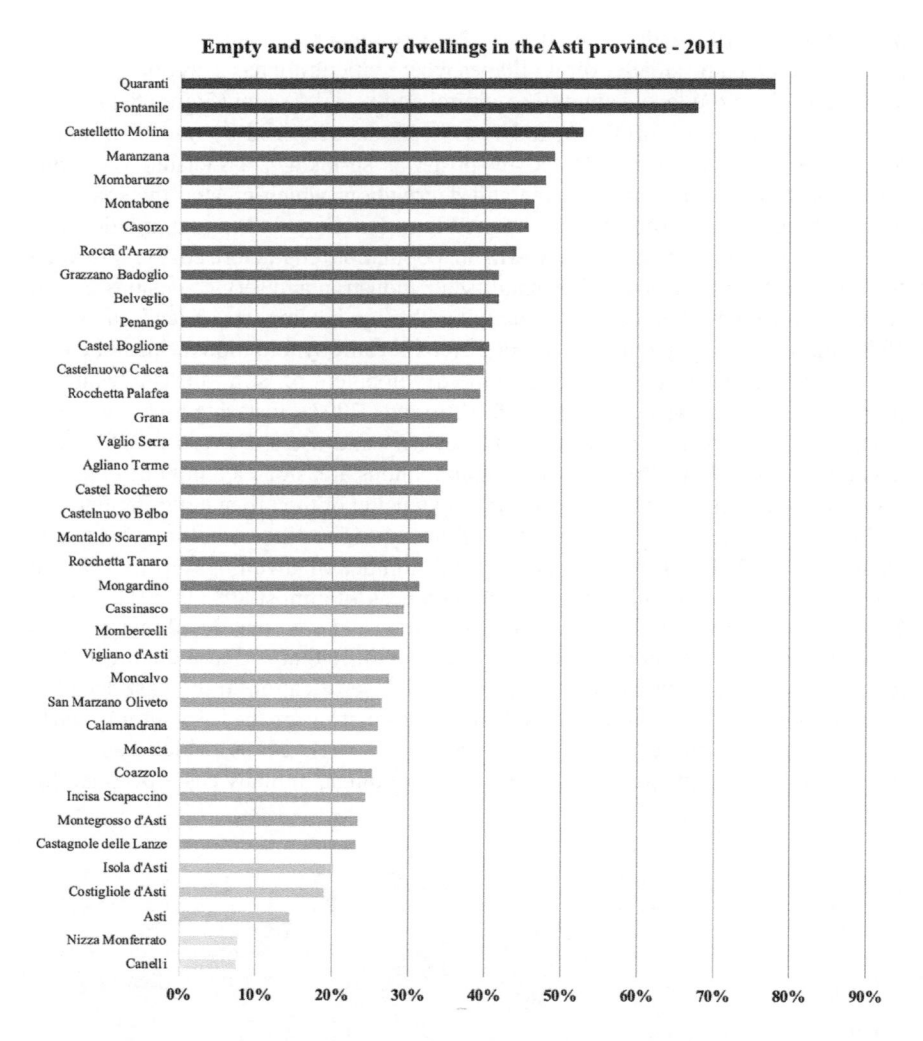

Empty and secondary dwellings in the Asti province - 2011

Figure 8.3 Percentage of empty and secondary dwellings in 2011 in the municipalities of the Vineyard Landscape of Piedmont: Langhe-Roero and Monferrato in the Asti province

Source: Author's elaboration on ISTAT data.

abandonment or conversion into new residences. This particular agricultural landscape and favourable weather conditions, especially during the summer season, supported the transition of empty farms and inherited family houses to holiday homes, whether rented or owned, in those municipalities in the countryside.

Climate change impacts on cultural landscape and viticulture

The Piedmont region is complex due to its orography, made up of the Alps, the hills and the Po Valley. For that reason, second home tourism takes on multiple varied forms: isolated mountain huts; entire villages specifically built for mass winter tourism during the 1960s and 1970s; renovated ruined buildings in the countryside; and inherited small apartments in medium and large cities. Similarly, the forecasts regarding climate change indicate non-homogeneous consequences for the regional territory. The Alpine area in Piedmont will potentially become a 'hot spot' of climate change, with the most evident being temperature increases. Heatwaves will most likely lead to an increase in forest fires (forest surface in 2016 in Piedmont amounts to 976,953 ha, and 17% of it is in hilly areas), while extreme events will alternate with periods of drought. Unexpected and intense precipitation will also increase hydraulic risks and the probability of landslides, exacerbating the already complex geo-hydrological instability (Spano et al., 2020), which affects the whole country but is also specific to the case study area (Figure 8.4). Most of the second homes located in isolated hamlets or historic countryside villages have been tackling the issues associated with hydrogeological instability in recent years, investing private resources to solve a collective problem. The effect of projected worsening hazards impacts tourism related to holiday homes, which may be discouraged in specific tourist destinations, and tourism linked to the so-called 'borghi' and inner areas.

Limitations or damages to the local infrastructure (such as roads or water supply services and private internet connection) would be crucial for rural inhabitants and tourists, with disruption peaks in the summer and autumn seasons. Moreover, the cultural landscape of Langhe-Roero and Monferrato will be subject to variations that will affect wine production and, therefore, the vineyard landscape. The agricultural landscape and high-quality wine production (D.O.C. and D.O.C.G.

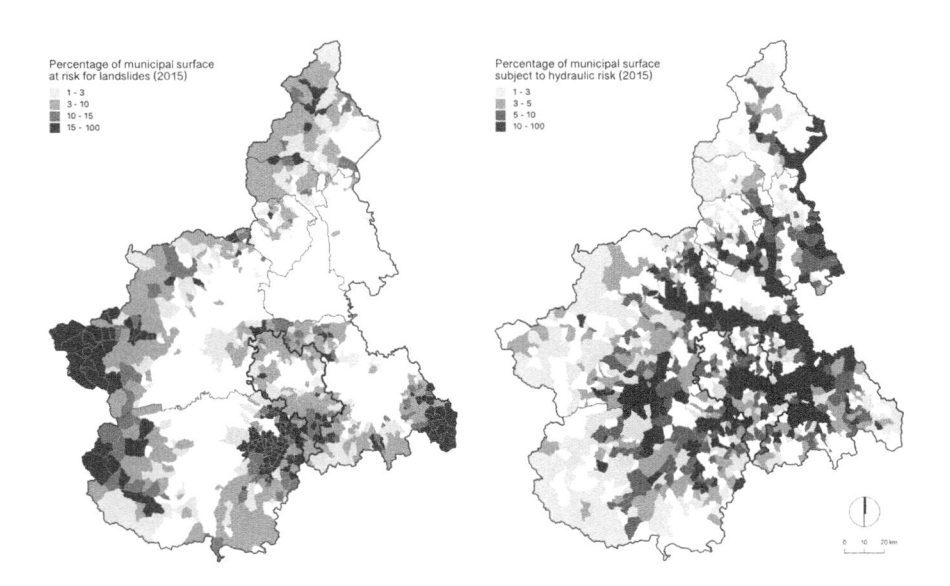

Figure 8.4 Percentage of municipal surface subject to landslides and hydraulic risks in 2015 in the regional context

Source: Author's elaboration on Italian government open data available at www.urbanindex.it.

wines) play a relevant role in the tourist patterns in Southern Piedmont, and it can be argued that significant climate change impacts might cause negative economic impacts on the tourism sector, similarly to what has been estimated for Tuscany (Nunes & Loureiro, 2016). The characteristics and qualities of wine are dependent on climatic aspects of the local region and environment, as well as on the soil, and cultural and management practices. Changes in temperatures and annual precipitation are already affecting the wine cultivation and production process, forcing small and medium producers to search for mitigation and adaptation practices. Studies have been conducted to assess how climate change will affect the identity and quality of some Italian wines in order to provide adaptation and mitigation strategies and to inform local policies (Bernetti et al., 2012). Results for the Piedmont region show a reduction in the optimal areas by 2100 according to both of the scenarios including or excluding mitigation actions (Spano et al., 2020). While a future shift of vine cultivation towards the Alps is predicted, for the south of the region, a considerable loss of suitable area for high quality wines is expected. The total area of vineyards in Piedmont is already rapidly decreasing as it has lost 40% of its surface area in only 30 years (Figure 8.5), which reflects an international trend shared with all the European countries. Thus, the geography of historical wine regions is already changing and will continue to be modified worldwide in the future by climate change, to face variations in the wine style and in the wine production process (Shultz & Jones, 2010). The regional map with the distribution of the vineyards shows that they are expanding closer to mountain and higher hilly areas, taking advantage of a cooler climate during the summer season, but globally

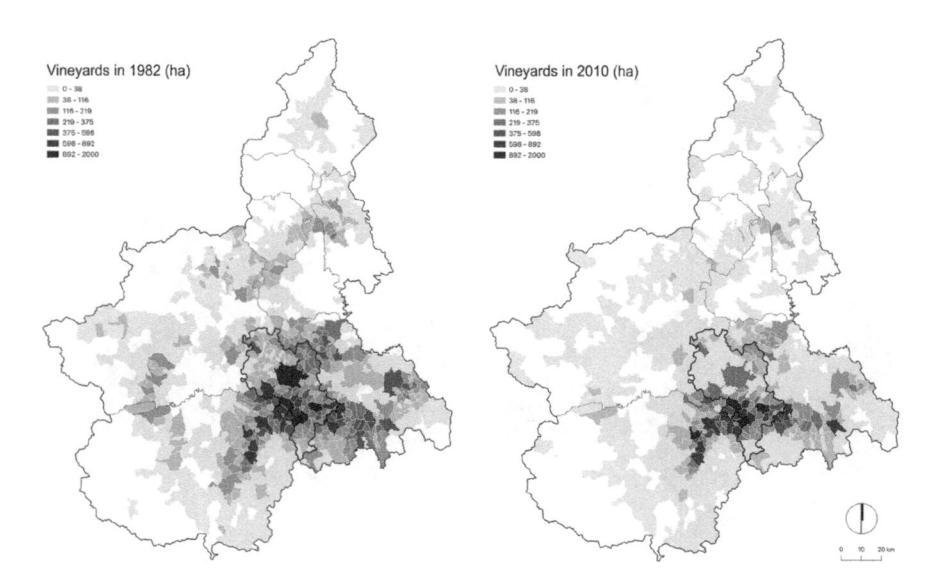

Figure 8.5 Vineyard area (ha) by municipalities in the Piedmont region in 1982 and 2010

Source: Author's elaboration on Piedmont region data available at www.regione.piemonte.it.

less hectares are dedicated to grapevine cultivation. Today the highest density are distributed in a smaller number of municipalities in the UNESCO site of Langhe-Roero and Monferrato, where the majority of the quality wine production (D.O.C. and D.O.C.G. wines) is concentrated, but future modifications may put economic and cultural sectors such as tourism at risk.

The landscape is therefore at the centre of the topic of climate change and its effects on second home tourism. The landscape is, on the one hand, the strength of the case study area, as the main attractive element, shaped over time by cultural and social practices, the foundation of local community identity. On the other hand, however, it also represents an element of extreme fragility, vulnerable to climate change, which could disturb not only the physical balance through changes in soil, water and air but which could also influence the evolution of socio-cultural phenomena, through direct and indirect effects on farming activities and on housing and tourist patterns.

Second home owners' perceptions of climate change

Evidence from the interviews reveals that the most visible climate change effect perceived by second home owners in the short term is related to extreme weather events, such as storms, continuous heavy rainfall, whirlwinds and floods, mostly occurring during the summer and autumn seasons. Damage to holiday properties affect buildings, rooftops, gardens and vegetable patches, resulting in unforeseen expenses for homeowners (Figure 8.6). As more economic effort is required, some homeowners may consider selling the property, especially when they already own

Figure 8.6 Damage reported by an interviewee to his holiday house during summer 2020. A violent storm uprooted the historic tree in the courtyard, causing damage to the roof and facade of the building.

multiple second homes and when those dramatic events are recurrent year after year. The extent of the damage is partially correlated to the fact that less extraordinary repairs rather than ordinary architectural maintenance are usually devoted to rural second homes, often old farmhouses converted into holiday retreats by those who inherited them. Moreover, in second home areas, often those located in small hamlets or isolated in the hills, inadequate attention is usually paid to woods, spontaneous vegetation or common lands, once safely managed by local farmers and today subject to abandonment by second home owners, thus contributing to the increase of landslides and hydraulic risks. Public infrastructure such as roads, the energy grid and telecommunications are frequently damaged or out of service due to flooding, landslides and storms, altering the regular activities and services available for second home owners and local inhabitants.

In the long run, as scientists have already predicted, climate change impacts on the agricultural sector will affect the cultural landscape of the vineyards, which is the crucial attractive element of the Langhe-Roero and Monferrato UNESCO site. Older vineyards that were more profitable in the past are now experiencing less favourable sun exposure in the summer season, with extreme heat scalding the grapes and leading to severe damage, which is sometimes even more extensive than that caused by storms and extreme weather events, such as hailstorms. Small producers are already experimenting with new strategies that might improve the diversification, and therefore the stability, of their businesses in the future, by replacing some vineyards already affected by grapevine diseases with hazelnut fields, where the fruits are destined for multinational companies in the confectionery field or for local processing and sale. As stated by some interviewees, several second home owners participate in the wine production sector by cultivating small segments of vineyards around the property or even producing a restricted quantity of wine. Others regularly enjoy rural tourism experiences connected to wine production, for example, harvest time or sharing it with friends and relatives visiting the holiday property. The majority of second home owners, as well as local inhabitants, are aware of the changing weather conditions occurring in rural areas. On average, while second home owners who have family ties to the place tend to be less disposed towards modifications to land use and management, foreigners and owners who bought their second home recently are generally more inclined to experiment with different crops, such as olive trees, and, in so doing, they are directly modifying the cultural landscape. Nevertheless, some of those actions might contribute to building new environmental and cultural conditions for a more resilient landscape and community in the face of climate change.

Ultimately, the increasing rise in heatwaves and higher overall temperatures that mainly affect the vulnerable population living in the metropolitan areas and urban settings during summer (Spano et al., 2020) is driving a significant number of citizens to temporarily but frequently move to their rural second homes, despite the possible and sudden extreme weather events that may occur, according to the interviewees. Holiday homes in rural environments are seen as havens, shelters for households, the elderly and children. Climate change is mitigated by local strategies and natural assets such as permeable soil and vegetation, with lower pollution concentration levels. Together with the isolated location factor that usually characterizes second homes in rural areas, the restorative value of living in a natural context is highlighted by the interviewees, that showed a new awareness about the potential effects on both mental and physical wellbeing as a result of the restrictions on mobility due to the 2020 pandemic (Pitkänen et al., 2020).

Second homes in the vineyards: a changing geography?

In the Mediterranean, the geography of second home tourism is related to the favourable climate, which is perceived as ideal for vacation periods. Among the most relevant intangible elements, family ties, place attachment and the vitality of the local community also play a significant role in the buying and selling patterns of second homes, especially in rural areas. However, in rural contexts, the landscape is a crucial determinant that has multiple meanings and cultural discourses attached to it (Pitkänen, 2008). Therefore, the effects of climate change on the landscape will most likely affect behavioural patterns and decision-making processes regarding the geographical location of second homes in the Italian countryside, both through direct and indirect impacts that are differently distributed and consistent.

The chapter presented the evolution of the interconnected relationship between the agricultural landscape and second home tourism in the UNESCO site Langhe-Roero and Monferrato, Piedmont, as well as the climate change perceptions of second home owners in this area. The study, through qualitative data, outlines three different scenarios of how different weather conditions will influence second home tourism in the coming decades. In the first scenario, some holiday home users will most likely be discouraged by the unpredictable financial resources required to cope with damage from extreme events (landslides, floods, storms). Both Italian and foreign owners will experience actual damage related to climate change during their lifetime as second home owners, dealing with the stress related to decision-making pathways. Secondly, others are likely to lose interest in the second home market in the area if the historical vineyards become subject to relocation, not only for the changing environment aesthetics but also for the consequent disappearance or weakening of cultural and traditional rural festivals and activities that animate the cultural landscape. As the geography of vineyards will likely change in the following decades, second home tourism will probably follow, as it is linked to the landscape and local cultural features. Lastly, a third opposite trend can be detected. A revival of residential tourism in rural Italy can be predicted, given how unbearable cities and metropolitan areas are projected to be in the future due to increasing summer temperatures. Together with the boost driven by remote working and multilocal living contemporary lifestyles, here lies the chance for a new wave of second home tourism in rural and peripheral areas that may lead to the renovation of abandoned farmhouses or empty second homes built in the 1960s and 1970s and to the recovery and enhancement of cultural traditions and festivals, unfortunately neglected by locals.

These preliminary conclusions are largely transferable to other contexts in the Italian countryside. The research may be relevant for different vineyard landscapes or rural areas where agriculture has a predominant role in the meaning and physical making of landscape, where the landscape is collectively recognized as a valuable asset to be consumed as a tourist attraction and sold as a territorial marketing brand (e.g. the olive tree landscapes in Apulia, Umbria and Liguria, the historical terraced landscapes in Cinque Terre, Valtellina and in the Amalfi Coast, the apple production landscape in Val di Non, Trentino). It is no coincidence that those territories are also renowned for being privileged destinations in the second homes market.

Even if second home users in rural areas might be seen as detached from their environment, they may be key actors who contribute to rural change (Müller, 2011) and thus influence the local community about both local and global issues, such as climate change. They can bring a 'resource potential' to rural communities (Gallent, 2015), leading the community towards greater resilience, often breaking some traditional customs related to living and agricultural practices. They could be involved in participation processes aimed at defining adaptation strategies with local stakeholders, such as wine producers, small tourist businesses or real estate agencies. Moreover, studying and monitoring the perceptions and actions linked to second home owners in the coming years could help strengthen tourism and housing policies and direct new possible patterns for holiday homes. Although uncertainties around climate change projections must be taken into account and individual and societal responses to it are still unpredictable, some outlines of future scenarios are already in place.

References

Abegg, B., Agrawala, S., Crick, F., & de Montfalcon, A. (2007). Climate change impacts and adaptation in winter tourism. In S. Agrawala (Ed.), *Climate change in the European Alps: Adapting winter tourism and natural hazards management* (pp. 25–60). OECD.

Alcamo, J., Moreno, J. M., Nováky, B., Bindi, M., Corobov, R., Devoy, R. J. N., Giannakopoulos, C., Martin, E., Olesen, J. E., & Shvidenko, A. (2007). Europe. Climate change 2007: Impacts, adaptation and vulnerability. Contribution of working group II to the fourth assessment report of the intergovernmental panel on climate change. In M. L. Parry, O. F. Canziani, J. P. Palutikof, P. J. van der Linden, & C. E. Hanson (Eds.), *Contribution of working group II to the fourth assessment report of the intergovernmental panel on climate change* (pp. 541–580). Cambridge University Press.

Bernetti, I., Menghini, S., Marinelli, N., Sacchelli, S., & Sottini, V. A. (2012). Assessment of climate change impact on viticulture: Economic evaluations and adaptation strategies analysis for the Tuscan wine sector. *Wine Economics and Policy*, *1*(1), 73–86.

Breil, M., Catenaccio, M., & Travisi, C. (2007). *Impatti del cambiamento climatico sulle zone costiere: Quantificazione economica di impatti e di misure di adattamento – sintesi di risultati e indicazioni metodologiche per la ricerca futura*. APAT and CMCC Report.

Brida, J. G., Osti, L., & Santifaller, E. (2011). Second homes and the need for policy planning. *Tourismos*, *6*(1), 141–163.

Carrosio, G., Magnani, N., & Osti, G. (2019). A mild rural gentrification driven by tourism and second homes. Cases from Italy. *Sociologia urbana e rurale*, *119*, 29–45. https://doi.org/10.3280/SUR2019-119003

Cosgrove, D. E. (1998). *Social formation and symbolic landscape*. University of Wisconsin Press.

Damm, A., Greuell, W., Landgren, O., & Prettenthaler, F. (2017). Impacts of +2 °C global warming on winter tourism demand in Europe. *Climate Services*, *7*, 31–46. http://doi.org/10.1016/j.cliser.2016.07.003

Demiroglu, O. C., Saygili-Araci, F. S., Pacal, A., Hall, C. M., & Kurnaz, M. L. (2020). Future Holiday Climate Index (HCI) performance of urban and beach destinations in the Mediterranean. *Atmosphere*, *11*(9), 911. https://doi.org/10.3390/atmos11090911

Dogru, T., Bulut, U., & Sirakaya-Turk, E. (2016). Theory of vulnerability and remarkable resilience of tourism demand to climate change: Evidence from the Mediterranean Basin. *Tourism Analysis*, *21*(6), 645–660. https://doi.org/10.3727/1083542 16X14713487283246

Elmi, M., & Perlik, M. (2014). Dal turismo alla residenza multilocale? *Journal of Alpine Research*, *102*(3). https://doi.org/10.4000/rga.2600

Ferrero, G. (1998). Seconde case, politiche urbanistiche e turismo nelle Alpi occidentali italiane. *Revue de Géographie Alpine*, *86*(3), 61–68.

Fraga, H. (2019). Viticulture and winemaking under climate change. *Agronomy*, *9*(12), 783. http://doi.org/10.3390/agronomy9120783

Fraga, H., Malheiro, A. C., Moutinho-Pereira, J., & Santos, J. A. (2013). An overview of climate change impacts on European viticulture. *Food and Energy Security*, *1*(2), 94–110. http://doi.org/10.1002/fes3.14

Galeotti, M., & Roson, R. (2012). Economic impacts of climate change in Italy and the Mediterranean: Updating the evidence. *Journal of Sustainable Development*, *5*(5), 27–41. http://doi.org/10.5539/jsd.v5n5p27

Gallent, N. (2015). Bridging social capital and the resource potential of second homes: The case of Stintino, Sardinia. *Journal of Rural Studies*, *38*, 99–108. https://doi.org/10.1016/j.jrurstud.2015.02.001

Gössling, S., Scott, D., Hall, C. M., Ceron, J.-P., & Dubois, G. (2012). Consumer behaviour and demand response of tourists to climate change. *Annals of Tourism Research*, *39*(1), 36–58. https://doi.org/10.1016/j.annals.2011.11.002

Hall, C. M., & Müller, D. K. (2004). Introduction: Second homes, curse or blessing? Revisited. In C. M. Hall & D. K. Müller (Eds.), *Tourism, mobility and second homes: Between elite landscape and common ground* (pp. 3–14). Channel View.

Hemming, D., Agnew, M. D., Goodess, C. M., Giannakopoulos, C., Salem, S. B., Bindi, M., Bradai, M. N., Congedi, L., Dibari, C., El-Askary, H., El-Fadel, M., El-Raey, M., Ferrise, R., Grünzweig, J. M., Harzallah, A., Hattour, A., Hatzaki, M., Kanas, D., Lionello, P., McCarthy, M., . . . Tanzarella, A. (2013). Climate impact assessments. In A. Navarra & L. Tubiana (Eds.), *Regional assessment of climate change in the Mediterranean* (pp. 61–104). Springer.

Jacob, D., Kotova, L., Teichmann, C., Sobolowski, S. P., Vautard, R., Donnelly, C., Koutroulis, A. G., Grillakis, M. G., Tsanis, I. K., Damm, A., Sakalli, A., & van Vliet, M. T. H. (2018). Climate impacts in Europe under +1.5∘C global warming. *Earth's Future*, *6*(2), 264–285. https://doi.org/10.1002/2017EF000710

Jones, M. (2003). The concept of cultural landscape: Discourse and narratives. In H. Palang & G. Fry (Eds.), *Landscape interfaces* (Landscape series, Vol. 1, pp. 21–51). Springer. https://doi.org/10.1007/978-94-017-0189-1_3

Koutroulis, A. G., Grillakis, M. G., Tsanis, I. K., & Jacob, D. (2018). Mapping the vulnerability of European summer tourism under 2 °C global warming. *Climatic Change*, *151*, 157–171. https://doi.org/10.1007/s10584-018-2298-8

Kovats, R. S., Valentini, R., Bouwer, L. M., Georgopoulou, E., Jacob, D., Martin, E., Rounsevell, M., & Soussana, J.-F. (2014). Europe. In *Climate change 2014: Impacts, adaptation, and vulnerability. Part B: Regional aspects*. Contribution of Working Group II to the Fifth Assessment Report of the Intergovernmental Panel on Climate Change [V. R. Barros, C. B. Field, D. J. Dokken, M. D. Mastrandrea, K. J. Mach, T. E. Bilir, M. Chatterjee, K. L. Ebi, Y. O. Estrada, R. C. Genova, B. Girma, E. S. Kissel, A. N. Levy, S. MacCracken, P. R. Mastrandrea, & L.L. White (Eds.),] (pp. 1267–1326). Cambridge University Press.

Lanzani, A., & Curci, F. (2018). Le Italie in contrazione, tra crisi e opportunità. In A. De Rossi (Ed.), *Riabitare l'Italia. Le aree interne tra abbandoni e riconquiste* (pp. 79–107). Donzelli.

Magnan, A., Hamilton, J., Rosselló, J., Billé, R., & Bujosa, A. (2013). Mediterranean tourism and climate change: Identifying future demand and assessing destinations' vulnerability. In A. Navarra & L. Tubiana (Eds.), *Regional assessment of climate change in the Mediterranean* (pp. 337–365). Springer. https://doi.org/10.1007/978-94-007-5772-1

Moreno, A. (2010a). Climate change impacts. The vulnerability of tourism in coastal Europe. In P. Martens & C. T. Chang (Eds.), *The social and behavioural aspects of climate change: Linking vulnerability, adaptation and mitigation* (pp. 30–47). Greenleaf Publishing.

Moreno, A. (2010b). Mediterranean tourism and climate (change): A survey-based study. *Tourism and Hospitality Planning & Development*, 7(3), 253–265. https://doi.org/10.1080/1479053X.2010.502384

Müller, D. K. (2011). Second homes in rural areas: Reflections on a troubled history. *Norwegian Journal of Geography*, 65(3), 137–143. http://doi.org/10.1080/00291951.2011.597872

Nicholls, S. (2006). Climate change, tourism and outdoor recreation in Europe. *Managing Leisure*, 11(3), 151–163. https://doi.org/10.1080/13606710600715226

Nunes, P. A. L. D., & Loureiro, M. L. (2016). Economic valuation of climate-change-induced vinery landscape impacts on tourism flows in Tuscany. *Agricultural Economics*, 47(4), 365–374. https://doi.org/10.1111/agec.12236

Padovani, L., & Vettoretto, L. (2003). Italy. In N. Gallent, M. Shucksmith, & M. Tewdwr-Jones (Eds.), *Housing in the European countryside. Rural pressure and policy in Western Europe* (pp. 91–115). Routledge.

Perlik, M. (2011). Alpine gentrification: The mountain village as a metropolitan neighbourhood. New inhabitants between landscape adulation and positional good. *Revue de Géographie Alpine*, 99(1). https://doi.org/10.4000/rga.1370

Perlik, M. (2019). *The spatial and economic transformation of mountain regions: Landscapes as commodities*. Routledge.

Perry, A. (2005). The Mediterranean: How can the world's most popular and successful tourist destination adapt to a changing climate? In C. M. Hall & J. Higham (Eds.), *Tourism, recreation and climate change* (pp. 86–96). Channel View Publications.

Pitkänen, K. (2008). Second-home landscape: The meaning(s) of landscape for second-home tourism in Finnish Lakeland. *Tourism Geographies*, 10(2), 169–192. https://doi.org/10.1080/14616680802000014

Pitkänen, K., Hannonen, O., Toso, S., Gallent, N., Hamiduddin, I., Halseth, G., Hall, C. M., Müller, D. K., Treivish, A., & Nefedova, T. (2020). Second homes during corona – safe or unsafe haven and for whom? Reflections from researchers around the world. *Finnish Journal of Tourism Research*, 16(2), 20–39. https://doi.org/10.33351/mt.97559

Plachter, H., & Rössler, M. (1995). Cultural landscapes: Reconnecting culture and nature. In B. von Droste, H. Plachter, & M. Rössler (Eds.), *Cultural landscapes of universal value: Components of a global strategy* (pp. 15–18). Gustav Fischer in Cooperation with UNESCO.

Romano, B., & Zullo, F. (2014). The urban transformation of Italy's Adriatic coastal strip: Fifty years of unsustainability. *Land Use Policy*, 38, 26–36. http://doi.org/10.1016/j.landusepol.2013.10.001

Schultz, H. R., & Jones, G. V. (2010). Climate induced historic and future changes in viticulture. *Journal of Wine Research*, 21(2–3), 137–145. http://doi.org/10.1080/09571264.2010.530098

Spano, D., Mereu, V., Bacciu, V., Marras, S., Trabucco, A., Adinolfi, M., Barbato, G., Bosello, F., Breil, M., Chiriacò, M. V., Coppini, G., Essenfelder, A., Galluccio, G., Lovato, T., Marzi, S., Masina, S., Mercogliano, P., Mysiak, J., Noce, S., . . . Zavatarelli, M. (2020). *Analisi del rischio. I cambiamenti climatici in Italia*. https://doi.org/10.25424/CMCC/ANALISI_DEL_RISCHIO

Teslić, N., Vujadinović, M., Ruml, M., Ricci, A., Vuković, A., Parpinello, G. P., & Versari, A. (2019). Future climatic suitability of the Emilia-Romagna (Italy) region for grape production. *Regional Environmental Change*, *19*, 599–614. https://doi.org/10.1007/s10113-018-1431-6

Torres, R. M., & Momsen, J. H. (2011). Introduction. In R. M. Torres & J. H. Momsen (Eds.), *Tourism and agriculture. New geographies of consumption, production and rural restructuring* (pp. 1–9). Routledge.

Trigila, A., Iadanza, C., Bussettini, M., & Lastoria, B. (2018). *Dissesto idrogeologico in Italia: pericolosità e indicatori di rischio – Edizione 2018*. ISPRA, Rapporti 287/2018.

UNESCO. (2014). *Vineyard landscape of Piedmont: Langhe-Roero and Monferrato*. Retrieved January 26, 2021, from http://whc.unesco.org/en/list/1390

9 The potential use pattern of second homes in response to climate change

The role of place attachment

Harpa Stefansdottir, Jin Xue, Rasmus Nedergård Steffansen, Petter Næss, and Timothy Kevin Richardson

Introduction

Climate change may have important effects on the potential use of second homes and their surrounding areas in the future. One important reason for this is that the outdoor recreational activities performed in such areas vary with opportunities provided by their location and are by nature dependent on seasonal changes and weather conditions. Although second home use has been widely studied from various perspectives internationally (Hall & Müller, 2018) and in Norway (Kaltenborn, 1998; Overvåg, 2009; Ericsson et al., 2011), more in-depth investigation is needed on climate change impacts on use patterns. Based on information about current use patterns of second homes in Norway, the purpose of this chapter is to unfold the role place attachment may have for the future use pattern in response to changing climate.

The concept of place attachment is relevant for this purpose because second home use is often of routinized character, and second home locations are part of the users' familiar environment (Hall & Page, 2014). Therefore, second homes can connect people to places, as they provide a sense of permanence, continuity, rootedness and belonging to those places (Stedman, 2006). Place attachments, which concern the positive emotional connections between people and their physical surroundings (Stedman, 2003), could influence action and clarify the nature of one's bond or interest in a particular location (Hashemnezhad et al., 2013; Mesch & Manor, 1998). The use pattern investigated in this chapter includes the visiting routine, where climate change may stimulate or diminish interest in visiting the place or in moving periods of visits between seasons. It also includes the types of recreational activities performed, their location, and an awareness or interest in the primary dwelling location or alternative locations that may meet aims for the intended activities at each time.

The structure of the chapter is as follows. Following this introduction, a brief literature review is given about second homes and climate change in Norway, followed by a theoretical perspective on the development and dimensions of place attachment. Then the method used in this study is described, involving qualitative interviews with second home users. This is followed by a presentation of the results

DOI: 10.4324/9781003091295-9

and a discussion of how different dimensions and degrees of place attachment play a role for the future use pattern with respect to climate change.

Second homes and climate change in Norway

Routinized use of second homes in natural surroundings plays an important role for the performance of various outdoor activities in Norway. Many Norwegian households own one or more second homes, or have access through their relatives. In 2020, there were nearly 440,000 second homes, or about one per 12 inhabitants at a national scale (Statistics Norway, 2020). Second homes in mountain areas in the country provide good access to skiing in winter and hiking in summer, while summer use is more common by the coast to perform, among others, water-based activities. Weekend trips to the second home in all seasons are common, in addition to week-long school holidays in autumn and winter. It is also usual to visit second homes during Easter and Christmas holidays, as well as for longer periods of time in the traditionally long summer holiday (school holiday in Norway is about two months).

Climate change is assumed to have a range of effects on future travel to and use of second homes in Norway, either positively or negatively (Aall & Høyer, 2005). These include more frequent floods, less snow and higher average temperature (Field et al., 2014; Hanssen-Bauer et al., 2009; Iversen et al., 2003). The sea level is also expected to rise, and extreme weather can damage waterfront buildings and facilities (Noregs Offentliga Utgreiingar (NOU), 2010). Warmer climate may at the same time contribute to increase the attractiveness of second home areas along the coast during summer because of more favorable conditions for swimming in the sea and other summer outdoor activities. Mountain landscapes will change, and the treeline will rise (Rauken et al., 2010). The ski industry is typically portrayed as a 'victim' of climate change (Steiger et al., 2019) as a few degrees of average increase in temperature are likely to shorten the skiing season considerably. This also includes traditionally snow-rich areas located at lower altitudes of the mountain regions in southern parts of Norway, or closer to the coast, which are the focus of this chapter in addition to coastal areas in the south. Worsened conditions, due to climate change, for skiing and other winter-based outdoor recreation activities in areas close to the largest cities may also increase the use of existing inland mountain resorts. Climate change may thus influence the opportunity for recreational activities in the second home areas in various ways. How place attachment affects use pattern of second homes due to climate change remains, however, unanswered.

Development and dimensions of place attachment

Places encompass the physical settings and the way they are experienced by people (Stedman, 2003). Place attachment is a positive emotional bond that develops between people and places. This relationship can be strong and tie a person to a certain place, meaning that it is special and distinguishable from other places (Hashemnezhad et al., 2013; Low & Altman, 1992). A place, by definition of the concept, is usually seen as having a certain location. However, various locations also may share common characteristics that have similar meanings, which may be seen as place attachment to multiple locations (Lin & Lockwood, 2014). When a person develops an attachment to a place, this is rooted in their previous experiences and satisfaction with the place (Hashemnezhad et al., 2013). As such, the diversity of meanings towards the place unfolds through long-term active use of the second home and activities in its surrounding area (Kaltenborn, 1997b; Stedman, 2006).

Place attachment has been conceptualized as comprising two main dimensions: the social and the physical (Hidalgo & Hernandez, 2001; Scannell & Gifford, 2010). The social dimension (also termed emotional attachment in previous literature) involves a deep tie to the social setting of the place, which can become significantly important as part of one's identity (Lin & Lockwood, 2014; Kaltenborn, 1997a; Hashemnezhad et al., 2013). The underlying factors that affect this kind of attachment include a history of social interactions that are important to a person. In the case of a second home as a place, the social dimension of place attachment can include a history of events and time together with family, friends and neighbours, such as a tradition of spending family holidays in the particular place (Hull et al., 1994).

Earlier studies suggest that the physical dimension (also termed place dependency in earlier literature) is grounded on the possibilities to fulfil a person's instrumental aims (Kaltenborn, 1998; Stedman, 2002), such as to perform recreational activities. Thus, this dimension may imply awareness of alternative places that share common characteristics that also satisfy needs or goals (Lin & Lockwood, 2014), meaning that attachment to a particular place may be weak. This could, for example, be the case if snow conditions for skiing are better close to the second home compared to the forest area near the permanent home. This could stimulate trips to the second home for the purpose of skiing, but the specific second home could be substituted with a second home at another location with good snow conditions. Use of second homes in natural settings in Norway is found to be strongly motivated by a wish to perform outdoor recreational activities (Overvåg, 2009). The types of recreation have been distinguished into various categories based on factors such as modern recreation, traditional outdoor life and socially anchored recreation (Ericsson, 2006).

Earlier studies on place attachment seem, however, not to have focused on experiences of nature that do not require the performance of any activity. This may be due to the lack of studies on the influence of the physical dimension on place attachment. Possibly, being unified with nature (Naess et al., 2008) in some way or another is also an important part of attachment to the place of the second home. The concept has not been used before to interpret the role place attachment may have for the future use pattern in response to changing climate. Place attachment may, for example, have distinct roles for different types of activities and thus be affected by climate change in various ways (Chen et al., 2022).

Place attachment can be felt to different degrees, where the highest commitment indicates wanting to sacrifice for the place (Shamai, 1991), meaning that the place has deep importance for the life of a person. The perceived quality of a setting may also result in satisfaction (or dissatisfaction), which is analytically distinct from attachment. A person may be satisfied with the setting, for example, physical attributes that satisfy a certain need, which results in a degree of like or dislike. Place attachment, however, implies how strongly a person perceives their linkage to the setting (Stedman, 2003). Attachment to the social dimension of a place has been reported as greater than the physical dimension (Hidalgo & Hernandez, 2001). However, it has also been pointed out that the physical dimension has been studied less in empirical research than the social (Hidalgo & Hernandez, 2001). Although social constructions are important, the local physical environment sets boundaries for possible social interactions and activities that can be performed (Stedman, 2003), meaning that the two dimensions are connected.

Methods

The analyses presented in this chapter stem from 18 qualitative interviews with second home users in Norway (see Figure 9.1). One of the second homes owned by one of the interviewees was located at the southern coast of Turkey and is not shown on the map. At three locations (Oppdal, Kragerø and Trysil), the number of interviewees with second homes within a concentrated area was too high to enable each such dwelling to be represented by a separate pin on the map. Seven of the interviewees were recruited among survey respondents to a larger study of climate change impacts on second home use patterns, all with a permanent address in the Oslo region. In addition, we selected 11 interviewees who owned second homes in three second home areas. Two of these are mountain areas in the municipalities of Trysil and Oppdal, whereas the third area is in the coastal municipality of Kragerø. Trysil and Oppdal are oriented mainly towards winter use (both alpine and cross-country skiing) and mountain-based recreational activities, such as mountain biking and hiking in summer. Kragerø is a typical coastal area for maritime and summer outdoor activities.

These two types of second home settings are expected to be affected by climate change in different ways. In addition, Oppdal and Trysil, although both are areas for mountain second homes, are affected to different degrees by warmer winter climate. The snow conditions of Trysil, given its inland location, will be affected to a lesser extent. Most second homes in the archipelago outside the coast of Kragerø are closed during winter because the weather often gets too harsh near the sea. The island of Jomfruland, where three of our interviewees have second homes, is now protected from second home developments because it is deemed special with a landscape and geological, ecological and cultural-historic qualities. The island is susceptible to strong winds and rising waters.

The interviewees cover an age range from 30s to 60s, representing different types of households (Table 9.1). Nine of them own one second home, and one has access to a second home through close relatives (IDs 1, 4, 6, 9, 11, 13, 14, 15, 17, 18). Six own or/and have access to two second homes each (IDs 2, 3, 7, 10, 12, 16), and two own or have access to three second homes (IDs 5 and 8).

The interview questions covered a wide range of topics related to the current use pattern of each second home and the surrounding area. The interviews were semi-structured and lasted about 60 to 90 minutes. They were audio-recorded and subsequently transcribed. An interpretation scheme was developed for the purpose of the larger study to analyze the interview data. This scheme included a number of

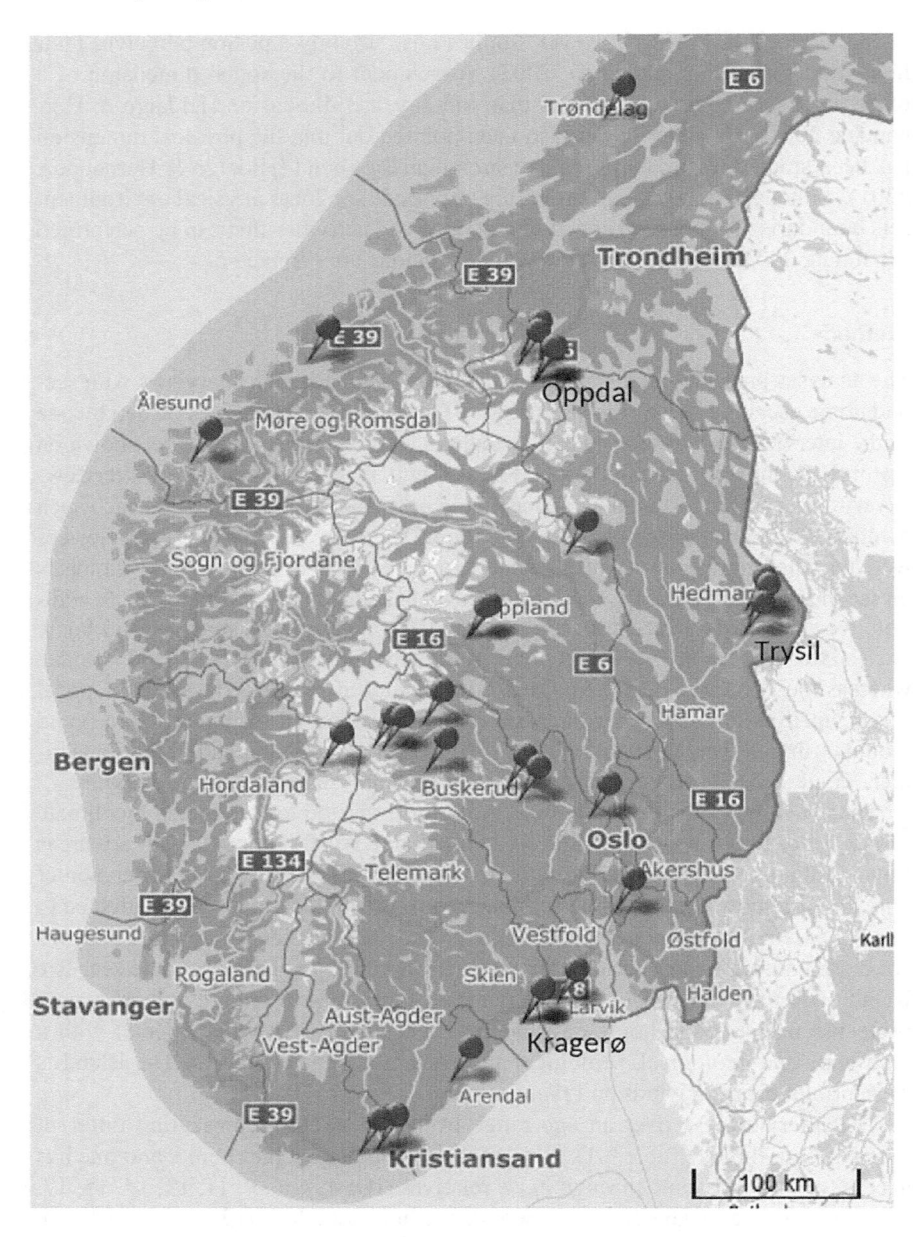

Figure 9.1 Locations of the second homes owned by or accessible for the interviewees

Table 9.1 Overview of interviewees, number of household members, permanent city and types of second home locations

ID	Age M (male) F (female)	Household members <18	Hosehold members >18	2nd home nr.	Type 2nd home location	Primary city
1	M52	3	2	1	Mountain	Oslo
2	F41	2	2	1	Mountain	Oslo
				2	Coast	
3	M55	1	0	1	Mountain	Oslo
				2	Coast	
4	F40	1	1	1	Coast	Oslo
5	F54	2	0	1	Coast	Oslo
				2	Mountain	
				3	Inmland	
6	F53	2	2	1	Mountain	Oslo
7	M71	2	0	1	Mountain	Oslo
				2	Coast (Turkey)	
8	F40	2	2	1	Coast	Oslo
				2	Coast	
				3	Mountain	
9	M70	2	0	1	Coast	Oslo
10	M58	2	0	2	Coast	Oslo
				3	Mountain	
11	F50	1	0	1	Coast	Oslo
12	F53	2	1	1	Mountain	Trondheim
				2	Coast	
13	F40s	2	2	1	Mountain	Trondheim
14	F40s	2	2	1	Mountain	Trondheim
15	M64	2	0	1	Mountain	Trondheim
16	M53	2	3	1	Mountain	Oslo
				2	Coast	
17	M34	2	1	1	Mountain	Oslo
18	M42	2	2	1	Mountain	Oslo

detailed research sub-questions to be answered by one member of the research team, based on the interview transcriptions, whereas another member acted as a quality checker. Synthesizing across the interviews was conducted separately for each of several question groups, among which a few themes are the bases for the main results of this chapter. These include the potential changes in activities and use pattern due to climate change, the motivations behind changes in activities and use pattern and the meaning of the location of the second home as place. The analysis aimed at how social and physical attributes of the place had meaning to the interviewees.

Climate scenarios were constructed for each of the second home areas of Trysil, Oppdal and Kragerø to use as a reference during the interviews with interviewees of the relevant areas. Based on results from a workshop with invited experts (a meterologist and professionals working with planning in two of the selected areas) and other available information about the climate in the areas (Norsk Klimaservicesenter, 2018; NCCS, 2015; Iversen et al., 2003), scenarios were generated by assessing how these changes in climate might affect the local physical conditions for second home related activities. Key information for the three scenarios, showing climate changes compared to the current situation, is presented subsequently.

Scenario 1: Climate change and physical conditions in Trysil in 2071–2100. (IDs 16, 17 and 18).

- Winter temperature will increase by 4–5°C (from average temperature (1961–1990) in Jan–Feb of −11°C, and in March −5°C). Period with snow cover 1–2 months shorter, reduction of max snow depth.
- Cross-country skiing will have shorter season in the lower areas, still good in the mountains.
- Summer temperature will increase, and more intense rain in shorter period is negative for paths.
- Growing season will be 1–2 months longer, leading to better conditions for vegetation – higher tree line.

Scenario 2: Climate change and physical conditions in Oppdal in 2071–2100. (IDs 12, 13, 14 and 15).

- Winter temperature will increase by 4.7°C (from average temperatures (1961–1990) in Jan–Feb −5°C, and March and −2.5°C). Periods with snow cover 2–4 months shorter, reduction of max snow depth.
- Cross-country skiing will have a shorter season, and there will be unstable conditions in the lower areas; still good in the mountains.
- Increased summer temperature. More rain in summer and risk of more frequent river flood may damage paths.
- Growing season will be 1–2 months longer, leading to better conditions for vegetation – higher tree line.

Scenario 3: Climate change and physical conditions in Kragerø in 2071–2100. (IDs 9, 10 and 11).

- Increase of temperature by 4–5°C will lead to a mean summer temperature above 20°C and higher sea water temperature (better bathing conditions).
- More days with stormy weather and intense rain. Can lead to sea-level rise and storm surges.
- More vegetation due to warmer summer and winter, drier summer.

Results

Based on interpretation of the interviews, both the social and the physical dimensions of places play important roles in influencing the future use pattern of second homes in response to a changing climate. The social dimension results in strong 'social ties' (5.1). The influence of the physical dimension is two-fold and results in different degrees of place attachment and distinct ways of responding to a changing climate: strong attachment to 'nature characteristics' (5.2) and evaluation of the place, based on its 'recreational opportunities' (5.3). This instrumental evaluation results in weaker attachment to the place and at the same time greater likelihood for changes in use pattern. These results will be explained further in the three following sections and summarised in Table 9.2. The results indicate that the use patterns of the interviewees may be influenced

Table 9.2 The dimensions of place, degree of attachment to place and potential changes in use pattern of second homes in response to climate change

Place dimension	Attachment to place	Interviewees	Potential changes in use pattern
Social setting	Strong	Coastal areas IDs 2, 3, 4, 8*, 9, 10, 11 Mountain areas IDs 2, 17	Adaptation to the climate conditions regarding recreational activities: choose activities possible under the conditions. Stable interest in visiting the place.
Physical, characteristics of nature	Strong	Coastal areas IDs 8**, 9, 10, 11 Mountain areas IDs 1, 3, 6, 12, 18 IDs 13, 14 also have high instrumental expectations.	Adaptation to the climate conditions regarding recreational activities: 1) choose activities possible under the conditions, 2) more travel within the local area to seek optimal climate-related conditions for recreational activities, for example, go more often higher up into the mountains to try to get above the treeline. Stable interest in visiting the place.
Physical, opportunity to fulfil instrumental aims	Weak	Coastal areas IDs 5, 7, 16 Mountain areas IDs 5, 7, 8***, 13, 14, 15, 16	Limited adaptation to the climate conditions regarding recreational activities. Increased or decreased interest in visiting the place 1) Decreased interest if the climate conditions are unsuitable for the aimed activities. 2) Increased interest in visiting the place if it better meets instrumental aims than before (in absolute terms or relative to areas closer to the primary dwelling).

*second home 1 and 2 by the coast **second home 2 by the coast ***second home 3 in mountain by both attachment to the social setting of the place as well as the physical characteristics of nature. The instrumental aspect of the place may overlap as well with attachment to the social setting or the natural characteristics of the place for some of the interviewees.

Social ties

Attachment to the social setting involves appreciation of the place because of long-term social interaction, memories and activities performed with others. In a few cases, these social ties and memories become very strong and part of one's identity (IDs 2 and 9), which results in stable interest in visiting the second home. For seven of the interviewees using second homes in coastal areas (IDs 2, 3, 4, 8, 9, 10, 11) and for two using second homes in mountain areas (IDs 2, 17), the social dimension is very important for their attachment to the place. The strong attachment to the social setting may be related to the fact that many of these second homes have been owned for a long period and used by the family, sometimes for generations. To keep the second home is mentioned as being very important in such cases.

From the perspective of attachment to the social setting of the place, recreational activities are performed to be with others and to socialize. Users will therefore adapt their choice of recreational activities to the climate conditions as far as there are not any dramatic climate changes. Although conditions for skiing in mountains may worsen and water-based activities by the coast get more difficult because of, for example, high waves, interviewees say they will choose activities that fit changes in the weather conditions. As explained by ID 17, the second home in the mountain of Trysil is an important meeting place for him and the greater family of his wife, a place "just (to) be away from everything else, and relax and, yes, have a good time and be together. So it's not like we don't go there if we can't ski, we go there all the same".

Strong attachment to the social setting will, according to our interviews, maintain the interest to visit the place despite climate change. ID 2 uses two second homes that have distinctive but important social meanings to her, which impact continuity in use. The small second home in Åfjord is important to keep, because it represents memories of her childhood and social attachment to the village where she grew up. It "isn't about having a cabin. This is about having this one. It is so important for the family". Her other second home, in Ål, is also a specific place with family history (back to the 1750s) and is thus very important for memories associated with the place. Because she will continue to keep both second homes in the future, it is highly likely that climate change will not dramatically change her use.

The Kragerø interviewees (IDs 9, 10 and 11) all tell about their strong attachment to the Jomfruland Island where they have their second homes and spend long parts of the summer holiday. Because of the strong place attachment, they seem likely to want to visit the place as much as they can, independently of climate change if the changes are not dramatic. This attachment is related both to the specific nature (see next section) and the strong social ties. ID 9 says the strong attachment to the place includes many components: "It's become a very big rucksack of many things. That's building up to my life history." Most importantly, the place is important for his life and identity, the relations to the people on the island and as a meeting place for the family through generations. The "place . . . is part of my childhood and upbringing, and it's a part of my children's childhood and upbring-ing, and indeed, it's actually now the grandchildren . . . Lots of social life, good friends and the ocean, all together. So it is a very strong place for many in the fam-ily". He states that this strong place attachment maintains his interest in the island, unless changes will be dramatic: "So that's the reason why I want to go back, even if it becomes harsh. It's my life . . . we are like the trees out there, because we have grown into this island . . . So it's not substitutable for someplace else".

Nature characteristics

Appreciation of the local nature and its characteristics, such as mountain landscape and vegetation, may lead to strong place attachment. From this perspective, activi-ties are chosen to help experience nature. Traditional outdoor activities, such as cross-country skiing and hiking in the mountains, provide a good opportunity for this purpose. Boat trips and walks could serve the same purpose in coastal areas, although not mentioned in the interviews. Five interviewees (IDs 1, 3, 6, 12, 18) using second homes in mountain areas illuminate their attachment to the places' natural characteristics. Two more mountain users (IDs 13 and 14), are also attached to the characteristics of the nature around their second home area in Oppdal. How-ever, they seem to simultaneously emphasize the place's opportunity to fulfil their instrumental aims to perform recreational activities (see Section 3). Possibly, Opp-dal interviewees talk more about the place's opportunity to meet their aims for out-door recreational activities compared to the Trysil interviewees because this area is at a lower altitude, and thus the skiing opportunities are already more affected by climate change. Four coastal users are attached to both the social setting of the place and the characteristics of nature (IDs 8, 9, 10 and 11).

From the perspective of attachment to the characteristics of the nature at the place, climate change is not likely to substantially change the attractiveness of visiting the second home. Rather, the users are more likely to change their choice of activities or adapt their outdoor recreational activities to the weather conditions. For example, by travelling more within the second home area to seek the locations with the best conditions possible (ID 12) or by buying innovative equipment (e.g. new skis) that add options possible under the new weather conditions (ID 13). The reduced skiing activity would, according to the interviewees, largely be replaced by other activities such as more walking trips on foot, biking, other bare ground activities, kiting or fishing.

To enjoy nature is most important while the type of outdoor activity comes second, as explained by ID 18 (Trysil): "It was very strange that people were doing cross-country skiing in places like the Ekebergsletta football field (in Oslo) because that was not a ski experience for me, it didn't give me anything at all. You need to go up in the mountains, unless you (only) do the technical training . . . For me it needs to have the nature". Artificial snow production may lengthen the skiing period. However, cross-country skiing seems to be connected with experiencing nature, and therefore artificial tracks as a solution have limits, as explained by ID 14: "When the snow has arrived very late or we have been to the cabin and there has not been snow here, then I have used the artificial snow track, but then I might as well be in the city and go skiing there in artificial track . . . I'd prefer to be on the mountain when there is proper snow".

Appreciation of the mountain nature characteristics and attachment to the place may increase over time as users get more familiar with the place, as is the case with ID 12: "I can walk in the same place a hundred times, and I see the same place in a new way each time, because there are different lights, and it's the colors and the odors, oh, that's so good." The way she has built up relation to the place enables her to perform her intended recreational activities under the best possible conditions of the area. When asked about the snow conditions, she says: "You can experience that you almost do not have snow in the ski slopes . . . , then you can go to the other side of the valley and then there's snow . . . , and it has to do with the mountains . . . , and this has very much to say about where the snow is lying in relation to the wind . . . , so it is a big difference". She says she will go all the same to the second home in the future despite a changed climate but will then drive to places further away from the second home to seek ideal conditions. It is also likely that climate change will influence them to go more often higher up into the mountains to try to get above the treeline, because the forest and the higher vegetation makes it difficult to walk uphill directly from the second home.

The appreciation of the Jomfruland Island (IDs 9, 10 and 11) as a place has, in addition to the social attachment, to do with its physical characteristics. The interviewees' description of nature illuminates emotional empathy and love for the place. At the same time, they do not talk much about their recreational activities. ID 11 says "it is the uniqueness of the nature of the place . . . , the property itself and the island as a whole." ID 10 talks about "the moon coming out of the sea . . . , it's very nice!" This appreciation of the nature, in addition to the social ties, which together result in a strong attachment to the place of Jomfruland Island, stimulates the interviewees to spend much time on the island and works as resilience for future use pattern. ID 10 says: "From midsummer to the first week of August is absolutely sacred. Then we do not go anywhere else". ID 11 says he "just loves the place, it can be rain, it could thunder, it can be a storm, it can be super boiling, it doesn't really bother me . . . That's not a question about the weather, because I go there anyway". ID 9, who is strongly attached to the place of Jomfruland Island, is very unlikely to change his use pattern in the future because the place is an important part of his identity. Being in this place, to him, "is like this rhythm of the ocean, these waves going in and out, are inside me . . . I'm a part of it very much".

Attachment to the specific characteristics of nature can also be separate from the location of the second home, as is the case with ID 3. Although the second home in Heggenes satisfies his love for mountain nature and demand for mountain-based recreational activities at weekends, he says there are also nice mountains further north where he would love to have a second home. He is not attached to the particular location of his second home but to the mountain region in general, and he would not feel sorry if he sold it. He has thought about replacing it with a caravan.

5.3 *Recreational opportunities*

The physical dimension includes the ways the place satisfies aims to perform outdoor recreational activities that may be dependent on climate conditions. For many of the interviewees, the second home serves as a pragmatic base to perform outdoor recreational activities, such as sports during winter (IDs 5, 7, 8, 13, 14, 15 and 16), or doing water-based activities (IDs 5, 7 and 16, with second homes by the coast). Some of these interviewees have more than one second home and use them in the different seasons, according to how each second home can best meet their aims for seasonal outdoor activities.

Weather conditions that are considered as preventing people from performing the intended activities may influence them to spend their time elsewhere, as explained by ID 16 (Trysil) who says, "If it would rain a lot more during the winter, then we wouldn't use it . . . I can go outside with rain boots on, but to do what? If it's raining during the winter, then I can't go skiing, and if it's really bad weather during the summer, then it's a lot less attractive to go biking or running, so the weather does influence". In Oppdal, the so-called 'middle period' in spring, a period in April–May, which currently lasts for about three to five weeks, can become longer. In this period, ID 13 says, they would rather drop going because "it is too rotten snow to make it possible to go skiing". When it rains very much, he says they normally just sit in the cabin and relax. "We are a bit like good weather people", he says. Similar is the case with ID 14, (Oppdal) who prefers to be in the city (Trondheim) if the weather is not good for outdoor recreation. "Yes, then it is not nice to go hiking, and it is not nice going skiing, so then we use the second home very little". He says bad weather forecasts, particularly high winds, might influence them to abandon the second home visit.

Year-to-year weather changes have affected ID 16's use of his second home in Trysil, depending on snow conditions, particularly in November and December. He also has another second home in Son (by the Oslo Fjord) for summer use, where he has a boat by the sea which he enjoys using. Both second homes are, to some extent, bases for performing his most liked outdoor activities of the season. However, he also says the second home in Trysil is a nice place to go to in the summer, and he plans to go there more often when he becomes retired. This may indicate that the second home in Trysil also has value as a place to be and is not completely thought of as a pragmatic base to perform outdoor recreational activities.

Second homes with a history of family use can also purely serve as a base to perform sport. Although the cabin in Vøringsfoss has been a family cabin since ID 5 was 15 years old, it does not seem that she is attached to this place, since she mentions several times the idea of selling this cabin due to poor road accessibility in the wintertime. Poorer skiing conditions could thus influence her to sell the cabin.

A shorter skiing season close to the primary home may also stimulate more frequent visits in periods of good skiing conditions in the second home area, as explained by ID 16: "Yes, you can say that. When the snow condition is good in Oslo, it's nice to stay in Oslo, and when the snow condition is very good here (at the second home) and not so good in Oslo, it's nice to go to Trysil". IDs 2, 5, 7 also state they will go more frequently to the second home in such cases.

Discussion

This study was aimed at unfolding the role place attachment may have for the future use pattern of second homes in Norway in response to a changing climate. Qualitative interviews with second home users in Norwegian mountain and coastal areas were interpreted regarding the role of both the social and the physical dimensions of places and possible attachment. The results illuminate that both dimensions play an important role for their use patterns and the way it is vulnerable to climate change. According to our results, the social dimension results in strong 'social ties' based on history of social interactions at the place. The outcome is twofold regarding the physical dimension, resulting in different degrees of place attachment and distinct ways of responding to a changing climate; attachment to the 'nature characteristics' at the place and evaluation of the place's 'recreational opportunities', where attachment to the place is weaker. Strong place attachment was linked with resilience in the interest of visiting the place. From the perspective of attachment to the social setting, users visit the place to be with other people, and climate conditions are thus not directly linked with the reason for the place attachment. When users are attached to the characteristics of the nature at the place, users choose recreational activities that help them to experience nature. Therefore, they tend to adapt their recreational activities to the climatic conditions. Experiencing different seasons and weather conditions are seen as part of an interesting experience rather than something to avoid. When place attachment is weaker, users from time to time consider whether a trip to the second home is worthwhile, based on the place's opportunity to fulfil their instrumental aims. In this case, weather conditions and possibilities to perform the intended outdoor recreational activities directly influence the decision whether to go. From this perspective, users tend to base their decisions on going to locations where they best can enjoy their intended outdoor recreational activities. This could be at the permanent dwelling if snow conditions are good in the close-by skiing area, or it could be at one second home rather than at another one, as is the case with ID 16 who has two second homes located in distinctively different natural settings.

The results support findings in earlier studies showing that the social dimension may contribute to a very strong attachment to the place (IDs 2 and 9) (Hidalgo & Hernandez, 2001). The physical dimension, however, results in two distinct ways of responding to changing climate, with different degrees of place attachment. The core issue of attachment to the characteristics of nature, in our case, involves love for nature to be in and experience it with the senses. The other kind of attachment is, however, directly linked with evaluation of the place's opportunity to meet desires for performing activities that are dependent on weather conditions, such as snow for skiing. This study shows that the twofold physical dimension of places can illuminate the role that place attachment may have in response to climate change.

Second home users in mountains may become more and more familiar with its varying landscape and micro-climate by time, as is the case with ID 12. This holds hand in hand with deeper place attachment and is in line with earlier findings by Kaltenborn (1997a). The familiarity of the place, the intention to both discover nature and perform recreational activities may, as a result of climate change, not only lead to resilience in the interest in visiting the second home but also lead to more travel within the second home area. If this travel is by private car, this relation to the place may actually lead to more encroachment on nature if it leads to an increase in built infrastructure for car driving, in addition to emissions.

There is an important difference in the two sides of the physical dimension regarding the meaning of the place and its link with outdoor recreational activities. When appreciation of nature as surroundings to experience is most important, then attractive locations or routes in nature are chosen first. Then possible equipment is chosen next, to be able to move along the routes, for example, on skis or foot, termed traditional outdoor activities by Ericsson (2006). On the contrary, when performing the outdoor activity is the main aim, the quality of the place is evaluated in line with its opportunity to meet this goal. This can not only lead to unstable interest in visiting the place of the second home but also lead to interest in locations or routes and activities that have little to do with experiencing nature and could as such be anywhere. In his journal chronicle about the new indoor arena for snow experiences in Oslo, Skjeldal (2020) writes about winter atmosphere, which he says is something you can't buy or solve by artificial snow and indoor arenas. To emphasize his message, he calls the new indoor arena a 'brothel' and says this kind of arena will not create love for the atmosphere linked with skiing, for example, among children. For the Norwegian nation, use of second homes in natural surroundings has a long history and is linked with traditional outdoor recreation which is distinct from newer modern activities (Ericsson, 2006). The three kinds of place attachment are in line with factors found by Ericsson (2006), who studied motivations for owning vacation homes in Norway. The mountain nature, as a place to be in and move through, has a symbolic meaning to the Norwegian nation and is part of the national identity (Åmås, 2014). Modern recreational activities, on the contrary, defined as those that require (extensive) constructions that might be harmful to the environment, such as alpine centers, golf courses, pools, entertainment and cultural facilities, are less intertwined with the experience of local characteristics. Such facilities are rather part of modernity and bear similar characteristics independently of their location and have even been termed as non-places (Auge, 2008) and compared to amusement parks (Steffansen, 2016).

If second home areas should become attractive in the future when climate change strikes, it is important that their surrounding areas portray and highlight the specific local characteristics of the place and the local identity (also called place-based development). The activities available should then relate to the characteristics and identity of the place. Such a development might stimulate a better sense of place attachment that is anchored in the natural surroundings, and possibly, in time, by a social dimension as well.

Conclusion

This chapter has illustrated the role place attachment has for the future use pattern of second homes in Norway with respect to changing climate. Strong place attachment, either to the social setting or the characteristics of nature, is likely to result in resilience in the interest in visiting the place of the second home in spite of climate change. In case of strong place attachment, users will adapt their choice of recreational activities to the climatic conditions. On the contrary, some users will base their decision to visit the place each time on its opportunity to fulfil their aims to perform the desired recreational activities. In Norway, some of the most popular outdoor recreational activities are dependent on climatic conditions. However, independent of type of activity, users may, through routinized use over a longer time, get more attached to the second home area based on positive memories about it.

References

Aall, C., & Høyer, K. G. (2005). Tourism and climate change adaptation: The Norwegian case. In C. M. Hall & J. Higham (Eds.), *Tourism, recreation and climate change* (pp. 209–221). Channel View Publications.

Åmås, K. M. (2014, October 10). Fjellet er symbol på det kjerne-norske [The mountain is a symbol of the core Norwegian]. *Aftenposten*. Retrieved from www.aftenposten.no/meninger/kommentar/i/BbVw/fjellet-er-symbol-paa-det-kjerne-norske

Augé, M. (2008). *Non-places: An introduction to supermodernity* (J. Howe, Trans.). Verso.

Chen, N. C., Hall, C. M., & Prayag, G. (2022). *Sense of place and place attachment in tourism*. Routledge.

Ericsson, B. (2006). Fritidsboliger – utvikling og motiver for eierskap. [Second homes – development and motives for ownership]. *Utmark*, *1*. www.utmark.org

Ericsson, B., Skjeggedal, T., Arnesen, T., & Overvåg, K. (2011). Second homes i Norge-bidrag til en nordisk utredning. *Geografisk Tidsskrift*, *51*, 187–198.

Field, C. B., Barros, V. R., & Intergovernmental Panel on Climate Change (IPCC). (2014). *Climate change 2014: Impacts, adaptation, and vulnerability: Working group II contribution to the fifth assessment report of the intergovernmental panel on climate change*. Cambridge University Press.

Hall, C. M., & Müller, D. K. (2018). Second home tourism. An introduction. In C. M. Hall & D. K. Müller (Eds.), *The Routledge handbook of second home tourism and mobilities* (pp. 3–14). Routledge.

Hall, C. M., & Page, S. (2014). *The geography of tourism and recreation: Environment, place and space* (4th ed.). Routledge.

Hanssen-Bauer, I., Drange, H., Førland, E. J., Roald, L. A., Børsheim, K. Y., Hisdal, H., Lawrence, D., Nesje, A., Sandven, S., Sorteberg, A., Sundby, S., Vasskog, K., & Ådlandsvik, B. (2009). *Klima i Norge 2100. Bakgrunnsmateriale til NOU Klimatilpassing*. Norsk Klimasenter.

Hashemnezhad, H., Heidari, A. A., & Mohammad Hoseini, P. (2013). "Sense of place" and "place attachment". *International Journal of Architecture and Urban Development*, *3*(1), 5–12.

Hidalgo, M. C., & Hernandez, B. (2001). Place attachment: Conceptual and empirical questions. *Journal of Evironmental Psychology*, *21*(3), 273–281. https://doi.org/10.1006/jevp.2001.0221

Hull IV, R. B., Lam, M., & Vigo, G. (1994). Place identity: Symbols of self in the urban fabric. *Landscape and Urban Planning*, *28*(2–3), 109–120. https://doi.org/10.1016/0169-2046(94)90001-9

Iversen, T., Førland, E. J., Røed, L. P., & Stordal, F. (2003). *Regclim. Regional climate development under global warming*. Final Report, Phase I, II. Á Meteorologisk Institutt, 71.

Kaltenborn, B. P. (1997a). Nature of place attachment: A study among recreation homeowners in Southern Norway. *Leisure Sciences, 19*(3), 175–189. https://doi.org/10.1080/01490409709512248

Kaltenborn, B. P. (1997b). Recreation homes in natural settings: Factors affecting place attachment. *Norwegian Journal of Geography, 51*(4), 187–198. https://doi.org/10.1080/00291959708542842

Kaltenborn, B. P. (1998). The alternate home – motives of recreation home use. *Norwegian Journal of Geography, 52*(3), 121–134. https://doi.org/10.1080/00291959808552393

Lin, C. C., & Lockwood, M. (2014). Forms and sources of place attachment: Evidence from two protected areas. *Geoforum, 53*, 74–81. https://doi.org/10.1016/j.geoforum.2014.02.008

Low, S. M., & Altman, I. (1992). Place attachment: A conceptual inquiry. In I. Altman & S. M. Low (Eds.), *Place attachment* (pp. 1–12). Springer.

Mesch, G. S., & Manor, O. (1998). Social ties, environmental perception, and local attachment. *Environment and Behavior, 30*(4), 504–519. https://doi.org/10.1177/001391659803000405

Naess, A., Drengson, A., & Devall, B. (Eds.). (2008). *Ecology of wisdom: Writings by Arne Næss*. Counterpoint Press.

NCCS. (2015). *Klima i Norge 2100. Kunnskapsgrunnlag for klimatilpasning oppdatert i 2015*. [Knowledge base for climate adaptation updated in 2015]. Report no. 2/2015. Retrieved 2023, from https://www.miljodirektoratet.no/globalassets/publikasjoner/m406/m406.pdf

Noregs Offentliga Utgreiingar (NOU). (2010). *Tilpassing til eit klima i endring*. Servicesenteret for departementa, Informasjonsforvaltning.

Norsk Klimaservicesenter. (2018). *Klimaframskrivninger*. Retrieved 2018 from https://klimaservicesenter.no/faces/desktop/scenarios.xhtml

Overvåg, K. (2009). *Second homes in Eastern Norway: From marginal land to commodity*. [Doctoral thesis, Norwegian University of Science and Technology]. Trondheim. https://ntnuopen.ntnu.no/ntnu-xmlui/bitstream/handle/11250/265331/311115_FULLTEXT02.pdf?sequence=2

Rauken, T., Kelman, I., Jacobsen, J. K. S., & Hovelsrud, G. K. (2010). Who can stop the rain? Perceptions of summer weather effects among small tourism businesses. *Anatolia, 21*(2), 289–304. https://doi.org/10.1080/13032917.2010.9687104

Scannell, L., & Gifford, R. (2010). Defining place attachment: A tripartite organizing framework. *Journal of Environmental Psychology, 30*(1), 1–10. https://doi.org/10.1016/j.jenvp.2009.09.006

Shamai, S. (1991). Sense of place: An empirical measurement. *Geoforum, 22*(3), 347–358. https://doi.org/10.1016/0016-7185(91)90017-K

Skjeldal, G. (2020). Eit horehus og ein hall med snø. [A brothel and a hall with snow]. *NRK*. Norway. www.nrk.no/ytring/eithorehus-og-ein-hall-med-sno-1.148

Statistics Norway. (2020). *Eksisterende bygningsmasse. Antall fritidsbygninger og fritidsbygninger per kvadratkilometer, etter region, statistikkvariabel og år* [Existing building stock. Number of leisure buildings and leisure buildings per square kilometer, by region, statistical variable and year]. www.ssb.no/statbank/

Stedman, R. C. (2002). Toward a social psychology of place: Predicting behavior from place-based cognitions, attitude, and identity. *Environment and Behavior, 34*(5), 561–581. https://doi.org/10.1177/0013916502034005001

Stedman, R. C. (2003). Is it really just a social construction?: The contribution of the physical environment to sense of place. *Society & Natural Resources, 16*(8), 671–685. https://doi.org/10.1080/08941920309189

Stedman, R. C. (2006). Understanding place attachment among second home owners. *American Behavioral Scientist, 50*(2), 187–205. https://doi.org/10.1177/0002764206290633

Steffansen, R. (2016). Critical realist methodology guiding theory development: The case of the Norwegian second home ownership paradox. *Journal of Critical Realism, 15*(2), 122–141. https://doi.org/10.1080/14767430.2016.1148375

Steiger, R., Scott, D., Abegg, B., Pons, M., & Aall, C. (2019). A critical review of climate change risk for ski tourism. *Current Issues in Tourism, 22*(11), 1343–1379. https://doi.org/10.1080/13683500.2017.1410110

10 Conclusions and future directions

Bailey Ashton Adie and C. Michael Hall

Introduction

Climate change is one of, if not the absolute, biggest threat currently facing humanity, and its impact will be felt by every single community on the planet. However, while the impact of climate change has been addressed in great depth across disciplines, including in housing studies, the literature on climate change and second homes is still in its infancy. This is especially problematic given that second homes are often located in areas which already face significant natural hazard risks. Accordingly, this book has sought to generate a discussion on this topic across a variety of contexts and from different theoretical perspectives. While all of these chapters are distinct in terms of their content, there are three clear themes that have emerged across this edited collection. The first looks at the planning processes related to climate change and second homes, emphasising the important role that second homes play within these planning contexts while often simultaneously being excluded from the conversation. The second theme is instead more locally focused and presents varied community responses to climate change, whether that be through in relation to pollution, changing landscapes, or natural hazard risks. This was the most common theme within this work and illustrates the importance of community-level research when discussing second homes. In comparison, the final theme looks at the more macro level impact of second homes on climate change, which contrasts with their frequent framing as eco-friendly holiday options that are an alternative to overseas trips.

Planning for climate change

Existential threats to second homes as a result of climate change are very broad in scope. This is particularly relevant for those used for the purpose of leisure, as is the case with the examples in this edited book, as these are often located in a variety of physical environments across the globe, each of which has its own unique associated risks. These climate change related risks, then, must be accounted for when developing local destination planning policies, but this can be exceedingly complex due to the aforementioned contextual complications. For example, in certain situations, the impacts of climate change can be felt immediately, as is the case

DOI: 10.4324/9781003091295-10

in natural hazard-related disasters following, for example, hurricanes, wildfires, or landslides. In contrast, other increasing climate change related natural hazard risks pose a much more long-term threat, as can be observed with sea-level rise, erosion, and changing weather patterns. However, even when the risks are known, planning for them can be very intricate as some longer-term threats may actually have fewer mitigation strategies, as has been observed in the case of heavy coastal erosion wherein planners may have no option other than to implement managed retreat (Abel et al., 2011; Bukvic et al., 2015). However, these planning responses can be further complicated by the broad array of policy arrangements under which they may fall as well as to whether or not any distinction is made at all between second and primary homes (Hall & Müller, 2018). Without a concerted effort by, and acknowledgement of, all relevant stakeholders, it will be exceedingly difficult to ensure an adequate response to associated risks, which will have a direct negative impact on community as well as overall destination resilience (Hall et al., 2017).

It is unsurprising, then, that the importance of planning for the impacts of climate change emerged as one of the key themes in this book. As has been highlighted, complications may arise within planning systems when there is a complex policy environment with which second home environments are managed. An excellent example of this is seen in the chapter by de Moraes and March (Chapter 2) which discusses the multi-scalar governance context of the Wye River Valley in Australia. Through an analysis of each policy level, from the macro to the hyper localized, their chapter illustrates the challenges of integrating climate change policies with emergency management systems in a natural hazard prone area that is also a popular tourism destination. They emphasize the difficulty in developing policies which address second home owners as a distinct group as the definition of second home owner is a fluid concept among both residents and non-residents. They suggest that place attachment may be a useful way to assess who is and is not a second home owner, which could, in turn, be used as an impetus to enhance community interconnectedness and, by extension, community resilience.

Another chapter focuses on planning for climate change shifts the focus to the northern hemisphere to discuss the Swedish second home context. Demiroglu, Müller, Back, and Lundmark (Chapter 3) begin with an overview of the current geographical distribution and usage of Swedish second homes before presenting a series of future hypothetical climate change projections which they highlight will potentially have a direct impact on second home ownership patterns in the future. They note that second homes will be at an increased risk natural hazard-related damage, in particular, that related to coastal erosion, flooding, and wildfires. Additionally, there is projected to be not only biodiversity loss but also changing weather patterns which may make certain areas, such as ski resorts, untenable for many current second home owners. However, they have emphasized that increasing temperatures in the region could also drive a growth in second home ownership as tourists shift their summer vacations northward. They end by stressing the need for consideration of second homes in local planning. This is particularly important given the noted shifts in second home ownership and usage patterns as the current infrastructure may be unable to cope with these changes.

Second home community responses to climate change

While planning forms the building blocks of resilience to climate change, resilience planning will only be successful provided that there is an in-depth understanding of the communities at risk as community resilience is strongly tied to overall destination resilience (Hall et al., 2017). Within the context of second homes, this element of community, particularly as it relates to homeowner awareness and response to change, has often been overlooked. This is due predominantly to the historical treatment of second home owners within local planning processes wherein they are equated with primary homeowners, if they have been included at all, as has been noted previously in this chapter. However, it would also be a fallacy to assume that all second home communities have the same needs, composition, or, indeed, the same concerns when it comes to the discussion of climate change. Community responses to change are complex, especially to sudden, dramatic change. For example, while place attachment has been identified as an element that can enhance community resilience to shocks (Norris et al., 2008; Zweirs et al., 2018), feelings of nostalgia, particularly as the result of sudden, drastic change (Boym, 2001), may result in differing responses from differently attached individuals (Adie & de Bernardi, 2020). Thus, the local second home community is not only potentially unique and distinct from the local population but also complex in and of itself.

In some contexts, the local composition of second home communities can influence responses to climate change while simultaneously creating schisms with the local resident population, as will be observed in the chapters in this section. This is clearly visible in the case of Italian second home owners in Tulum, Mexico in the chapter by Velázquez (Chapter 6). His study focuses on the differing responses to plastic waste, specifically in the form of plastic drink bottles, between the local indigenous population, the Mayans, and a specific subset of the Tulum second home community, Italian nationals. In contrast to their American and Canadian counterparts, the Italian second home community considers itself more environmentally conscious, and they are more visibly environmentally active at the local level. However, these local activities are considerably problematic with the Italian second home owners engaging in neo-colonial paternalistic behaviour towards the local Mayan community. While the Italian community has been organizing awareness raising art events and attempting to influence local authority waste planning measures, the Mayan population highlighted their lack of agency in discussions around responses to plastic waste and an overall unwillingness by the second home owners to understand the structural inequalities faced by the local community. Thus, local climate change initiatives have become a platform by which a portion of the second home population has effectively prioritized their own interests over those of the local community, whose voices are often excluded from the conversation, limiting the actual effectiveness of any local pro-environmental policy making.

Responses to the impact of climate change, however, do not always pit local populations against second home owners. Place-based attachments can be a determining factor in climate change action, with those with stronger local attachments behaving more similarly to primary residents. Toso (Chapter 8) emphasises this in her exploration of second home owners' perceptions of and responses to climate change in a UNESCO World Heritage listed cultural landscape in Northern Italy. In general, this second home population is aware of climate change impacts, particularly as a result of damage to their own properties and surrounding infrastructure due to an increased number of storms and related natural hazards. However, there are additional climate change related issues in the region due to the importance of local viticulture. More specifically the shifting weather patterns are leading to a decrease in viable grape crops. Local homeowners as well as second home owners with family ties to the region are both pre-disposed to preserve this existing agricultural landscape, which leaves vineyard owners particularly vulnerable in the face of climate change induced alterations in growing conditions. In comparison, both foreign and domestic owners, especially those who have purchased their properties more recently, are more inclined to experiment with other crop types, such as olive trees, which are better suited to the new climatic conditions. While this may be viewed as a threat to the cultural landscape, it does result in a more economically resilient population, although it may, in turn, impact negatively on the attractiveness of the region as a second home destination.

The issue of attractiveness can be a significant problem, particularly when taking into account long-term planning for second home destinations. However, again, place attachment appears to play a significant role. In Norway, Stefansdottir, Xue, Steffansen, Næss, and Richardson (Chapter 9) found that second home owners who were more strongly attached to their second home locations were also more likely to adapt their activities to changing climatic conditions. This willingness to adapt occurred regardless of whether the place attachment was derived solely from the physical location or from the local community. In comparison, second home owners who viewed their homes through a strictly utilitarian lens wherein the home was merely a base from which to engage in specific recreational activities were significantly more likely to indicate that they would be willing to relocate should it become more difficult to engage in their preferred activity in the second home destination. This is in line with previous work by Adie (2020) which postulated that place attachment was the dominant factor in the post-disaster decision-making process of second home owners. In particular, the utilitarian viewpoint of less- or non-attached individuals was highlighted as a rationale for non-maintenance of a second home after hazard-related damage either to the actual property or to the wider environment.

Natural hazard-related damage and resultant disasters are a major risk factor for second home owners. However, while the chapter by Toso (Chapter 8) did touch on natural hazard-related impacts of climate change, the three previously discussed chapters have been predominantly focused on more general alterations to the local landscape due to climate change impacts. In comparison, the final two chapters discussing second home community responses to climate change are specifically focused on natural hazard risk awareness and risk-related adaptation. The first of these looks at second home owners at a coastal destination in the USA that experienced significant damage from Hurricane Sandy in 2012. In this study, Adie (Chapter 5) emphasizes the importance of place attachment as a lens through which risk awareness and mitigation are mediated. Due to the highly place-attached nature of the second home owners in this study, there were two identified responses to natural hazard risk wherein actual risk mitigation was tied directly to past experiences of hazard-related damage. More specifically, barring financial difficulties preventing action, only those who had experienced significant damage from the storm or repeated flood damage implemented mitigation and/or adaptation measures. Interestingly, while all of the interviewed homeowners were highly risk aware, those who had no past experience of damage to their own property had a marked tendency to minimize the potential impact of that risk and accept it as an inevitability of owning a coastal home, regardless of the level of damage to the overall coastal environment from natural hazards.

High levels of risk awareness were also observed in Czarnecki, Dacko, and Dacko's (Chapter 7) mountain second home owners in Poland, who face increased risks of, in particular, landslides. In general, more than half of the second home owners in this region appeared to note an overall increase in extreme weather events while over two-thirds were aware of the threat that these weather events posed to their property. Interestingly, most second home owners in this area did engage in some form of adaptation, but this was directly influenced by the second home owners' overall sense of community belonging, particularly as faith in the response capability of the local authority was generally low. While physical adaptation was the most common response, regardless of the homeowners' sense of community belonging, a higher sense of community belonging was more likely to lead to an additional adaptation measure wherein there was a reliance on local support networks to respond to potential risks. Given the emphasis on community, these results may indicate the impact of community-derived place attachment in the Polish second home owners' risk adaptation responses, similar to those noted in the study by Adie (Chapter 5). Although not present in all responses to climate change, it is clear, based on the majority of the chapters in this section, that place attachment has a role to play in the understanding of second home community's responses to climate change.

The impact of second homes on climate change

While much of the existing literature on second homes and climate change is focused on the impact of climate change on second home owners, there is significantly less written on second homes as potential net contributors to climate change (Adamiak et al., 2016; Naess et al., 2019; Scott et al., 2023). Second homes contribute to greenhouse gas (GHG) emissions via the construction and use of second homes, including the clearing of properties of vegetation to build and service a home, and by the travel of people using a second home. In the case of the latter, Hiltunen's (2007) examination of the environmental impacts of rural second home tourism in Finland estimated that, on average, 1264 kg CO_2 was emitted per year per car and 599 kg CO_2/year per person. Also in Finland, Ahlqvist et al. (2008) estimated that 1999 trips to second homes resulted in 0.4 million tons of CO_2, with trips to second homes accounting for 7% of all distance travelled by private cars. Interestingly, in analysing data from 2004–5 Ahlqvist et al. (2008) suggested that the annual energy consumption of second home related mobility was approximately

1070 GWh, equivalent to about 0.26 million tons of CO_2. In contrast, the use of electricity at second homes was only 500–900 GWh a year, highlighting the importance of mobility as a factor in second home related GHG emissions.

Much of the contribution of second homes to climate change is from the travel to and from second homes, which is primarily car driven. In a study of Finnish second homes, Adamiak et al. (2016) found that second home owners visit second homes, on average, 25.9 times a year and users 10.3 times a year, with the mean distance between the place of permanent residence and the second home being 167 km for second home owners and 229 km for users. The car is also the most important mode in terms of distance traveled for trips to and from domestic second homes located in Norway and accounted for about 240 kg CO_2 emissions per year per respondent in Naess et al.'s (2019) survey. However, when overseas second homes of Norwegians are considered, the amount of GHG emissions generated changes substantially as use of airplane as the main travel mode generated nearly 1650 kg CO_2 per capita over the 12-month period. As Naess et al. (2019, p. 4) note, "The per capita CO_2 emissions for respondents' travel by airplane and car to and from second homes abroad amounts to one fourth of the per capita CO_2 emissions among Norwegians for all purposes, excluding oil and gas production".

While it is then clear that second homes can be viewed as net contributors to overall emissions, there is little research into public information on the topic. This is the key focus of Pitkänen and Rantanen's (Chapter 4) study on media discourses of second homes and climate change in Finland. Their research indicates a generally positive or neutral stance on second homes, with a small proportion of media coverage even suggesting that climate change could lead to a positive increase in second home ownership in Finland due to a potentially more temperate climate. Finnish media discourse predominantly frames second home ownership as a good alternative to more carbon-intensive international travel while acknowledging the need for adaptation to increased climate change related risks, such as those observed by Czarnacki et al. (Chapter 7) and Adie (Chapter 5). In contrast, while some articles do emphasise the negative impacts of second homes on the climate, the majority tend to do it in such a way as to provide technological solutions to increase the efficiency of second homes, thus reinforcing second homes as a more eco-friendly leisure option in comparison to traditional holidays. While it is, perhaps, not surprising that Finland, a country with a history of second home usage, generally presents second homes in, at worst, a neutral light, media discourse can shape overall perceptions of climate change. Thus, without a full acknowledgement of the negative impacts of second home usage, there is a risk of an overall inability to then later introduce more restrictive controls on second homes as this may be seen as an overreaction to a leisure activity which the general public views as a green alternative to other forms of travel.

Avenues for future research

As has been observed, research into this area is still embryonic, and thus there are a myriad of directions for future research. However, what this work has provided, through a variety of climate change related contexts and international case studies, is a collection of clear threads emerging from within the small current body of research on the topic. In particular, and perhaps unsurprisingly, given the negative impacts of climate change in many second home destinations, there is an emphasis on governance, planning, and eventual climate change-driven adaptation and mitigation. While research into planning and governance of second home destinations is not a new subject (Hall, 2015; Hall & Müller, 2018), it is important to understand how newer climate change policies are being implemented at the local second home community level as well as what is being done to address new or increased hazard risks faced by homeowners. Additionally, given the renewed emphasis on rising inequalities due to the changing climate, there is a significant need for research which critically engages with the concept of second homes as symbols of displacement. In this context, second homes can not only effectively force out local populations through leisure-driven gentrification but also potentially reorient policy and hazard mitigation funding to these second home areas. This is due to the fact that these second homes are often assessed as higher-value properties that are owned by individuals with significantly more socio-political capital than the average citizen. It should be noted, however, that this does not describe all second home owners, as has been observed throughout this book, which further emphasises the need for context specific research. This is especially necessary given the diverse ways in which second homes are interpreted and legislated throughout the world.

In addition to these varied policy environments, second home communities themselves are often wildly different between contexts, not only in terms of their socio-demographic characteristics but also in the ways in which they view the world and their place in it. It has become clear that there is a general dearth in community-centred second homes research and, in particular, a focus on the psychological elements which drive both individual and community responses to climate change. It is necessary to not only understand how second home owners and second home communities adapt but also to understand *why* they make the decisions that they do in regard to climate change. For example, as was observed in several chapters in this book, one clear element impacting certain responses to climate change has been place attachment. However, there is relatively little engagement with this topic in the second homes literature. Therefore, there is an evident need for this to be researched further, especially in contexts wherein physical adaptation measures need to be implemented as a response to hazard risks. Similarly, although not addressed in this work, nostalgia may also play a role in the willingness to engage in mitigation and adaptation measures, especially in second home communities with long-term residents or where homes are often inherited. Overall, it is essential to better understand the myriad of different ways in which second home owners and second home communities understand their environment and how they both impact on and are impacted by climate change.

Both a renewed focus on planning practices as well as a better understanding of communities and individual homeowners will assist in the advancement of scholarship in this area beyond mere responses to climate change and shift it towards a better understanding of how second home communities can become more resilient. This, in turn, requires a more comprehensive policy environment which is inclusive of not only the myriad of individual stakeholders and local communities but also the physical realities of climate change impacts. The implementation of more context-specific resilience development policies within these second home communities may then not only create stronger community responses to change, both incremental and sudden, but also potentially create a feedback loop wherein these responses to change further reinforce local resilience. However, it needs to be noted that resilience is only a viable response to climate change provided that the existence of the community in a specific location is still viable. Thus, in addition to a focus on resilience, there is a renewed need to understand second home owners' willingness to relocate or abandon their properties should there be no further available adaptation measures. It is in this research area that the psychological factors of second home ownership may well play a significant role.

Given the increasingly negative impacts of climate change, the question may soon arise as to whether or not second homes are still a viable leisure pursuit. Currently framed as an eco-friendly alternative to traditional travel, second homes are still net contributors to individual emissions. It is difficult to see what the future may hold for these properties given the scale of global change that humanity is facing, but, whatever happens, second homes play a significant role in several cultures and are having a growing impact on others. Consequently, the need to understand the intersection between these leisure properties and climate change has never been greater.

References

Abel, N., Gorddard, R., Harman, B., Leitch, A., Langridge, J., Ryan, A., & Heyenga, S. (2011). Sea level rise, coastal development and planned retreat: Analytical framework, governance principles and an Australian case study. *Environmental Science & Policy, 14*, 279–288. https://doi.org/10.1016/j.envsci.2010.12.002

Adamiak, C., Hall, C. M., Hiltunen, M. J., & Pitkänen, K. (2016). Substitute or addition to hypermobile lifestyles? Second home mobility and Finnish CO_2 emissions. *Tourism Geographies, 18*(2), 129–151. https://doi.org/10.1080/14616688.2016.1145250

Adie, B. A. (2020). Place attachment and post-disaster decision-making in a second home context: A conceptual framework. *Current Issues in Tourism, 23*(10), 1205–1215. https://doi.org/10.1080/13683500.2019.1600475

Adie, B. A., & de Bernardi, C. (2020). 'Oh my god what is happening?': Historic second home communities and post-disaster nostalgia. *Journal of Heritage Tourism*. https://doi.org/10.1080/1743873X.2020.1828429.

Ahlqvist, K., Santavuori, M., Mustonen, P., Massa, I., & Rytkönen, A. (2008). *Vapaa-ajan asumisen ekotehokkuus (VAPET) Mökkeily elämäntapana ja ekotehokkaiden käytäntöjen hyväksyttävyys* [Eco-efficiency of leisure housing (VAPET) Summer cottages lifestyle and the acceptability of ecoefficient practices]. TTS tutkimuksen raportteja ja oppaita 36. Työtehoseura.

Boym, S. (2001). *The future of nostalgia*. Basic Books.

Bukvic, A., Smith, A., & Zhang, A. (2015). Evaluating drivers of coastal relocation in Hurricane Sandy affected communities. *International Journal of Disaster Risk Reduction, 13*, 215–228. https://doi.org/10.1016/j.ijdrr.2015.06.008

Hall, C. M. (2015). Second homes planning, policy and governance. *Journal of Policy Research in Tourism, Leisure and Events, 7*(1), 1–14. https://doi.org/10.1080/19407963.2014.964251

Hall, C. M., & Müller, D. (2018). Governance and planning for second homes. In C. M. Hall & D. Müller (Eds.), *The Routledge handbook of second home tourism and mobilities* (pp. 17–26). Routledge.

Hall, C. M., Prayag, G., & Amore, A. (2017). *Tourism and resilience: Individual, organisational and destination perspectives*. Channel View.

Hiltunen, M. J. (2007). Environmental impacts of rural second home tourism Case Lake District in Finland. *Scandinavian Journal of Hospitality and Tourism, 7*, 243–265. http://doi.org/10.1080/15022250701312335

Naess, P., Xuea, J., Stefansdottir, H., Steffansen, R., & Richardson, T. (2019). Second home mobility, climate impacts and travel modes: Can sustainability obstacles be overcome? *Journal of Transport Geography, 79*, 102468. https://doi.org/10.1016/j.jtrangeo.2019.102468

Norris, F. H., Stevens, S. P., Pfefferbaum, B., Wyche, K. F., & Pfefferbaum, R. L. (2008). Community resilience as a metaphor, theory, set of capacities, and strategy for disaster readiness. *American Journal of Community Psychology, 41*, 127–150. https://doi.org/10.1007/s10464-007-9156-6

Scott, D., Hall, C. M., Rushton, B., & Gössling, S. (2023). A review of the IPCC Sixth Assessment and implications for tourism development and sectoral climate action. *Journal of Sustainable Tourism*, https://doi.org/10.1080/09669582.2023.2195597.

Zwiers, S., Markantoni, M., & Strijker, D. (2018). The role of change – and stability-oriented place attachment in rural community resilience: A case study in south-west Scotland. *Community Development Journal, 52*(2), 281–300. https://doi.org/10.1093/cdj/bsw020

Index